perfect parties

perfect parties

the ultimate step-by-step guide

Alison Price

CREATIVE PUBLISHING international

MINNETONKA, MINNESOTA

First published in the USA and Canada in 2001 by
Creative Publishing international, Inc.

President/CEO David D. Murphy
Vice President/Editorial Patricia K. Jacobsen
Vice President/Retail Sales and Marketing Richard M. Miller
Executive Editor/Lifestyles Department Elaine Perry

First Published in Great Britain 1999 by **Kyle Cathie Limited**
Text © 1999 Alison Price
Photography © 1999 Jeremy Hopley except as credited below

Editor Sophie Bessemer
Copy-editor Samantha Grey
Design Vivid
Home Economist Dave Withers
Stylist Wei Tang
Production Lorraine Baird and Sha Huxtable

Printed and bound in Singapore by Tien Wah Press Pte. Ltd

10 9 8 7 6 5 4 3 2 1

ISBN 0-86573-165-9

Additional photographic acknowledgements
page 14: Hulton Getty; page 26: Marc Staines; page 37: Hulton Getty; page 54: Bill Batten; page 55: Bill Batten; page 59: Superstock; page 61: Hulton Getty; page 65: Superstock; page 67: Bill Batten; page 77: Hulton Getty

Dedication
To my mother for teaching me the love of good food, to my father for teaching me to be practical, I thank you.

Contents

Foreword
by Sir Elton John

When you've been to as many parties as I have, you tend to think you've seen it all before. Over the years, I've found that perfect and memorable parties require the host to blend the comfort of tradition with a fresh inventive spirit. It's where the expected and the unexpected meet. A successful party makes a guest feel completely comfortable yet never bored.

Alison Price has been responsible for some of the best parties I've ever given. She never ceases to amaze me. She always knows exactly what I want, yet never makes it feel stale or predictable. Whether it's a simple dinner for eight or a huge 50th birthday extravanganza for 400, her parties are always perfect.

With this book, Alison can help make your parties perfect too. I suppose I should be worried that she's given away her trade secrets. I'm not. I know that she will never run out of ways of creating the perfect party.

introduction

From a very early age, encouraged by my mother and father, I devoloped a great love for food, setting tables, making decorations and arranging flowers. To this day, I can recall the flavors of the wonderful soft summer fruits my grandfather grew, especially his loganberries. I remember sitting in his summer house in a garden full of scented flowers, surrounded by sweet-smelling summer jasmine, having afternoon tea. I also recall parties given by my mother. For Christmas, there were home-baked hams with roast capons and fresh vegetables, followed by Christmas puddings. I remember the wonder of watching my father light the brandy over the puddings and the bowls of brandy butter and homemade mince pies, filled with my mother's own mincemeat that I had eagerly helped her to make. On family picnics, there were flasks filled with homemade lemonade and bottles of ginger beer. Home is where I learned about entertaining and the art of sharing.

I started Alison Price and Company in 1981 with my business partner, Terry Shaw. Our aim was to create a different style of food that would excite and amaze. Years of discovery followed, as well as extremely hard work. Terry and I would cook, wash up, deliver, do the accounts, write the menus and plan everything down to the last detail – all from a small flat in Bayswater, west London. Soon the business began to grow from personal recommendations and Gary Withers of Imagination offered us our first professional kitchen in his new offices. We have moved since then several times – we just keep outgrowing places!

We have always enjoyed running our business and have met enchanting people who have been generous in giving us the opportunity to be creative. Parties have taken us not only around Britain, but also abroad. What started as a two-person business has grown into a dedicated and loyal team of more than 20, who all contribute ideas, menus and planning.

We are perfectionists about food, wines and service and do not believe in gimmicky ideas – simple, elegant entertaining is our company philosophy. Attention to detail is one of the most important pieces of advice I can give. We always say failure is not an option.

Of course, at the beginning of our business venture, we had the odd disaster. I remember a wedding that we catered for in the country where the water supply was from a well which ran dry halfway through the evening, leaving no water for coffee or to flush the toilets. On one occasion, power failed just as 350 guests sat down for dinner. We have even set off fire alarms when sautéing foie gras. (These days we make provisions for such eventualities!) We have, however, had years of great enjoyment creating memorable parties, every day bringing new ideas and ways for the team to express their creative talents. In this book, you will find a wealth of practical advice resulting from all our experience.

Giving a perfect party is not difficult to do. Careful planning is required, whether you are giving a small dinner for 10 or a large party for 100 guests or more. It is enjoyable, too, to write a guest list matching new friends with old, think of different designs for invitations and create table settings that will amuse and delight your guests. Choosing the food is an excitement in itself. You may also want to create a memorable theme, in which case you will find lots of ideas on pages 16–23. Remember that entertaining is your opportunity to be as individual as you want to be.

I hope this book will give you all the ideas and enthusiasm you need. Whether holding an impromptu supper in the kitchen with bowls of simple pastas, homemade sauces and fresh salads or planning a grand dance, you will experience the unique pleasure of seeing your guests having a fabulous time – and, what is more, you will have great fun doing it.

pre-party

If you have ever wondered what makes a successful party, the anwer is detailed planning and preparation. Remember the rule of the six 'p's, prior proper planning prevents poor performance; and think ahead to what must be done. For a party to be under control, someone must be in charge to make decisions.

prepare to party

If you have asked family or friends to help, be very clear what their responsibilities are. They can then proceed with as much enthusiasm as you, and listening to their ideas may help you to decide your plan of action. By devoting time and energy to organizing a party, you will ensure that it runs as smoothly as possible.

Be Aware of Your Budget

The budgets required by different styles of parties vary greatly, and it is vital to set a realistic budget for the type of party you are planning. Allocate the main part of the budget to the aspect of the party that is most important to you. For some people this is the wine and food, to others it is the decorations and entertainment. If you are planning a large, sit-down dinner, the cost of renting tables and chairs can be very expensive. A drinks party is probably the least expensive form of entertaining. If you are providing the drinks, allocate half the cost of the food budget, although this will alter if you plan to serve expensive wine and champagne. Renting a room may be necessary for some parties. Party rooms come in a wide variety of forms and sizes, at vastly varying costs. You need to find one appropriate for the style of event you are planning, and allow for the rent cost in your budget. Always allow a little extra in the budget for unforeseen costs, too. Once you have finalized your budget, be very strict about keeping to it and do not be persuaded to spend more.

Perfect Planning

If you are planning a relatively large-scale party, such as an anniversary dinner dance, start by making a detailed list of the party requirements. These will include some or all of the following: invitations; food; drink; china; cutlery; glassware; furniture (also any furniture that must be removed from your home); location; flowers; decorations; entertainment; staff. Write a schedule of events for the day, including at what time various deliveries are expected. Map out a sequence of events, such as the time allocated to pre-dinner drinks and when to announce dinner, allowing time for guests to be seated before serving. Dinner should take about one and a half hours. If your party includes speeches, decide how many there will be and how long they are likely to take. If the meal is followed by dancing to a band or DJ, your schedule must include what time they will play until. Allow about half an hour to three quarters of an hour for guests to leave. Making a detailed pre-party plan with a schedule that includes the timing of events will be of enormous help to you on the day.

The organization of an occasion such as a lunch, cocktail party, tea party or dinner may not be as structured, but most of the elements remain the same.

Setting the Date

Plan the date of the party as far in advance as possible. The dates you will celebrate important events, such as a 50th wedding anniversary or a 21st birthday are obviously set in stone. Otherwise, you need to take the following points into consideration when choosing the date.

Consider whether the date falls in the school holidays, as many families take the opportunity to vacation together. If you are planning a party during the holiday season, remember that it is a busy social time and people's schedules fill up early. Final days of major sporting events are good dates to avoid, unless you want to hold a party to celebrate the event. Bear in mind, however, that while you may not want to watch a final, the chances are that some of your guests will. One customer

of ours actually rented large television screens so guests could watch the World Cup final.

Good months in which to give a party are February and March since with Christmas and New Year behind them, people are refreshed and eager to enter the social scene again. Parties during these months are a great success with very few refusals.

BEST FOR BUSINESS

DIFFERENT STYLES OF PARTIES ARE OFTEN BEST HELD ON DIFFERENT NIGHTS OF THE WEEK. WHILE FAMILY EVENTS OR WEDDINGS ARE POPULARLY HELD ON SATURDAYS, DID YOU KNOW THAT ONE OF THE MOST POPULAR NIGHTS OF THE WEEK FOR CORPORATE ENTERTAINING IS THURSDAY?

to hire a band. Choose the style of music for your party carefully, discussing your expectations with the band leader. Make your booking as soon as you have made your choice. This applies to a DJ and any other form of entertainment, too.

Food for Thought

Once you have decided on the date and location for your party, start to plan the menu and wines within your budget. Discuss the intended menu with your wine supplier, who will be able to make recommendations. When giving a dinner party, plan your menu wisely, thinking especially about what food will be in season. Think also of the dishes that you enjoy – tried and tested menus that you know work well and that guests will appreciate. Make sure that they can be prepared in advance. Always have a fall-back menu, too, in case certain foods are not available.

The Hardware

Once you have planned your menu, look carefully at your china, cutlery, glassware and linen. Decide on the plates, serving dishes, and so on, that you will use for each course. If you have silver cutlery, polish the pieces and buy tarnish-proof bags to store them in to prevent them from discoloring. Count your glasses to be certain that you have enough. Check that your linen is clean and pressed, then wrap it in acid-free paper and store in a bag laid flat in a cupboard or drawer. Alternatively, roll the linen and store it around a cardboard tube.

For Rent

You may not want to use your own china, glassware and so on for your party, or simply do not have enough. In this case, there are many excellent rental companies offering a wide range of china, glassware, cutlery, linen, chairs, and even ovens and microwaves. Place your order as soon as you have decided on the style of your party and the number of guests.

A Location to Remember

If your home is not large enough for the number of guests you wish to invite, you may consider holding the party at a different location. Discover whether rooms in local museums, art galleries or large houses, or barns, boats or empty warehouses are for hire. We have even carried out the catering for parties in an unused Underground station in central London! Interesting and unusual locations are to be found everywhere – it just takes a little research. Make a list of suitable options, then make appointments to view the rooms and discuss arrangements. Most locations have an experienced events manager, who will be of great help to you. When you have made your choice, book as far in advance as possible because popular locations become booked up early.

Timely Invitations

Once the date and location for your party have been decided on, invitations need to be organized. Although for weddings and dances you ought to send invitations out two months before, for drinks parties and formal dinner parties, four weeks is enough. Indeed, particularly when it is a relatively informal affair, most people prefer to invite guests to dinner simply by telephoning them.

A HINT OF FUN TO COME

When giving a large party, such as a dance or birthday party, it is a lovely idea to send a 'save the date' teaser card to be followed at the appropriate time by the invitation.

A Musical Accompaniment

Music is essential to any party. For a drinks or dinner party, a compact disc player with suitable music can be all that is required. If you have a piano, you may like to engage the services of a piano player. It is worth contacting your local music school as many have students who, by arrangement, play at parties and other events. When planning a large dance, you may want

Thinking Ahead to Table Settings

Making your own tablecloths and napkins can give your table a really special touch, but do this with plenty of time to spare. If you are arranging your own floral decorations, buy flowers that will be perfect on the day. Allow a few days in the warmth to open buds and bring blooms to perfection. Choose flowers that are in season and, as with the menu, have an alternative plan. Consider containers, too, and select a style that will complement the table and the flowers.

The Morning After

When every detail of your party is planned – the invitations sent, the food, drinks, flowers and staff arranged, the house prepared, silver and glassware gleaming, garden tidied up and paths swept – have you thought of the next day? Do you want to be faced with a lot of dirty glasses and plates? Some people do not mind at all – I know a couple who enjoy post-party cleaning, when they like to discuss the night's events. Others recoil at the thought of facing the mess with a hangover. I recommend arranging for the house to be cleaned the next day – you will usually be able to find a local agency. Book a realistic time because you will not appreciate jolly cleaners turning up at 6.30am when you have only been in bed for an hour or two.

HELPING HANDS

IF YOU NEED TO EMPLOY HELP, BOOK EARLY TO AVOID DISAPPOINTMENT – ESPECIALLY DURING BUSY PERIODS SUCH AS SUMMER AND CHRISTMAS.

party plan checklist

Three to six months ahead
- Book location if required

Ten to twelve weeks ahead
- If invitations are to be printed, start organizing them now

Four weeks ahead
- Invite your guests
- Decide what sort of food you will be serving. Will it be just canapés or will you be planning a full dinner?
- Book any help
- Make a detailed list of all the items you require
- Plan any decorations; if you plan to rent any props, start looking now

Three weeks ahead
- Start to plan the menu, remembering the pre-dinner nibbles
- Check if any of your guests have special dietary requirements
- Order wines, decide on cocktails and soft drinks
- Make a time plan for the day before and the day of the party

Two weeks ahead
- Make sure the table linen is clean and pressed; wrap in acid-free paper

- Start chasing guests who have not replied to your invitation
- Check your tableware; now is the time to ask friends or arrange to rent
- Make a detailed shopping list for food, buying any unperishable items
- Make and freeze food that can be prepared in advance
- Start to make any decorations

One week ahead
- Chase any guests who still have not replied

Five days ahead
- Clean silver and wrap it in tarnish-proof bags
- Check that you have ordered everything
- Buy flowers, cut the stems and store in a cool place in water
- Write your food shopping list
- Keep chasing those guests who have not replied

Two days ahead
- Make any dishes that can be refrigerated in advance
- If you are employing help, write a list of what you would like them to do
- Place wines, champagne and soft drinks in the refrigerator

- Finish making any decorations
- Order the ice

Day before
- Remove and store any furniture.
- Write your table plan – memorize it if possible; if not, make a neat card for reference
- Write place cards and set the table
- Arrange the bar
- Prepare cocktails or fresh-fruit drinks if serving and place in the refrigerator to chill
- Prepare canapés if serving
- Organize hand towels for the bathrooms and a coat storage area
- Arrange flowers

On the day
- Remove canapés from the freezer
- Finish preparing canapés and drink garnishes

Two hours before
- Remove corks from white wine bottles and the foil from champagne tops
- Chill the drinks
- Check that bathrooms have soap and hand towels
- Brief staff or helping hands
- Have a bath and relax

Before any of the practicalities it is vital to decide what, if any, theme your party will have. A little thought in this direction is well worth it – creating a theme for a party gives it an element of fun and can even add a sense of magic to an occasion.

fantasy themes

enthusiasms each person has. For a birthday party with a host who has a passion for musicals, we decorated each table in the style of a current West End show. These provided a wonderful talking point, and at the end of the evening, most of the table decorations had disappeared – taken home by guests as keepsakes of a great party! On the following pages you can see what can be achieved at home for three very different themes. I hope they fire your imagination to make your party that little bit more memorable.

Style on a Shoestring
You do not have to spend a fortune to create a spectacular themed party. I find a glue gun and a staple gun are very handy for making decorations, and then you can do a lot with attractive leaves, pretty branches and pinecones. Other useful items to collect include cards, ribbons and tissue paper. Fabric remnants are wonderful for making your own tablecloths and napkins – even if you do not have a sewing machine, a friend will. All it takes is a little imagination and planning.

Think carefully about your chosen theme to be sure that it is the right one for you and will not place too much demand on the time you have available or over-stretch your budget.

Look in books and magazines and draw or make photocopies of ideas for room decorations, table settings or costumes. If the party you are planning is to celebrate a special occasion such as a birthday or wedding anniversary, think what particular interests and

Circus Skills

A children's, or even an adult's, birthday party could be enlivened by creating a circus theme with brightly colored balloons, clowns' wigs and theatrical masks for guests to try on. Provide an assortment of items such as jack-in-the-boxes, juggling balls and hoops. Serve popcorn, toffee apples and colored candies to children and adults alike – most adults enjoy reliving the fun times of childhood.

Themed Table Settings

It is easy to create table settings that enhance your theme by using different tablecloths and tying or folding napkins in various styles. You could use carpets, brightly colored blankets or quilts instead of tablecloths. For a 'last days of the Raj' party, we covered tables with lengths of jewel-colored silks and used sari fabric for runners.

A French Feast

For people with an enthusiasm for the south of France, we have brought to life a French theme by recreating their favorite restaurant simply with red and white checked tablecloths and large white napkins. In the center of each table, baskets filled with crudités were surrounded by bowls of olive oil and French bread tied in cloths, country-style. The room was lit by candles in hollowed-out artichokes and the music was typically French. Guests feasted on bouillabaisse served in large white bowls, followed by tarte tatin and crème fraîche. The evening was not only a great success, but the decorations and food easy to prepare.

Color Coordination

It can often work well to plan a party around one color, such as white, using white linen and white china with arrangements of white flowers in white or glass vases – even the guests can be asked to wear white. For this theme, simplicity will achieve the most elegant effect. Take care not to include food in such themes – it must look appetizing.

Summer Magic

Take inspiration from a summer garden for a natural theme, creating beautiful table settings with baskets or plant pots overflowing with summer flowers, herbs and fruit. Be inventive, perhaps using small garden forks and trowels (make sure that they are new and gleamingly clean) to serve food from a buffet. You could also bake bread in plant pots. Weave strings of tiny white lights through shrubs or trees.

Pool Party

For a pool party, cover tables with aquamarine-colored tablecloths and place goldfish bowls in the center – these could contain goldfish if you already keep them or have a suitable home for them after the party. Or, make centerpieces with piles of shells and pebbles covered with sand.

FESTIVE FIREPLACES

COLLECT PINECONES TO FILL FIREPLACES THAT ARE NOT IN USE – THEY NOT ONLY LOOK DECORATIVE BUT GIVE YOUR HOME A WARM AND WELCOMING FRAGRANCE.

merry christmas

We all love to decorate our homes at Christmas, hanging wreaths on doors and garlands on mantelpieces. The decoration of the tree tends to be the most popular activity of all, and adorning it with homemade cookies shaped into stars and half-moons looks particularly festive. Other favorite tree decorations include colored glass balls and sparkling white fairy lights wound around the branches. Make leftover lengths of ribbon into garlands or tie them in bows on the branches. My friend Clare Signy searches antique markets for chandelier drops and balls to create wonderful decorations, and you can do the same.

Christmas is also the time to entertain family and friends over dinner. I like to spray nuts and fruits gold then place them in bowls on the table. I tie my napkins with dark green velvet ribbon and make bread rolls in the shape of garlands. Prepare pomanders of oranges and lemons studded with cloves and pile them high on side tables; long cinnamon sticks arranged in vases also look festive. For a really enchanting display, place frosted pears on glass cake stands. If you have a glue gun – a useful tool for many crafts – make pyramids and balls of nuts to place around the house.

If you do want an ultraviolet effect, just replace ordinary lightbulbs with ultraviolet bulbs – the room will come to life. Food can be eaten off colored plates or in napkins that harmonize with the colors of the paint. If you like, you can extend the input your guests have in creating the scene for their own party by letting them paint up their own original designs on the plates using the popular ceramic paints now available.

It is the application of a theme to the smallest details that really makes a spectacular party. For this street scene, we wanted the serving dishes to have an industrial, down-to-earth feel to them. Consequently, the beer and soft drinks stand in galvanized steel trays and even the salt and pepper (and, of course, mustard) are served from unfancy but utilitarian plastic containers.

street smart

This idea was developed for a party for teenagers a few years ago. The aim was to design something hardwearing yet suitably 'iconoclastic' and different. On that occasion the walls were splashed with ultraviolet paint. In fact, as these photographs show, with just a little artistic inspiration you can splash ordinary paint onto canvas draped over the tables and walls. It is most fun when you leave one wall or canvas free for guests to unleash their own creativity upon.

silks and spices

Inspired by the brightly colored silks and aromatic scents and spices of the east, this room setting has a romantic mystery about it. Wooden bowls placed in the center of the tables hold a selection of spices or fruit which not only look exotic but also release fine scents which can pervade a room (it is important to appeal to all the senses when creating a theme). As a further original decoration, we filled silk bags with pebbles painted in colors that complement the color scheme used for the napkins and the rest of the room. The hearts by every gleaming bowl then can be written upon to provide stunning name cards. To complete this theme, we removed the curtains from the windows and in their place hung generous lengths of pinkish silk (below) which can then catch the wind (and any drafts) to create a gently moving backdrop to the room. Using an inexpensive fabric such as colored muslin would create the same effect.

Where are you going to hold your party? Will you be entertaining at home or at an outside location? If your party is to be at home, then take some time to work out how to arrange the space you have available. This may not always be readily obvious and involves a careful, lateral look at all areas of your home.

home or away?

Look at familiar, useable spaces with a critical eye to see how they could be arranged differently and how many guests they could accommodate comfortably. Changing rooms from their normal daily use is fun for the host and an interesting talking point for guests. Be inventive, using a large cupboard for a bar, placing tables in bedrooms, or a buffet or long dinner table in a large hall. Ask yourself practical questions: Where can you store coats for the evening? Is it possible to allocate separate bathrooms to men and women? For a large party, I would suggest putting up signs for men's and ladies' bathrooms so that you are not continually asked where they are. Also consider whether there is enough space in your kitchen to prepare the food you plan to serve, and whether your oven and refrigerator space will allow you to cater for the number of guests you want to invite. Plan where you will stack dirty plates, glasses and empty serving dishes.

Clearing to Create Space

If space is tight in your home, I advise removing some furniture and storing it in a room (that you will not be needing), or in a cellar, garage or garden shed. If it is not possible to store it yourself, there are numerous furniture removal companies that will take away your furniture for a night and return it the following day.

Room to Move

For a cocktail party, arrange a few seats for guests, and make sure that there are clear surfaces to put down glasses. Do not place bars or buffets in areas that could easily become congested. If you are planning a garden party in the summer, place blankets and chairs on a lawn.

Sometimes the best solution is to reinvent space by turning a garage into a disco, or even a kitchen, for the day. For a disco, use ultraviolet lighting and cover the existing lights with colored gels. In a garage, you can be adventurous with the decorations, draping the walls with fabric splashed with paint (see pages 20–21 for how we created the street effect with paint). Alternatively, rent a dance floor and supply your own music, perhaps with the help of enthusiastic family members.

LOOKING AFTER EVERYONE

REMEMBER WHEN PLANNING COCKTAIL PARTIES OR BUFFETS TO LEAVE SOME SEATING IN THE ROOMS FOR ELDERLY OR INFIRM GUESTS.

Cocktail Parties and Buffets

For cocktail parties and fork buffets, allow a space of 5ft (1.5m) per person. This takes into account a bar that will probably be in the same room and the removal of some of the furniture. For smaller parties you can get away with less than 5ft (1.5m) per person.

Are We Sitting Comfortably?

When planning a dinner party at home for a large number of guests, it is a good idea to make a basic scaled-up plan of the room, or rooms, you have chosen to use. Draw the shape of the room on a piece of paper, noting the measurements of its width and length. Indicate the positions of any obstacles, such as fireplaces, bay windows, recesses, immovable pieces of furniture, suspended light fittings and doors that open into the room (most do). Try to ensure that the windows are accessible so that they can be opened.

Take an average-sized reception room of 18 x 14ft (5.5 x 4.25m). In a room of this size, with no obstacles except for the door, it would be possible to sit up to 20 guests at two 5ft (1.5m) round tables, seating up to 10 guests per table. This would be cozy, but not uncomfortable. If you wish to have one long table, the important measurement to consider is that of the space between the floor edge and the open door. On some occasions, with space at a premium, we have removed the door for the evening. Ideally, the table should be 4ft (1.2m) wide to allow 1.5ft (50cm) depth for the place settings each side, leaving 1ft (30cm) for decorations and serving bowls placed along the center of the table. Allow 2ft (60cm) width of table for each guest, with 2ft (60cm) more

The following is a guide to fitting guests at different-sized tables (at a rectangular table assume a width of 4ft (1.2m) with two people seated either end).

Table Size	Maximum Number of Guests
Round Table (diameter)	
3ft (1m)	6
4ft (1.2m)	8
5ft (1.5m)	10
5ft 6in (1.7m)	11
6ft (1.85m)	12
Rectangular Table (length)	
4ft (1.2m)	8
6ft (1.85m)	10
8ft (2.4m)	12
10ft (3m)	14
12ft (4m)	16

Plan showing use of space when seating guests at rectangular tables or round tables.

behind the chairs to give space for serving. The maximum size that the table should be in the average-sized reception room is 12 x 4ft (4 x 1.2m); with two guests at each end, this seats a maximum of 16 guests. It is worth noting that long tables tend to take up more space than round ones, so if you are trying to fit the maximum number of guests into an odd-shaped room, use a combination of different-sized round tables to utilize corners.

Glorious Garden Parties

For a summer party, set up a garden table as a bar to serve drinks from. Your yard may present other possibilities, too, whatever the season, such as a greenhouse or conservatory for serving coffee and desserts. A candlelit summerhouse could provide an idyllic romantic hideaway. For outdoor parties, the weather plays an important role so listen to forecasts beforehand and make sure you have drawn a contingency plan to cope with unwanted surprises. It may be possible to cover a garden terrace with a canopy or you may need to move everything inside – be open-minded about adapting your plan.

Playing Away from Home

If you are not able to accommodate the number of guests you would like to invite at home, you could consider a tent in the yard if there is sufficient space, or look for a suitable location.

Tremendous Tents

Tents can become an extension of your home, with the house used for serving pre-dinner drinks and canapés and guests having direct access to the tent through doors that normally lead to the yard. Sometimes, guests may not even be aware that they are sitting under canvas.

If you have decided on having a tent in the yard, start your search for a tent company by asking friends and family for recommendations. All tent companies will make a site visit, armed with photographs and samples of lining – some even supply furniture. Ask if they are erecting a tent with similar specifications to yours in the near future that you could visit. Take into consideration the area over which the tent will be positioned. Some sites may require a scaffold structure to create an even floor. Tents today are extremely sophisticated, with

heating controlled by a thermostat, air conditioning, windows and patio doors. The color and type of lining depends on your preference.

With the number of guests you are inviting in mind, decide how much space is required for a reception area, bar, buffet and dance floor. The tent company will be able to supply a scaled-up plan setting out the different elements as you want them. If you are engaging the services of a catering company, they will require a service tent large enough for cooking and clearing away dishes to; also consider a separate staff area and a storage area for coats and bags.

The Light Fantastic

Lighting in a tent can include night-sky ceilings, pin-spotted tables, and bars and buffets bathed in pools of light. Decorative features can be spot lit to bring them to life. If you want these effects, ask the tent company to recommend a specialist lighting firm. It may be necessary for power to be supplied by generators, but these are now almost silent. It is worth the investment for peace of mind.

Practical Matters

Try to ensure that the tent has windows on to attractive features of the yard, such as a beautiful flower border, pond or fountain. These could also be highlighted with outside lighting. You may need to arrange with the tent company to have additional bathrooms. These can now have luxurious touches, from designer wallpaper to scented candles and linen hand towels – your choice will probably be dictated by budget.

Expect your life to change while the tent is being erected, bearing in mind that some take up to a week to assemble and two days to dismantle. Check when the company will arrive to dismantle the tent – you do not want to see them at six in the morning following the party. I would suggest a midday start, which gives you time to recover from the night before. Try to ensure that all equipment is removed from the tent before they start to dismantle it. In addition, it is a good idea to have previously arranged insurance to cover any accidents, and most tent companies offer this.

Bien Venue

The thought of having your home life disrupted for up to 10 days by a tent company may lead you to decide to look for a rental location. Your budget will point you in the direction of the appropriate place for you, from a grand house to the local village hall. The best space should be flexible but the more popular locations are booked months ahead. Most locations have an experienced events manager who can give you advice. To help you to arrange the practicalities, make a list of questions that you need to ask (see right). Do be warned for the budgeting stage that some locations have lists of approved caterers and florists that they like to use who are accustomed to organizing food and flowers in a very tight time frame. This can be very important when you are, for example, renting rooms in museums or art galleries that close at 6:00pm, with

your guests invited for 6:30pm. When you have made your choice of location, write to confirm the booking as soon as possible and send your deposit. In most cases, you will be sent a contract detailing your arrangements. Check this carefully as you do not want any surprises on the day.

Asking the Right Questions

To help you choose the right location, these are the questions you need to ask yourself and the location manager:
• Will the location hold the number of guests you are inviting?
• Are there any restrictions to activities such as smoking, drinking red wine in certain areas or dancing?
• Is there easy parking – if not can it be arranged?
• Are there telephones available (to call for taxis)?
• Is there cloakroom space for coats?
• If you are having a dinner, can pre-dinner drinks be held in a separate area?
• If using them, are you allowed to bring in an outside caterer and florist?
• Are there kitchen facilities and what are they like?
• Is there a food preparation area?
• Are you allowed to bring in ovens or hot cupboards, and is the power rating able to cope?
• What types of entertainment are allowed?
• What time can you start setting up?
• When are the guests expected to leave and will overtime be charged for late departures?
• Is the lighting appropriate (some places have much more sophisticated systems than others) – if not, would candles enhance the interior?
• Finally look at the bathrooms and if they are not very attractive, make them more welcoming with floral arrangements, fragrant soaps and hand towels

ENCHANTED EVENINGS

IF YOUR PARTY IS IN THE EVENING, ARRANGE A VISIT TO SEE THE LOCATION AT NIGHT TO MAKE AN INFORMED JUDGEMENT ON WHETHER THE MOOD WILL BE SUITABLE.

invitations

The success of a party depends upon attention to every detail. Well-designed invitations, in keeping with the style of your party, sent out in good time will encourage guests to look forward to the event. Organized records of expected guests and an efficient seating plan will ensure that the occasion runs smoothly.

Making your Guest List

When making your guest list, you have to be sure that the number you wish to invite will fit in the space where you are planning to hold your party. As a host, inviting guests into your private world calls for you to be very thoughtful. You want to create a lively party with an interesting collection of guests that may include family members, friends and business colleagues. Choose guests who will be lively and even some with controversial views and conflicting interests to encourage discussion and debate. These days it is not so important to have a strict 50 percent male to female ratio, and you can mix age groups. For last-minute cancellations, have a list of friends who you know will not be offended if they are invited to make up the numbers.

Invitations

These days we live in a world where faxes and e-mail are dominating our communications. However, receiving a written invitation remains an important part of social etiquette. The thrill of opening an invitation followed by the anticipation of going to the party is something we all love.

Your chosen invitation design will set the style of your party. It can be traditional, but if you are giving a party with an unusual style or theme, try to be original with the design of your invitations, too. Interesting ideas include a tin can with an invitation label tied onto it, a CD or tape with a recorded invitation, a cigar tube holding an invitation, and a small piece of glass with the invitation etched on. The invitation could also be added to fluorescent light sticks, a sheet of transparent film or an archive photograph. A simple and fun option is to fill the envelope with confetti, glitter or paper shapes that will spill out. People can become excited about going to a party that they know will be special simply because you have followed through the style of the party with your chosen invitation.

The invitation must include all the information your guests need to know: date, timing, dress, the type of hospitality being provided and where to reply. Enclose an RSVP card as this acts as a prompt for guests to reply. Some people can still be very slow in replying so, to be sure of numbers, do not be shy about telephoning them. Indicating to guests the style of the party will be appreciated as there is nothing worse than arriving in black tie to find that the remainder of the guests are in casual wear. If parking is almost impossible for your guests, give that information as well.

Rules to Remember

On formal invitations, the guest's name is always written by hand with a fountain pen, as is the envelope. Full titles, rank and any decorations are used when writing on the envelopes but not on the invitation.

Timing

Timing for sending invitations is as follows:
Two months before a wedding or a large dance;
Six weeks before a special celebration;
Four weeks before a formal dinner, drinks or buffet party.

right size. Read the printer's proofs carefully, checking that the information is correct. Try not to agonize too much over the look of the invitations as changing your mind will mean a delay in sending them, and by then you may find that your guests have other social or business commitments.

The 'Yes' or 'No' List

I recommend that you compile a 'yes' and 'no' list for replies, making a note of daytime and evening telephone numbers for contacting people when you need to. Guests' names should be checked off once they have been invited and replied. If you know about, or are told about, any special dietary requirements, write these next to the guest's name for later reference.

Allowing for Refusals

When more parties were given 30 years ago, 33 percent refusals were allowed for. These days fewer parties are given, so you can expect more acceptances. For private entertaining, allow 15 percent refusals for a cocktail party and 5 percent for a dinner. Refusals for business can be up to 30 percent for a cocktail party and 10 percent for a dinner. Refusals will vary depending on the time of year, the day of the week, and when invitations were sent.

MAPPING THE WAY

IF YOU LIVE IN THE COUNTRYSIDE OR YOUR HOME IS DIFFICULT TO FIND, HAVE A MAP PRINTED EITHER ON THE REVERSE OF THE INVITATION OR ON A SEPARATE CARD.

To invite friends to a dinner party, a telephone call is sufficient. Do this three weeks before, and if you like, follow with a card or letter confirming the arrangements. If the dinner is for business, keep to formal invitations.

The Printed Word

Plan your invitations as soon as you have decided on the date for your party to allow yourself time. Printers will need at least four to six weeks before they are able to deliver printed invitations. During this time, after about two to three weeks, you will approve the design, style of the type and your copy. Ask for the envelopes before you receive the printed invitations as these can be written in advance. If the invitations will not fit in standard-sized envelopes, ask how long it will take to make them to the

Planning menus, no matter how simple or grand, requires thought. I always prefer to use fresh ingredients that are in season; then flavors are at their finest and prices at their most economical. Seasonal produce is also the most readily available and of course it gives you a starting point to your menu planning.

menu planning

When choosing ingredients, think about an interesting range of colors and textures. Imagine tasting all the elements you would like to serve, then consider whether they mix well together. Classic combinations, for example, include fresh mint with new potatoes and strawberries with cream. Deciding what will complement each element is a good starting point when planning a menu. Try to keep the dishes you plan to serve simple, full of flavor and easy to prepare.

Tasting as Good as it Looks

Consider the visual appeal of the combination of dishes on your planned menu. For example, I would not advise serving scallops, followed by chicken with creamed potatoes and a dessert such as crème brûlée. Although each dish on its own is delicious, served as a dinner they are all the same color. Think about how the colors and textures of the ingredients in each course will complement one another.

Perfect Presentation

When preparing and serving food, it is worth giving everyday meals a slight twist in the way they are presented. For a classic dish, such as a Caesar salad, try replacing the traditional croûtons with long, spicy ones. A casserole becomes hearty made with whole vegetables or delicate when the vegetables are cut into small dice.

Buying the Best Ingredients

When buying food, take time and care choosing each ingredient. Check for freshness and do not be forced into buying any item you are less than happy with. In large cities, it is becoming increasingly difficult to find a local butcher, fishmonger or green grocer – where I live in central London I have managed to find local shops and markets, where I have developed good relationships, but it takes time. Most of us are left to shop under one roof in large supermarkets. These generally have specialist fish and meat departments, so make the most of their staff's expertise by approaching to discuss what you would like to buy.

Be Kind to Yourself

These days we are bombarded with cooking programs and new books, putting pressure on us to prepare food like three-star Michelin chefs. Be practical and accept that this is not realistic. Do not feel that you should prepare dishes that you sense are not going to work for you in the time you have available, otherwise you may be in the kitchen all night. Choose a menu that can be prepared ahead, that will require only minimum attention before serving. If you do not have time to prepare all the courses, visit a local delicatessen or bakery for the starter or dessert. As long as the food you serve is fresh, why feel guilty?

BUDGET BLUES?

IF YOUR BUDGET ONLY RUNS TO A SIMPLE DINNER, SERVE A HEARTY SOUP WITH LOVELY WARM BREAD. FOLLOW WITH ONE CHEESE AND HOMEMADE OATMEAL COOKIES, OR A FRUIT TART. GUESTS ALWAYS ENJOY GOOD, HONEST FOOD.

Variety is the Spice of Life

The best menus have a varied mix of flavors, ingredients, colors and textures. Try not to repeat any of the elements within a dinner menu. For a buffet or cocktail party, you can repeat some flavors and textures. If serving canapés before dinner, try not to include any of the dinner ingredients. For a buffet, remember those guests who may not be meat eaters, and always allow a few dishes that do not contain any dairy products, fish or meat. You can be bold when planning the menu and amaze your guests with bright and beautiful garnishes and serving dishes, but don't forget that classic simplicity can look effective too. Just keep within your own capabilities and choose a style which suits you and with which you are comfortable.

BREAK WITH TRADITION

DO NOT FEEL THAT YOU MUST ALWAYS FOLLOW TRADITION. THINK OF IMAGINATIVE ALTERNATIVES TO POTATOES LIKE RISOTTO, BEANS OR GNOCCHI.

No-Fuss Canapés

If serving canapés, plan bite-sized ones with no messy bits to drop onto carpets or spill onto guests' clothes. They should be easy to prepare and serve, and not so elaborate that they can only be assembled at the last minute. Also take into consideration your range of kitchen equipment and the storage space in your refrigerator. Calculate that you are not over-stretching yourself budget-wise. If serving only a very few canapés, make them memorably exquisite! (Try a boiled quail's egg with celery salt!)

Remember the Vegetarians

Most parties nowadays will probably include non-meat eaters and as host, you do not want them to feel left out. Before you start planning your menus, ascertain how many, if any, of the guests are vegetarians and then consider whether to adapt a dish for them or cook a separate course.

WINES WITH FOOD

FORGET ANY 'RULES' ABOUT THE COLOR OF THE WINE YOU SHOULD SERVE — WHITE AND RED CAN BOTH BE DELICIOUS WITH FISH.

Summing Up

Planning menus is enjoyable, and your party is sure to be a success so long as you keep within your time frame, capabilities and budget. Take time to present each dish with care and perhaps a little wit. Consider the plates or bowls best for serving each course. Also take into account practicalities, such as the room you will serve your guests in, and do not plan elaborately arranged food that must, for example, be transported from the basement up three flights of stairs – your beautiful presentation could suffer!

If you are like me, you will have a diverse collection of serving dishes, plates, bowls, cups, cutlery and glasses – what I call hardware. I enjoy mixing and matching china, and seeing the effect of combining different side plates with main-course plates to create an inviting table setting.

the hardware

Multi-Purpose Styles

I like to collect useful items that can have dual functions. Many years ago in Boston, I found jam jars that work really well as glass tumblers to serve beers or soft drinks in. Large white bowls can be used to serve pasta, a substantial main-course salad or a comforting winter soup. Bowls for vegetables or salads are also useful for desserts, such as a crumble or brûlée. Beautiful, painted Italian pottery is perfect for summer lunches in the garden, but also looks wonderful for serving breakfast in the kitchen or dining room. Most invaluable of all is simple white china, which fits any food and allows you to use tablecloths and napkins in a greater range of color.

Mix and Match

It is not necessary for all your china to match, as different shapes and color shades can complement one another. This is worth bearing in mind if you are giving a large dinner party, when you may want to borrow plates from family or friends. Try to collect pieces of china that will not date, keeping in mind your preferred style of table settings and food. I am always on the lookout for new pieces and find that antique fairs are an excellent hunting ground. It is worth having a store of glass plates as they are ideal for serving desserts. I never buy anything that I cannot put in the dishwasher; this rule applies even to my collection of early blue and white china, which I use with great regularity.

BEAUTIFUL BUFFETS

To present plates in style at a buffet, layer them with napkins or tie up piles of plates with large linen napkins.

Choosing Cutlery and Glassware

The type of cutlery and glassware you choose should depend on your lifestyle. Even if you love silver, consider how much time you wish to devote to keeping it highly polished. This said, over the years I have put together a wonderful collection of beautiful silver cutlery from my various visits to antique markets and fairs. Using items collected abroad can bring back happy memories – I have some pretty silver and mother-of-pearl fruit knives that always remind me of time spent in New England. When friends ask what you would like for a birthday present, why not ask for a silver dessert fork or spoon to add to your collection? The gift will last a lifetime.

Fortunately these days there are no set rules on which pieces of cutlery to use for certain dishes, although fish knives and forks have gone out of fashion, to be replaced by dessert knives and forks. Be imaginative – for example, horn spoons are ideal for boiled eggs. Serving spoons and forks will add interest to your table settings, and come in a variety of designs. Likewise, cutlery old and new can be found with classic wooden or bone handles, or jazzy plastic ones.

From stemmed glasses to tumblers, there is a bewildering amount of glassware of all shapes and sizes to choose from – plain or decorative, it is up to your personal taste.

Serving

Collect serving dishes in interesting shapes and styles. Look around the house for large bowls, vases, flowerpots, baskets or any other item. Large fish platters, for example, allow wonderful arrangements of vegetables or salads. Steamer baskets look effective when piled high and topped with a bowl of noodles or rice. Footed bowls look delightful filled with salads, and hollowed-out Parmesan wheels, available to order from cheese merchants, are an imaginative way to present pastas or risottos. A one-pot dish, such as a cassoulet, is best served from the pot in which it was cooked – just clean around the edges first and check that your table or serving surface is heat resistant before you put it down.

ICE SPECTACULAR

Ice creams or sorbets look magnificent served in ice bowls. Pile these high up and watch them catch the light.

Stand and Deliver

Finally, if you do not own a large amount of hardware or do not wish to use your own plates, glasses, cutlery and serving dishes for a party, then renting is the answer. There are many companies that specialize in renting these items and it is worth arranging an appointment to see what is available. Ask if prices include delivery and collection, whether you will be able to return your rented items dirty, and if so, at what extra charge. Times you arrange for delivery and collection are, as usual, important – I suggest asking the company to deliver on the morning of your party and to collect the following day (allowing you time to recover). Bear in mind that if any equipment is damaged or lost, a replacement charge will be made. (It is important to make this clear to any staff/helpers for the event.)

Frequently the number of guests you have invited to a party is too many to cope with single-handedly. In this case, your thoughts may turn to hiring waiting staff or asking friends and family if they are willing to lend a helping hand. Most people will be honored and flattered to help, so do not be afraid to ask.

helping hands

Parties are, by their nature, a social occasion, so even a hard-pressed cook can usually find an extra pair of hands to help. Perhaps a family member or friend excels at cooking a certain dish – if so, they may be willing to make this for your party. Always make it clear exactly what help you need. For example, if you have a particular style of setting your table, demonstrate one place setting. As a professional, I always offer to help friends if they are giving a large party; sometimes they welcome the idea, but there are also occasions when they prefer to organize the evening themselves. The golden rule is never be afraid to ask for help.

Professional Help

When hiring waiting staff, I would suggest that you contact a reputable agency or ask friends whether they can recommend reliable staff – word of mouth is the best recommendation. If you contact an agency, it is important to be clear about what type of party you are giving and what you expect the staff role to be. Plan timings precisely so that staff have sufficient time to set the table and prepare the bar. For dinners and buffet parties, arrange for the waiting staff to arrive two hours before the guests and to continue for about half an hour after the last guest has departed. For drinks parties, the staff should arrive one and a half hours before guests arrive.

What to Expect

Give staff clear instructions – do not just expect them to start cleaning the silver and pressing linen on arrival. Be clear as to whether you would like them to wash up or load the dishwasher. If you are giving a dinner party, show them where the china, glassware, cutlery and linen are stored, and tell them what pre-dinner drinks and snacks you are serving. Experienced waiting staff will run your party, not only opening doors, taking coats and serving drinks, but helping you to place canapés on trays and perhaps even doing the last-minute cooking of vegetables, dressing salads, preparing cheese baskets and making the coffee and teas. Remember that they are there to help you.

LOOKING AFTER WAITING STAFF

IF EMPLOYING STAFF FOR OVER FOUR HOURS, PROVIDE A LIGHT SNACK. YOU CANNOT EXPECT STAFF TO WORK LATE WITHOUT FOOD. IF YOUR PARTY FINISHES AFTER THE LAST TRAIN OR BUS, IT IS STANDARD PRACTICE FOR THE EMPLOYER TO ARRANGE AND PAY FOR A TAXI.

Paying Practices

Waiting staff are paid by the hour to work a minimum of four hours. If using an agency, you can receive a bill or pay the staff directly, with the commission charged separately. If you hire staff without an agency, discuss fees first.

BEHIND THE BAR

WHEN GIVING A DRINKS PARTY WITH MORE THAN 25 GUESTS, I WOULD RECOMMEND HIRING AN EXPERIENCED BAR PERSON, WHO WILL BE WORTH THEIR WEIGHT IN GOLD. AS WITH WAITING STAFF, ALWAYS PROVIDE AS MUCH INFORMATION AS POSSIBLE.

Chefs and Cooks

When finding good chefs or cooks, the same principles apply as for finding waiting staff. Discuss with them your ideas for the menu as well as what dishes they like to prepare. They will be clear about the service that they will provide and what you will be expected to supply. Take time to show them the china and serving dishes you wish to use. They need to know in advance how many guests are invited, timings, how formal or informal the party will be, and whether there will be help serving the food and washing up. Charges are arranged in one of two ways – a flat fee plus the cost of food, or you can be charged on a per-head basis. Most chefs and cooks know good waiting staff that they work with regularly, so it is worth asking for their recommendation.

Mission Impossible

Do not expect cooks or chefs to create a dinner without proper ovens and so on. If you cannot prepare dinner without certain equipment, then neither can they. Remember that, if necessary, you can rent equipment. Be realistic about your chosen menu, too. In a small kitchen, serving three hot courses may be very difficult.

The Morning After

We have all given parties, gone to bed then awakened faced with the prospect of cleaning up. If you are giving a party without any staff, it may well be worth arranging for a cleaner on the morning after – not too early, as the chances are that you will have had a very late night. Contact cleaning agencies about two weeks beforehand, giving details about what you require. Cleaners generally charge by the hour.

Dressed for Success

For formal dinners and receptions, butlers dress in striped trousers, a black jacket and vest, with a white shirt and silver and black tie. For less formal occasions, the dress code, which applies to both men and women, has changed. It includes a black jacket, trousers, vest and bowtie with a long white apron. If your party has a theme, the staff could dress in accordance with this – although they must still be comfortable. Theatrical costume rental agencies generally have an excellent range of outfits.

Suggested Staff to Guests Ratios

Dinners One waiting staff per 10 guests
Drinks Parties One bar person and three waiting staff per 50 guests
Informal Fork Buffet Party One bar person and two waiting staff per 30 guests
Formal Seated Buffet Party One waiting staff per 10 guests
Afternoon Teas Two waiting staff per 30 guests

Information to Give Waiting Staff

• Timings, including arrival of guests and when the party is expected to finish
• Number of guests
• Menu
• Drinks and wines (do they need decanting?) and how they will be served
• Any guests who require a special diet or drinks
• Where the linen, china, cutlery and glassware are stored
• How you would like tables and bars to be set
• Where coats and bags should go
• Instructions to clear ashtrays regularly and replace them with clean ones
• Where the bathrooms are for the guests, with instructions to maintain their tidiness during the party
• Instructions to tidy the reception area during dinner and to clear everything away and wash up
• Where coffee is to be served

In the decoration of the party space – be it a room or rooms at home, a tent or a rented location – your dreams and desires can begin to take shape. Much depends on the style or theme of your party which can be brought to life by your chosen decorations.

room transformations

In the early planning stages you will have started to think about possible themes for your party. If you are unsure about what might work well, discuss your plans with family and friends – they will enjoy sharing ideas. For example, you may like to recreate a style from a bygone era. Ask friends to give practical help, too, in decorating the party space. Most people welcome the chance to be creative, and if you give them clear instructions as to what you want, you will be amazed at the results. For ideas, look in magazines and books where a wealth of inspiration is to be found. In the midst of this planning do not forget your budget – if it is realistic, keep within it.

Changing Rooms

One of the easiest mistakes to make when decorating for a party is to get carried away with ideas and tend towards over-decorating a space. Be aware that you do not want the finished room to look fussy and become overpowering to guests. There are infinite ways to adapt any room very subtly with only a little bit of effort – for example, a Moroccan-style party is created by dispensing with chairs and replacing them with large cushions covered in richly colored fabrics for guests to sit on. For any theme, draw attention to interesting areas, such as windows and pretty corners of the room, by placing candles

and small pots of flowers or plants on windowsills or other surfaces. For children's parties, cover the table with thick, plain white paper and fill paper cups with crayons so that children can amuse themselves by becoming artists. You may also like to write their names on balloons tied to the backs of chairs.

Magical Transformations in Tents

Most tents tend to be decorated with flowers. If you want to create a theme, a prop-rental company is a good source of interesting pieces. Take a look around at what they have in stock and it is bound to give you some ideas – you will be surprised at the effects that can be achieved. Around the walls of a tent, branches of trees cut and arranged to represent a wood or hedge look extremely attractive, as do climbing plants entwined around trellis – the plants can be transferred to the garden after the party.

Dance floors must be well defined, with small, round tables and chairs placed around them and the areas divided with a device as simple as low picket fencing or as grand as statues at each corner and an arbor of flowers. By scattering the floor of a tent with lavender flowers or dried herbs, the scent will be released as guests walk over them.

WINDOWS ON THE WORLD

WINDOWS OF A ROOM OR TENT CAN BE TRANSFORMED BY DRAPING INEXPENSIVE COLORED FABRIC ACROSS THEM. IF YOU WANT TO PERSONALIZE THE MATERIAL, GLUE ON FAKE JEWELS OR STENCIL AN INTERESTING DESIGN ONTO IT.

Food and flowers are two great passions of mine. Flowers bring warmth and life into the home. It is not necessary to have grand, costly arrangements – a single vase with a perfect bloom is just as pleasing. You can always gather up branches of blossom or put out small posies of fresh herbs to scent and brighten a room.

flower festival

Think carefully about the style of arrangement you prefer and your budget. There are many inexpensive ways to use plants, flowers and foliage to decorate a room. Try visiting flower markets early in the morning (one of my great joys) to see what is available. If buying from florists, place your order ahead of time to make sure that you have the flowers you want on the day of the party. Remember to allow time for the blooms to open, so that they are perfect on the day. Do not buy flowers on the day of your party that are not yet open because they will be at their best five days later. Always cut and split the stems, then place the flowers in fresh, clean water in a cool place until you are ready to arrange them.

SEASONAL SPECIALS
MAKE THE MOST OF YOUR MONEY BY ALWAYS BUYING FLOWERS AND PLANTS THAT ARE IN SEASON. THE EXCEPTION IS A SPECIAL OCCASION FOR WHICH YOU MAY WANT TO BUY SOMEONE'S FAVORITES.

Blooming Beautiful
Garden roses arranged informally in bowls and silver beakers set a romantic scene at any table. Cut the roses on the day and scatter on the table any petals that have dropped. In spring, decorate the table with pots of bulbs such as paper whites, hyacinths or crocuses – these will continue to brighten up your home long after

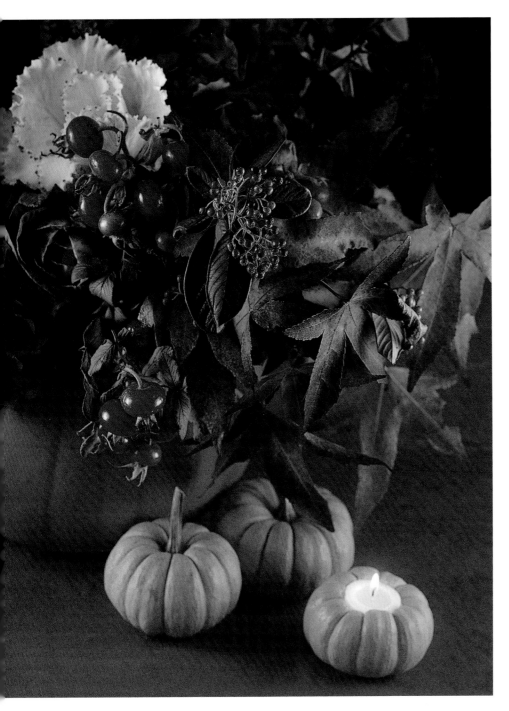

with small pots or posies of sweet-smelling flowers. In a bathroom, too, you can add sea shells and pebbles which will last long after the party.

Garden Glories

If you have a garden, look not only for flowers but for interesting foliage that could be used in your centerpieces or to create displays around the room. For example, berries, fruits, nuts and ornamental corn with colorful foliage make enchanting autumnal arrangements displayed in pumpkins, which can be surrounded by hollowed-out baby squashes with votive candles glowing inside. Ask yourself whether any of your friends or family have a large garden that you could raid.

Pots of Style

Small terracotta pots filled with a mixture of inexpensive plants or herbs look stunning placed along the center of the table. Grouping together pots of herbs in saucers or baskets also looks very attractive. In summer, try trailing geraniums or lavender, or a foliage plant such as Mind Your Own Business. After the party, they can be transferred to the garden or to window boxes.

Hiring a Professional

If you are planning a grand party or wedding for which you need the services of a floral decorator, discuss in detail the type of flowers and arrangements that you would like. A good floral decorator will be very creative and stay within your budget, no matter how large or small. If you are holding the party in a tent, discuss the color of fabrics you will use and have a sample of the lining available. Remember that flowers must complement the style and colors used for table settings and interiors.

PRACTICALLY SPEAKING

WHILE TALL LUXURIANT ARRANGEMENTS ARE FASHIONABLE ON A TABLE, YOUR GUESTS WILL BE HAPPIER IF THEY CAN SEE TO TALK TO THE PERSON SEATED OPPOSITE.

the party. The very reliable and flamboyant gerbera looks stunning in a single vase or try an assortment grouped in a few narrow vases for a colorful effect. A wonderful, and inexpensive, idea of Simon Lycett's for displaying gerberas is to wind colorful pipe cleaners around the stems and group them in the center of the table –

they look like they are on springs! For flowers with bare or unattractive stems, glass cube vases are very versatile. Fill them with gravel or small stones to hide the stems, add water, then arrange your chosen flowers or plants. Aside from the room in which the festivities are held, guests will also visit the bathroom so think of adorning this

During the last decade, candles have once again come into their own. Who cannot recall the joy of lighting candles during a power outage and seeing pools of glowing light transform the room?

candlelight

In the 1980s, I worked with the floral designer Ken Turner and found using candles within displays an education in the romance of candlelight for parties. Today candles are available in many styles and colors, with a vast range of pretty containers. The effects that can be created are almost infinite – but it was Ken who first lit the way!

A NECESSARY NOTE OF CAUTION
REMEMBER NEVER TO LEAVE CANDLES UNATTENDED, ESPECIALLY INDOORS.

Candlelit Dinners
When planning your party, consider using candles to light rooms and tables. Their flickering light dances over table settings and interiors to give a warm, sensuous and magical atmosphere. For formal dinners, long candles in tall candlesticks with small shades on top look wonderfully elegant. They cast a warm glow over the table, creating reflections on the silver and glassware and bringing them to life.

CREATING A CENTERPIECE
FOR AN ENCHANTING FOCAL POINT, GROUP CANDLES IN VARIOUS SHAPES, SIZES AND COLORS IN THE CENTER OF THE TABLE.

Scents of Occasion
For a dinner party, it is best not to use heavily scented candles on the table as they will interfere with delicious food smells. On the other hand, lighting scented candles does help to neutralize any tobacco smells if you have smokers at a party. Scented candles also make a world of difference in a tent, since they can complement the fragrance of flowers and remove the musty smell that sometimes pervades a tent.

Clever Candleholders
Ideal candleholders can be made by cutting patterns in hollowed-out fruit and vegetables. Try with oranges, lemons, apples, artichokes, pumpkins

or squashes. Such candleholders will add wit and humor to a table or terrace. Other decorative options include wrapping thick pillar candles with sheets of sushi seaweed (nori) secured with raffia or pins, or placing small candles in your favorite shells or inside hollowed-out coconut shells. At Christmas, surround candles with cinnamon sticks tied in place with gold cord. For a soft, feminine effect, wrap candles with paper doilies tied with ribbon. Alternatively, to create a tropical look, cut snake grass into lengths and tie it around candles using thick garden twine. For further impact, make holders from thick bamboo cut into varying lengths to surround the bases of tall candles.

THEATRICAL EFFECTS

To create a sense of drama, stand tall, wrought-iron candelabras in corners of the room or on tables. (Use only non-drip candles, and keep them a way from drafts.)

Outdoor Lighting

Using candles along paths and drives is a wonderful way of welcoming guests. We place thick pillar candles inside brown paper bags filled with fine builder's sand to light the way. Or, on a summer's evening, hang lanterns from trees. These are easy to make from tin cans in which you pierce holes to form a pattern of perforations. Place a votive candle inside each one, attach loops of wire to the tops and hang them from trees and shrubs to create areas of glowing light in the garden.

Extra-Special Candles

When using votive candles in glass holders, try wrapping the holders with pretty leaves, flower petals, grasses or herbs. Or, spray the holders with glue so that you can decorate them with nuts, spices, and dried lemon and orange slices. To create lively splashes of color, wrap cellophane around the holders. For table settings, place cards tied around votive candles look very pretty.

Flowers and candles bring a touch of enchantment to table settings. Cover uninteresting tables with attractive cloths that you already have at home. Look in cupboards and drawers for interesting fabric items such as a pretty sheet, blanket or rug if you are short of ideas – it is surprising how good these can look.

table settings

Gather together your favorite pieces of china and glassware and arrange them on the table to see the effect. If you have a long table use lengths of fabric as a runner down the center, or along the sides to replace traditional place-mats. You could take the theme further by tying napkins with fabric strips to match the tablecloth or runner. Napkins can be cut in any shape or size from matching or contrasting fabrics. Other options for improvised napkins include scrim, jacquard tea towels, or scarves – let your imagination run riot (see page 57 for more ideas). Large tropical leaves, such as banana leaves, can replace placemats.

PLACE CARDS

ONE FUN WAY TO PERSONALIZE YOUR TABLE IS TO PREPARE PLACE NAMES FOR EACH GUEST SO THEY KNOW WHERE THEY ARE SITTING. KEEP IT LEGIBLE AND YOU CAN BE AS ORIGINAL AS YOU LIKE – WRITE NAMES ON LUGGAGE LABELS, GLOSSY LEAVES, MASKS, BALLOONS OR PIECES OF PAPER TUCKED NEATLY INTO FOLDED NAPKINS.

Ringing the Changes

Sometimes when entertaining informally, I get inspired to do something out of the ordinary with my table setting – some ideas take very little effort (and can be surprisingly practical). Why not use different china, glassware and cutlery for each course. If you need extra linen or tableware, ask friends if they could lend items that will match your theme. In place of flower arrangements on dining tables, piles of smooth pebbles with tiny candles look delightful and create a soothing mood. In winter, make piles of spices such as star anise, cinnamon and cloves, placing candles inside hollowed-out oranges. For an autumn theme, fill bowls with polished horse chestnuts, some still in their prickly, citrus-green shells, and golden leaves.

Edible Decorations

Baskets of vegetables and herbs or figs and whole or halved pomegranates look stunning, or in summer, pile glowing, deep-red cherries in bowls. Alternatively, bowls of sweets in myriad colors, shapes and sizes look fun and attractive. Salt and pepper can be presented in an assortment of interesting containers, from shells and tiny flowerpots to large wooden bowls and hollowed-out miniature vegetables. Butter can be rolled into balls, mixed with herbs if desired, and placed on edible leaves or small, round glass coasters, or smoothed into colored-glass candle holders. On buffet tables, use fruit and vegetable decorations to emphasize the food you are serving. Tall glass vases filled with lemons and limes enhance bars greatly. Hollowed-out pumpkins make enchanting natural holders for food; warm them in the oven for hot food. Banana leaves look stunning shaped into serving bowls, but do not use them for liquid food as they will leak. I also love disguising serving bowls inside baskets.

ORIENTAL SETTING

MATCH YOUR TABLESETTING TO YOUR FOOD – AT AN ORIENTAL MEAL, SUBSTITUTE CHOPSTICKS AND RICE BOWLS FOR CUTLERY AND PLATES AND PLACE SAUCERS OF SOY AND CHILI SAUCE ALONG THE TABLE.

formal dining

For a large, formal dinner party, display table numbers, letters or names on stands so that guests can identify their table. If you are theming your party, you can have fun naming the tables and designing the name cards. We arranged a July 4th party for which each table was named after an American state and the name cards on the tables were shaped like the state they identified.

You may have a friend or relative who has wonderful handwriting, or wish to engage the services of a calligrapher to write the cards. Ask how long they will take to complete the job, and as for the printing of invitations, allow for this in the time plan for the party. Supply the correct information for guests' names. A copy of your guest list is useful. Remember to give guests their full names, not simply 'Mr and Mrs William Smith' – give Mrs Smith's name. The style of place cards and menus should complement that of the invitations.

A STEP TOO FAR
NEVER THEME FOOD COLORS TO MATCH THE TABLEWARE AND LINEN. DO YOU REALLY WANT TO EAT PURPLE FOOD OFF A TABLE SET WITH PURPLE TABLEWARE AND DECORATIONS? I KNOW I WOULD NOT!

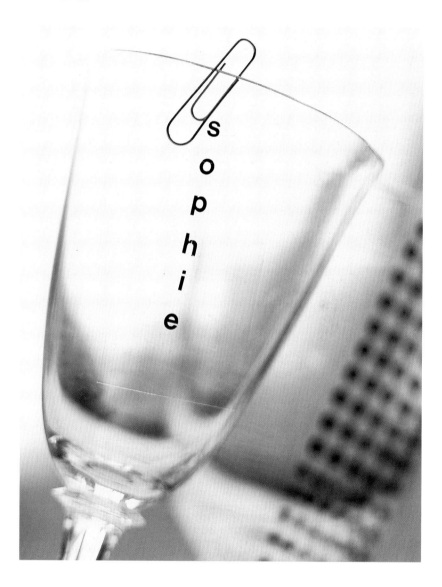

Successful Seating
Seating cards are essential for large parties. Write the guest's name on a small envelope and place a card inside indicating the table where they are seated. Arrange the seating cards on a reception table or counter in alphabetical order so that, as guests arrive, they are given or pick up their own card. In this way, guests can keep their card in a pocket or bag to refer to and there is no crowding around seating plans causing congestion at entrances. Giving out seating cards also provides a good guide to the number of guests that have arrived. If you need to make any last-minute changes to the seating plan, nobody will be the wiser if you write some new seating cards, whereas changing names on seating plans can look a mess.

ON THE MENU
FOR A FUN TALKING POINT AT THE START OF THE MEAL, GIVE YOUR GUESTS A MENU WRITTEN WITH GOLD OR SILVER MARKER PEN ON BRIGHTLY COLORED, THICK CARD.

Menus
When arranging menus for the tables, allow one between two guests. If it is a very special occasion, give the date, and if appropriate, the hosts' names or the name of the person that the celebration is for. If grace is being said, the name of the person saying grace should be included. Other menu information that can be included are the wines to be served, food courses, including coffee, and the speeches (with names of speakers).

classic elegance

To create an elegant and opulent table setting for a truly formal dinner, it helps to stick to a fairly simple scheme based on classical colors and styles. Here, on top of a beautiful white Italian linen tablecloth, the fine gold and white china is picked out by the sparkling gilt-tinged crystal glasses and the rich gold napkin rings. These rings can be made very easily with tassels and cord from any fabric shop, and for your own fabulous fine linen tablecloth to use again and again, just edge good quality linen sheets with runners of lace. To echo the gleam of the polished silverware, you can offer all sorts of accoutrements for the traditional dinner table such as silver salt cellars and pepper pots, candles and beakers. Any manner of personal touches may be added to suit the mood of the occasion – the gorgeous full-blown roses in this case offer glorious luxury and romance while, to me, the wistful young boy gazing into the salt (below) injects a mischievous sense of humor. Once the candles are lit, you can be sure that a table like this will positively shine.

contemporary chic

There are times for a less formal occasion when you can create a setting made up of very individual place settings. A genuinely contemporary table need follow no rules and you can achieve a fantastic explosion of pattern, style or color – the choice is endless. It is easy to mix and match plates and cutlery and you'll find that with just a little care to the juxtaposition of colors you will still achieve a brilliantly coherent setting.

Wooden handles of inexpensive cutlery can be dipped in paint and then you can have great fun painting your own designs or a single-color wash on the plates and bowls with ceramic paints. Why not get each of your guests to design their own plate – it is easy to arrange. Plates lined with tropical leaves or bowls adorned with a single flower will ensure each guest feels his or her place is special.

mostly moroccan

Sometimes you may want to do something a little bit different with your table setting. This table shows how, with a little thought to the theme and style of your party, you can create a stunningly evocative table that can become a talking point in itself.

Inspired by the wonderful flavors and colors of Djiery's Moroccan food on page 100, we have chosen here to recreate the vibrant originality of North African eating. Blue and green tiles on the floor replace the traditional table, and plump cushions make a comfortable alternative to chairs. If you are unwilling to eat off the floor, then a low coffee table could be just as effective.

Colorful Moroccan plates and tea glasses can be rented, but are worth purchasing since they are beautiful and original enough to use when serving any food or drink. If serving Moroccan food, then you could also provide small clay bowls on the table filled with appropriate 'extras' – not just salt and pepper but also almonds, prunes, olives, and of course, harissa. Finally, a few rose petals scattered around the table or in a bowl on the table can be a sensuous touch of decadence.

new ways with napkins

Napkins can change the look of your table setting in almost an instant to create a formal or informal, witty, colorful or even daring statement. To enliven your table settings and complement different themes, try some of the following ideas: tie napkins with ribbons, raffia, lengths of ivy, skeins of hops, gold cord with a fake jewel or heavy cord in a nautical knot, or decide on a style and vary it slightly for each.

There are many types of napkin to buy or make yourself, including traditional linen napkins with hemstitched borders, antique giant French damask napkins, scarves, scrim, tea towels, bandanas, or even pieces of fabric trimmed into shape with pinking sheers. You can fold napkins into elegant shapes such as fans or tall cones, drape them or tie them in one of the ways suggested

earlier, stand them in glasses or make huge piles of bright colors. Whatever you do, the secret of success is to ensure that they are in keeping with the table setting.

HAPPY BIRTHDAY

MAKE A BIRTHDAY LUNCH OR DINNER EXTRA SPECIAL BY FOLDING THE NAPKINS TO LOOK LIKE PRESENTS.

Selecting the right entertainment for your party will set the mood for the night. The choice depends on your budget and the style of your party – you may want to enhance a relaxed atmosphere or create an upbeat mood that could be witty and even a little daring requiring your guests to enter into the party spirit.

it's showtime

Whether it is playing charades or booking a 14-piece dance band with singers to supply the music at a grand dance or wedding, consider what is appropriate to your party. If you are looking for music there is much on offer, from a string quartet, jazz trio, wind quintet, a piano player creating subtle background music or strolling players catching guests' attention to a lively dance. Musical quartets and pianists set the scene perfectly for larger drinks parties. If the room is small, a quieter form of live music, such as a harpist, is recommended.

SETTING THE MOOD

WHEN I GIVE A DINNER PARTY, I CHOOSE THE CDs WITH CARE – JOLLY BUT NOT LOUD AS GUESTS ARRIVE, EBBING TO A QUIET CALM DURING DINNER. IT IS NEVER SO INTRUSIVE THAT GUESTS ARE UNABLE TO CONVERSE.

A Walk on the Wild Side

For table entertainment, magicians are popular, as are caricaturists, palm readers and even face painters. This style of entertainment also helps to break the ice. To make a large event even more memorable, look-alikes to the famous are very amusing and circus performers such as jugglers, fire-eaters, hot-coal walkers and stilt walkers can greet your guests on arrival. A display by tango or salsa dancers, with the great rhythm of the music, is ideal for persuading guests onto the dance floor.

Finding a Disc Jockey

Choosing a DJ is just as important as selecting a live band. The disc jockey needs to be experienced enough to judge the mood of the party. Carefully discuss the music that you would like and be prepared to accept advice. Disc jockeys know the popular music that makes parties go with a swing and keeps guests dancing through the evening. The best means of finding a good disc jockey is always personal recommendation, although it may take some time, energy and research. When planning a large party, such as a wedding or dance, start your search as soon as you have finalized the date and the party location. A location's events manager should help – seeing more acts than most, they are in a unique position to offer advice.

Finding a Band

In your search for a band or any forms of other entertainment, you could consult an entertainment agency who can suit your budget and taste. When considering a band, to see how they present and hear their style of music, try to see them performing, or ask if they have a demo tape or video. Discuss your taste in music with the bandleader – check that your favorite tunes are easy to dance to. Most bands and entertainers have a list of past customers and it is a good idea to contact one to confirm your choice.

Asking the Right Questions

You will be asked to sign a contract, so make sure that you have discussed every detail and check that you know the answers to the following questions:
• What time does the band start and finish playing?
• What time do they intend to set up?
• Will they require a sound check? If so, when? (Not in the middle of pre-dinner drinks!)
• How long is each set, when are the breaks and how long will they last?
• Can the music continue during the breaks with just a few band members playing, or music from a stereo?
• How much will it cost to extend the entertainment beyond the agreed time?
• Are the singer or singers you have chosen named in the contract with the number of band members?
• Does the band require a sound system, and if so, who supplies this?
• Who decides on the playlist and can you order the songs to encourage people onto the dance floor?

Looking After Entertainers

Most entertainers will require plenty of soft drinks and food, as well as an area to change. Locations normally have a designated space for this. If the party is in a tent, arrange for entertainers to have the use of a small area behind the stage. At home, set aside a room large enough for a few people and specify whether smoking is allowed.

The etiquette of party giving and going can send terror into the strongest hearts. For a party to run smoothly and for an atmosphere of conviviality to remain throughout, it helps for host and guests to bear in mind some basic rules of etiquette and good manners. These are some of the more common dilemmas.

party etiquette

Duties as a Host

Your main duty is to give your guests a relaxed and enjoyable party. Some guests will arrive early, and if you have not finished in the kitchen, invite them to join you, give them a drink and finish those last-minute jobs with relaxed conversation. You must be confident, never apologize for yourself, the food or draw attention to guests who do not drink alcohol or are vegetarian. Never drink too much before guests have arrived or before you finish cooking – you need to be in control. If you appear relaxed and confident, then this will rub off on your guests.

Arriving Late

As a guest, always try to inform your host if you are delayed and give an indication of your expected arrival time. As a host, if you know the guest is going to arrive later than the time you planned to serve dinner, I suggest you carry on with your original time plan – people are very understanding.

Making Introductions

We can all recall times when we have walked into a room of strangers and discovered that there is no one to introduce us to other guests. I know some people who have left parties because they have felt excluded. As a host, the importance of introducing your guests to each other cannot be underestimated. At a large party, make your introductions early. Use your ingenuity to introduce people with common interests and remember which guests have professions, friends or relatives in common. Start your party near to the front door so that you can greet each guest and facilitate introductions. A good host is able to put guests at their ease by being a good listener and supplying relaxed and amusing conversation. If you have one guest who does not know many people, wait for an appropriate break in conversation and introduce them to a group, staying for a while to make sure that he or she feels comfortable. If you see that a guest is overwhelmed by someone and feeling trapped in an unwelcome situation – you may receive pleading 'help me' looks – wait for an appropriate moment to rescue them by saying something such as 'You must come and say hello to George. He has been asking if you have arrived.'

Awkward Silences

It is the duty of the host to overcome those moments of awkward silence when a few seconds can feel like hours. A useful 'trick' is to remember an interesting item of news that could be of common interest to one or more of your guests. Alternatively, suggest a suitable, reasonably light-hearted subject, directing it back to a guest to carry on.

Including Children

If are totally against having children at your party, I advise you to write on the invitation that you are unable to accommodate children. If you are inviting them, it is best to arrange some form of entertainment – perhaps a face painter, clown or magician. Alternatively, organize some form of child care. I am strongly of the opinion that no special arrangements should be made for children's food. Just serve the same as you do for the adults only on a smaller scale. Also, be warned – people often tell me that their teenage children can help serve the food or do extra tasks, but in 18 years' party giving, I have rarely found young teenagers to be really willing to help. If you are inviting teenagers, make sure that they have some friends to socialize with – they will probably use another room.

REMEMBERING WHO

I CONFESS THAT I AM NOT VERY GOOD AT REMEMBERING NAMES. I CAN TRY SEVERAL DIFFERENT NAMES AND STILL NOT HAPPEN UPON THE RIGHT ONE. MY TRICK IS TO SAY, SIMPLY, 'IT IS RATHER NOISY IN HERE AND I DID NOT QUITE CATCH YOUR NAME.'

Replying to Invitations

Invitations should be replied to as soon as you have checked your commitments. Do not put off replying until the host has to telephone you.

A HOST PUTS LOTS OF TIME INTO CREATING A MEMORABLE PARTY, SO SHOW YOUR APPRECIATION BY WRITING A 'THANK YOU' NOTE WITHIN THREE DAYS.

Drunken Guests

Dealing with drunken guests is probably one of a host's most difficult tasks. We know that some people have a tendency to drink just a little too much and your duty to your guests is to ensure that the intoxicated person is not a nuisance. Make sure that the person is not driving home – order them a taxi or perhaps offer a bed for the night. Try to be discreet when handling the problem – this is easier in a large crowd than at a smaller party.

The Smoking Dilemma

You can expect some of your guests to smoke and it may be impolite to tell them not to. Most smokers will ask if they can smoke, so if you feel very strongly, request that they smoke in the yard or on the terrace. If you allow them to smoke in the house, open a window, offer plenty of ashtrays and change them frequently. Scented candles help to neutralize the smell.

How Do I Ask My Guests to Leave?

For a dinner party, serve coffee in a separate area or room to encourage guests to move around. Reduce the amount of drink served, and if some people are still there at 3am, offer to start booking taxis. If all else fails, say good night and go to bed! Even the hardiest party animal should take the hint. Our experience is that as soon as the bar closes, guests depart very quickly, so my advice is, if you want guests to leave, stop offering drinks. (The reverse applies too – a steady supply of alcohol will ensure your party continues through to the small hours!)

food & drink

For a party, drinks require as much planning as the menu. Like the food, they need to be carefully thought out to echo the mood of the party. Think about how you will present them, whether you will need garnishes, what sort of glasses will be most appropriate and who is going to serve them.

the party spirit

Large Parties

Make sure that the bar is positioned in a convenient area that is easily accessible and will not become congested with guests. Protect the floor around it with a waterproof floor covering, taping it down to prevent anyone tripping over a corner or edge. Choose a table that is at least 6 feet (2 meters) long and 3 feet (1 meter) high. Cover it with a cloth to the ground as it is useful to be able to store spare glassware and ice coolers under the table. If you are using an electric blender at the table for making cocktails, make sure that there is an electrical outlet near that area of the bar. Tape down the base of the blender to prevent any accidents. If you not want to rent glassware for a large number of guests, consider plastic glasses. These are now available in many wonderful shapes and colors, and most can be used many times.

Small and Informal Gatherings

Enliven the room by making the drinks table or bar look attractive. Cover the table or serving top with a pretty or exotic-looking cloth, and scout around your home to find an unusual and decorative container for the ice. Arrange the glasses in matching rows, each glass complementing the other. If serving fruit juices or fruit cocktails, pour them into jugs or jars and place a ladle next to them. It is a good idea to tie labels around the handles or lids, to

remember which is which, and to allow guests to serve themselves at any time. For an informal party, I like to use fun glasses with wonderful garnishes, such as stems tied with ribbons, ivy or raffia. If there are just a small number of guests, make fruit or herb ice cubes by adding pieces of fresh fruit or herb sprigs to the water in each compartment of the ice tray before freezing. These decorative ice cubes look particularly lovely in glasses of mineral water. For a summer party outdoors, half-fill a large terracotta pot or wooden barrel with ice and use to chill and serve bottled or canned beers. Place the beers on the ice and cover with more ice, leaving a few beers on top – guests will be able to help themselves.

What Drinks to Serve

Appropriate drinks to serve will depend on the style of party, with occasions varying from a formal champagne or cocktail reception to a more casual party with a choice of wines and soft drinks, a barbecue with beers and a bring-a-bottle party. It really depends on what you feel would work for you. For example, you could serve pitchers of Bloody Marys and homemade fruit coolers at a brunch party. When budgeting, a good rule of thumb is to allow half the cost of the food as the budget for the drinks. The drinks you serve should be within the budget you have allowed for.

Setting Up a Bar

Blender
Bottle opener
Cloth for mopping up spills
Cocktail shaker
Corkscrew (a good one)
Crushed ice
Cutting board and knife
Drink napkins to wrap around glasses
Ice bucket or bowl (one for ice cubes and one for crushed ice)
Ice cubes
Ice tongs, or spoon
Jugs, glass and metal
Long spoon
Olives
Slices or twists of lemon, lime and orange
Stirrers
Strainer
Straws
Can opener

Cooling Drinks

To cool champagne, wines, beers and soft drinks, find a large waterproof container – such as a trash can, a galvanized container, a plastic toy box, a large cooler or a wooden half-barrel. When using coolers like these in the home, place inside a large trash bag to protect the floor from condensation. Put in enough ice to cover the bottom of the container, place the bottles in the cooler and cover with ice. If you do not have enough ice, fill the container

with cold water. Once the bottles are submerged they will quickly chill. For larger parties, I would suggest you use separate containers for champagne, wines, beers and soft drinks. To make serving guests quicker and easier, when preparing the drinks, loosen the foil on champagne bottles and remove and replace the corks in white wine bottles. Place the drinks in the ice at least 2 hours before guests arrive.

For a dinner party, place the drinks that require chilling in the refrigerator 2 days before the party and turn the refrigerator to almost the coldest setting. Make your ice cubes at the same time, using trays or bags. You may find that once you have started the food preparations for the party that your refrigerator is not quite big enough to hold all the drink and the food. In the winter this is not a problem – drinks can easily be kept cold outside, but in the summer you may have to be a little more inventive. Fill a sink with cold water and ice for the drinks or be ruthless in removing items from the refrigerator that either are not needed for your party or will not deteriorate at room temperature. Remember the food hygiene rules however (see A Good Cook's Kitchen Guide page 79).

Quantity of Ice Required

For a cocktail party of 50 guests, the amount of ice required for cooling drinks and using in glasses is four 30-lb (13.6kg) bags. You can divide or multiply this number to assess quantities required for different numbers of guests. If the weather is very hot, add 2 more bags.

Glamorous Glassware

There is a wonderful range of glassware available today, both to buy and rent, ranging from classic to fun and even garish. The style you choose will depend on your taste and the type of party you are giving. It may well be worth renting glassware as many rental companies have exciting ranges. The advantage of this, too, is that you can send back dirty glasses for a small extra charge.

Quantity of Glassware Required

When serving champagne, wine or cocktails at large drinks parties and buffets, allow for 2 glasses per person. Some of your guests will then go on to soft drinks, so in addition, allow for 2 glasses per person for soft drinks.

Quantity of Drink Required

FOR A COCKTAIL PARTY (2 HOURS)
Wine or champagne Allow half a bottle per person (to provide $2^1/2$ glasses each)
Cocktails Allow 3 glasses per person
Soft drinks, mineral water allow 2 cups ($1/2$ liter) per person

FOR PRE-DINNER DRINKS
Wine or champagne Allow a third of a bottle per person (to provide $1^1/2$ glasses each)

FOR A DINNER PARTY
White wine Allow a third of a bottle per person
Red wine Allow half a bottle per person
Mineral water Allow a liter per person

I have chosen the cocktails and fresh-fruit drinks on the following pages for their enduring popularity – when we create a party with a cocktail bar, these are the most requested. You will also find that they are relatively easy to make up in jugs for large numbers.

In the recipes, I use freshly blended fruit juices. These will not give the bitter aftertaste that prepared juices can, and the colors are much more vibrant. Most of the cocktails can be prepared in advance, then stored in the refrigerator or on ice. Pour the prepared cocktails into jugs or containers and label with hand-written stickers. Why not also make fun garnishes and look for interesting stirrers and straws to add to the party spirit?

coolest cocktails

Bellini

This delicious summer drink is made with fresh, ripe peaches, which give it its delightful color. To be really authentic use white peaches. MAKES 10

12 ripe peaches, for 3 cups (750ml) juice
1 bottle chilled semi-sweet, good sparkling white wine, or Prosecco

To remove the skins from the ripe peaches, first pour enough water to cover the peaches into a large pan and bring to a boil. Lower the heat, place the peaches in the water and count to 10. Remove them with a slotted spoon and place in a bowl of ice-cold water. Drain, then peel off the skins with a sharp knife. Cut the peaches in half, remove the pit and slice. Place the peach slices in a blender or food processor, and blend to a smooth purée. Strain over a bowl. Pour into a jug, then cover and refrigerate. Chill the sparkling wine for 1 day before serving. To serve, stir the peach juice and pour into a large jug. Add the sparkling white wine and stir until blended. Pour into elegant glasses.

Bloody Mary

This is my favorite recipe of several available, and is definitely worth trying! MAKES A LARGE JUG

1¼ cups (300ml) plain, pepper, chili or lemon-flavored vodka, placed in the freezer
2 cups (500ml) tomato juice
½ cup (100ml) Clamato juice
juice of 4 limes
1½ tsp celery salt
freshly ground black pepper to taste
pinch of sea salt & pinch of sugar
10 drops of West Indian pepper sauce, or 20 drops of Tabasco sauce
2 tbsp Worcestershire sauce
2 tsp freshly grated horseradish
ice cubes
long celery sticks & lime wedges to garnish

Mix together all the ingredients in a jug. Fill a tall glass with ice cubes, pour in the Bloody Mary, and garnish with a celery stick and a wedge of lime. If you prefer a hotter Bloody Mary, add more pepper sauce. To make a Virgin Bloody Mary, mix as above but omit the vodka.

BEST TOMATO JUICE

MAKE YOUR OWN TOMATO JUICE BY BLENDING FRESH TOMATOES IN A BLENDER, OR BUY A GOOD BRAND, TO ENSURE A REALLY GOOD BLOODY MARY THAT HITS THE SPOT INTENDED.

Winter Whisky Warmer

We made this delicious drink for a cocktail party on a freezing January night. It proved very popular, particularly as guests arrived in from the cold – what better way to warm up! MAKES 8

peel of 1 orange & 1 lemon
five 2.5in (5cm) cinnamon sticks
2 cups (½ liter) good Scotch whisky
½ cup (100ml) lime juice
2 tbsp brown sugar
cinnamon sticks, to garnish

Peel the orange and lemon, place in an airtight container and refrigerate. Break the cinnamon sticks into small pieces. Place a stainless steel saucepan over low heat and pour in the whisky. Add the lime juice, sugar, orange and lemon peels, and cinnamon sticks, and stir until the sugar has dissolved and the punch is warm. Do not boil as you will lose the alcohol. Pour into the punch bowl. Ladle the Warmer into a glass and garnish with a cinnamon stick.

PRESERVING PEELINGS

IF CONVENIENT, YOU CAN PEEL THE ORANGE AND LEMON 2 DAYS IN ADVANCE AND STORE THE PEEL IN AN AIRTIGHT CONTAINER IN THE REFRIGERATOR.

Bellini

West Indian Rum Punch

My friend, Steve Camacho, makes the best rum punch I have ever tasted. It takes time to mature but it is well worth the wait! MAKES 12

2½ cups (600ml) light brown rum, such as Mount Gay or Cavalier

7fl oz (200ml) freshly squeezed lime juice (about 12 limes)

1⅔ cups (400ml) sugar syrup made with Demerara raw sugar or any light brown sugar (see page 74)

freshly grated nutmeg

Angostura bitters

ice cubes

lime, to garnish

Mix the essential first 3 ingredients in a large jug, then add the nutmeg. Cover and refrigerate for 36 hours. Add the bitters to the punch and stir. Fill the glasses with ice and pour in the punch. Garnish with a slice of lime. Now put your feet up and enjoy!

CARIBBEAN COCKTAILS

RUM IS A STAPLE INGREDIENT IN THE COCKTAILS OF THE CARIBBEAN AND EACH ISLAND HAS ITS OWN METHOD FOR MAKING A PUNCH. THESE VARY BUT THE GENERAL RULE OF MEASUREMENTS IS 1 OF SOUR, 2 OF SWEET, 3 OF STRONG AND 4 OF WEAK (A GLASS TOPPED WITH ICE).

Champagne Cocktail

I love the French term *eau de vie* (water of life) for fruit-distilled alcohol. All variations combine well with champagne to make unusual champagne cocktails. Experiment, using Kirsch (cherry), Poire William (pear), Mirabelle (plum) or Fraise (strawberry). 1 BOTTLE OF CHAMPAGNE MAKES 5 GLASSES

small sugar lump

Eau de Vie de Framboise (raspberry)

chilled champagne

Place a sugar lump in a tall, elegant champagne flute, then cover with the Eau de Vie, top up with champagne and serve.

West Indian Rum Punch

DAMPING DOWN

ABOUT 30 MINUTES BEFORE IT IS REQUIRED, POUR A LITTLE CHAMPAGNE INTO THE GLASS. THEN WHEN YOU POUR THE CHAMPAGNE (OR OTHER SPARKLING DRINK), IT WILL NOT OVERFLOW THE GLASS.

Piña Colada

The most famous of all cocktails, made well it should be smooth and easy to drink – sometimes too easy! If possible, use fresh pineapple. Have fun serving the drinks in non-traditional 'glasses.' MAKES 16

3¼ cups (800ml) rum, preferably a white rum such as Bacardi

6 cups (1.6 liters) fresh pineapple juice

3 cups (750ml) coconut cream

crushed ice

toasted coconut curls, to garnish (see page 126)

Place all the ingredients in a blender, blend for about 10 seconds, add a handful of crushed ice, then blend for 5 seconds more. Pour into glasses or containers such as hollowed out baby pineapples or coconuts; garnish with coconut curls and serve with straws.

Watermelon Margarita

A drink that looks wonderfully decorative and is delicious made with either tequila or vodka. For a refreshing soft drink, you can omit the tequila. MAKES 20

7½lb (3.5kg) ripe, seedless
   watermelon, rind removed & cut into
   pieces, for 2 quarts (2 liters) juice
10 juicy limes
salt
crushed ice or ice cubes
2 tbsp ginger cordial
3 cups (750ml) tequila or vodka
wedges of watermelon or slices of lime,
   to garnish

If you cannot find seedless watermelon, remove the seeds before blending. (Unfortunately there is no easy way to do this. I advise slicing the watermelon into manageable triangles and then, with the point of a sharp knife, picking out as many as you can. You could also gently shave the most seed-dense areas – this can dislodge quite a few. Place the pieces of watermelon in a blender or food processor, and blend well. Pour into a jug. Cut the limes in half and squeeze out the juice, strain, then add to the watermelon juice. Refrigerate. Salt the rims of the glasses, then half-fill with crushed ice or ice cubes. Add the ginger cordial and tequila to the juice, stir, and pour into the glasses. Garnish with a wedge of watermelon or a slice of lime. The watermelon margarita can be mixed and placed in the refrigerator, or on ice, about 2 hours before serving.

TO SALT THE RIM OF THE GLASS

THIS IS THE REV. FRANK MERCURIO'S FOOLPROOF METHOD. POUR LIME OR LEMON JUICE ONTO A PLATE, THEN COVER WITH AN UNFOLDED TEA TOWEL. SPRINKLE ENOUGH FINE SALT OVER A SECOND PLATE TO COVER IT. MOISTEN THE RIM OF EACH GLASS ON THE TEA TOWEL, THEN DIP AND TWIST BRIEFLY IN THE SALT.

Watermelon Margarita

Strawberry Daiquiri

Strawberry Daiquiri

The first frozen Daiquiri was created in Cuba early this century. Always use fresh strawberries for this drink, and serve in large cocktail glasses with a straw to slurp it up. If you want to garnish it, a slice of strawberry and and some fresh mint, look and taste wonderful. MAKES 7

⅔ cup (150ml) light rum
3 tbsp strawberry liqueur
2 tbsp fresh lime juice
12 large strawberries
5 handfuls of crushed ice
strawberries & mint to garnish

Place the rum, liqueur, lime juice and strawberries in a blender and blend for about 10 seconds, then add the crushed ice and blend for 4 seconds more. Pour into glasses, garnish and serve with straws. Alternatively, blend all the ingredients but omit the crushed ice, then pour into a jug or container. Be careful not to overblend the strawberries as you want to retain a certain amount of texture in the drink. Store in the refrigerator, or on ice, for at least 2 hours before serving. Stir well, then fill glasses with crushed ice and pour in the drink. Garnish with strawberries and mint and add straws.

Classic Margarita

One of the simplest and most refreshing of all cocktails, it is no wonder that the Classic Margarita is one of the all-time favorites. MAKES 25

fine salt for the rims of glasses
1 quart (1 liter) tequila
2 cups (½ liter) triple sec
1 quart (1 liter) fresh lime juice
ice cubes
lime wedges, to garnish

FROZEN MARGARITA

FOR A FROZEN MARGARITA, BLEND ALL THE INGREDIENTS WITH CRUSHED ICE IN A BLENDER. THE RESULT IS SIMPLY THE MOST PERFECT COCKTAIL FOR A SUMMER'S DAY – SALT IN THIS CASE IS NOT NECESSARY.

Salt the rims of the glasses (see page 70). Pour the tequila, triple sec and lime juice into a jug or container and stir. Place in the refrigerator, or on ice, at least 2 hours before serving. To serve, fill medium-sized glasses with ice cubes, pour in the drink and garnish with wedges of lime.

Mai Tai

I first tasted this mouthwatering cocktail in Hawaii – its wonderfully exotic flavor will transport you to the tropics. It is also deceptively alcoholic – a fact the sweetness covers up. MAKES 6

7fl oz (200ml) dark rum
7fl oz (200ml) golden rum
3½fl oz (100ml) triple sec
3½fl oz (100ml) orange-flavored liqueur
3½fl oz (100ml) almond-flavored syrup
juice of 4 limes
1 dash of grenadine
ice cubes
orange slices, to garnish

Pour all the ingredients into a shaker and shake for about 10 seconds, then strain into the glasses. Add ice cubes, stirrers and straws, then garnish with the orange slices.

Moscow Mule

A combination of lime and ginger beer makes this drink extremely refreshing, and it is one of my favorites. It is actually an excellent blend to drink without the alcohol – the ginger beer gives it that essential bite. MAKES 18

3 cups (750ml) vodka
1½ cups (375ml) fresh lime juice
6 cups (1.5 liters) ginger beer
ice cubes
lime wedges to garnish

Mix the ingredients in a large container and pour into jugs. Serve in tall glasses filled with ice, add a stirrer and garnish with a wedge of lime. All the ingredients, apart from the ginger beer, can be mixed at least 2 hours before serving, then placed in the refrigerator or on ice.

Long Island Iced Tea

An innocent-sounding name for a delicious mixture of alcoholic drinks, this is one of the most frequently requested cocktails. Beware though – one glass is usually enough! MAKES 14

7fl oz (200ml) Bacardi or white rum
7fl oz (200ml) gin
7fl oz (200ml) vodka
7fl oz (200ml) Cointreau
7fl oz (200ml) tequila, preferably gold label
7fl oz (200ml) lime juice
1 quart (1 liter) cola
ice cubes
lime wedges to garnish

Pour the rum, gin, vodka, Cointreau and tequila into a jug or container. Place in the refrigerator, or over ice, for at least 2 hours before you plan to serve the drink. Then, when ready, pour the lime juice and cola into the blend of alcohols and stir. Pour into tall glasses filled with ice cubes, then add stirrers and straws and garnish with lime.

Cosmopolitan

This popular drink looks most stylish served in classic cocktail glasses. Before serving, chill the glasses as well as the vodka in the freezer. MAKES 16

2 cups (500ml) vodka
3½fl oz (100ml) Cointreau
3½fl oz (100ml) cranberry juice
3½fl oz (100ml) fresh lime juice
twists of lime, to garnish

Pour all the ingredients, except for the twists of lime, into a jug or container and stir well. Place in the refrigerator, or on ice, at least 2 hours before serving. To serve, pour into iced cocktail glasses and add a delicate twist of lime into each glass.

Terry's Dry Martini

A classic cocktail, the Dry Martini is always in great demand. The best are made by first chilling the gin and glasses in the freezer. Stir or shake to mix – as demonstrated by James Bond – or pour directly into chilled glasses. Garnish with a twist of lemon. If you prefer your Dry Martini made with vodka, choose a good Polish brand. MAKES 10

3⅔ cups (900ml) gin
1 tsp dry vermouth
10 twists of lemon, to garnish

Pour the gin into a jug, then add the vermouth. Stir and place in the freezer at least 2 hours before serving. Pour into classic chilled cocktail glasses and finish with a twist of lemon.

VERMOUTH VARIATION

FOR JUST A HINT OF VERMOUTH IN YOUR MARTINI, MAKE IT IN A COCKTAIL SHAKER. SHAKE ICE AND VERMOUTH TOGETHER WELL THEN STRAIN OUT THE VERMOUTH, PLACING A SLOTTED SPOON OVER THE TOP OF THE SHAKER. NOW ADD THE GIN TO THE SHAKER, SHAKE VIGOROUSLY AND POUR THE FLAVORED GIN INTO CHILLED GLASSES.

Singapore Sling

The origins of this famous cocktail lie in Raffles Hotel, Singapore. Its bright orange color is testament to the fact that it was originally intended as a woman's drink. Today, however, it is very definitely a drink enjoyed by all. MAKES 12

7fl oz (200ml) gin
7fl oz (200ml) cherry brandy
3½fl oz (100ml) cointreau
3½fl oz (100ml) lemon or lime juice
2⅓ cups (600ml) fresh orange juice
2⅓ cups (600ml) fresh pineapple juice
ice cubes
pineapple slices and cherries, to garnish

Place all the ingredients in a shaker and shake for about 10 seconds. Strain into tall glasses filled with ice cubes. Add stirrers and straws, and garnish with pineapple slices and cherries. Alternatively, place all the ingredients in a container, omitting the ice, and stir. Cover and place in the refrigerator.

BRAZILIAN NIGHTS

FOR THE AUTHENTIC BRAZILIAN EXPERIENCE (SEE RIGHT), SEARCH OUT REAL BRAZILIAN RUM — IT HAS A UNIQUELY PIQUANT FLAVOR — AND SERVE YOUR CAIPIRINHA VERY COLD ON A VERY HOT NIGHT. THEN PARTY UNTIL DAWN!

Caipirinha

A Brazilian speciality, this cocktail is my editor's favorite and is easy to make. Since it must be mixed in the glass, the quantities given are for an individual drink. MAKES 1

1 fresh lime, skin well washed, then cut into small segments
1½ tsp sugar
3 tbsp Brazilian rum

Place the lime segments and sugar in an old-fashioned glass. Crush the lime with a spoon to release the juice and stir to dissolve the sugar. Fill the glass with ice, add the rum and stir.

fresh fruit drinks

Sugar Syrup

Most of these fruit drinks, and some of the cocktails, require sugar syrup – you can, if necessary, use a low-calorie sugar substitute. MAKES 1 QUART (1 LITER)

1 quart (1 liter) water
4½ cups (1kg) sugar

Place the water and sugar in a saucepan and bring to a boil. Reduce the heat and stir until all the sugar is dissolved, then remove from the heat and let cool. Pour into a clean container, cover and refrigerate. Sugar syrup will last for a long time chilled.

Watermelon & Lime Cooler

Mexico is known for its fruit coolers – this one reminds me of Mexico's jewel-like colors. MAKES 12

2 quarts (2 liters) watermelon juice (see page 70)
1 cup (250ml) fresh lime juice
3½fl oz (100ml) sugar syrup (left)
ice cubes
melon & lime slices & mint to garnish

Pour the watermelon juice into a jug or large container, add the lime juice and sugar syrup, then stir well. Pour into glasses filled with ice. Garnish with mint and a slice of melon or lime.

Raspberry & Red Currant Frappé

Melon, Apple & Lime Coolade

This fresh combination of flavors makes a truly mouthwatering drink. MAKES 6

2 ripe green melons, sliced, seeds & skin removed, cut into small cubes
1¼ cups (300ml) fresh apple juice, a sharp variety
2 tbsp lime and ginger cordial
ice cubes
melon & lime slices & sprigs of mint to garnish

Place the melon in a blender and process until smooth, then pass through a sieve. Pour the melon juice into a large jug, add the apple juice and the lime and ginger cordial, then stir well. Cover and refrigerate. Pour into glasses filled with ice. Garnish with a melon or lime slice, and a sprig of mint.

Raspberry & Red Currant Frappé

When raspberries and red currants are plentiful, this makes a very refreshing soft drink. MAKES 6

sugar syrup to taste (above left)
4½lb (2kg) raspberries, fresh or frozen
1¼lb (600g) red currants with stalks removed
ice cubes
1¼ cups (300ml) mineral water
sprigs of raspberries, red currants, mint, or basil to garnish

Make the sugar syrup and chill. Place the raspberries in a blender and blend until smooth. Pour this purée into a fine sieve, then use a ladle to press the juice through it until only the seeds remain; repeat with the red currants, blending in the same way. Pour juices into a jug and refrigerate. Fill glasses with ice. Add the mineral water and sugar syrup to the frappé and garnish with fruit or herbs.

Banana & Coconut Sunset

I first tried this soft, creamy drink in the Caribbean, sitting by the sea watching the sun go down and nibbling toasted coconut curls. (They seemed so perfect for the drink that I added them to my recipe.) For me, the splash of grenadine at the top represents the sun setting through the clouds. MAKES 12

6 ripe bananas
4½ cups (1.2 liters) fresh pineapple juice
2 cups (500ml) coconut milk
ice cubes
splash of grenadine
toasted coconut curls (see page 126)

Process the bananas, pineapple juice and coconut milk in a blender until smooth. Pour into a tall glass filled with ice, pour a little grenadine on top and sprinkle with coconut curls.

FREEZING FRUIT

YOU CAN MAKE THE FRUIT PURÉES WHILE FRUIT IS IN SEASON AND FREEZE FOR LATER, BUT DO NOT REFREEZE IF USING FROZEN FRUITS.

Banana & Coconut Sunset

Mango & Passion Fruit Cooler

For me, the mango is a favorite fruit. I had an aunt who used to say that the only way to eat a ripe mango is sitting in the bath or in the sea. It can be quite messy, but there is no need for anyone to sit in the bath or sea to enjoy this drink. Sweet and luxurious, it captures beautifully the taste of the tropics. MAKES 6

4 ripe mangoes, skinned & the flesh cut
   away from the pit
16 ripe passion fruits, flesh scraped away
   from the husks & strained to remove the
   seeds
1¼ cups (300ml) mineral water
sugar syrup to taste (see page 74)
crushed ice or ice cubes
mango slices to garnish

Blend the mango flesh and strain the juice into a jug. Then blend the passion fruit, and strain into the jug of mango juice. Add mineral water and sugar syrup to taste; stir well. Cover and refrigerate. Pour into glasses filled with ice and garnish each with a mango slice.

Pawpaw & Pineapple Cooler

This is a very refreshing drink – if the pineapple juice is a little sharp, add some sugar syrup. MAKES 7

2 pawpaws or papayas, each weighing about
   1lb (450g), skinned, seeded & chopped
   (makes about 2 cups/½ liter)
2 cups (½ liter) fresh pineapple juice
7fl oz (200ml) mineral water
ice cubes
pineapple slices, to garnish

Process the pawpaw in a blender until smooth, then pass through a sieve and pour into a jug. Add the pineapple juice and water; stir well. Cover and refrigerate. Pour into glasses filled with ice. Garnish with pineapple slices on the sides of the glasses.

FRESH FRUIT DRINKS

WITH THE EXCEPTION OF THE BANANA & COCONUT SUNSET, WHICH SHOULD NOT BE MADE MORE THAN 2 HOURS AHEAD, ALL THESE DRINKS CAN BE PREPARED A DAY IN ADVANCE AND THEN CHILLED.

Mango & Passion Fruit Cooler

When you know how many guests to expect and have read the section on Menu Planning (page 32), you need to address the cooking and preparation of the food in a practical manner. Think about the people invited. Are they young or old? Will there be children? Are there special dietary requirements or dislikes?

practical cooking

It's All in the Preparation
All the menus in this book are planned to give you time to be a host as well as the chef. Most can be prepared in advance, with only a little assembling required before serving. Follow the timing guides and you will be able to entertain with great confidence. The guides give the maximum time in advance you can prepare each element of the meal – watch out for marinating however, because this ideally does need to be done at the time specified and not on the day. (If you are very rushed, most marinades will produce a good enough flavor after 2 hours.)

Golden Rules
Give yourself time to read through the recipes before preparing them to familiarize yourself with what is required. I would not advise you to cook any meal for a party that you have not tried before. Friends and family will be more than happy for you to practice on them and may also be good critics. If your timing begins to slip a little on the day do not worry, just carry on; if your guests see that you are anxious, it will make them feel uncomfortable whereas no one minds food served a little later than expected in a relaxed atmosphere.

Food Quantities
The numbers each recipe or menu serves have been worked out on the basis of the average numbers at each sort of party – therefore the dinner and supper menus serve 10 guests while each cocktail food recipe makes enough for 30. With twice or half the number of guests, doubling or halving the recipes will work. Any more or less and you should refer to the chart on food quantities (page 79). When arranging food for buffets using a variety of dishes, you may not be confident as to whether there will be the right amount. In this case, train yourself to imagine an amount of 20 smallish portions – you will soon become expert at it.

MAKING THE MOST OF THE MENUS
THE MENUS ARE DESIGNED TO GIVE A BALANCE OF FLAVORS AND TEXTURES SO IT IS BEST NOT TO MIX AND MATCH. IF THERE IS ONE INGREDIENT THAT YOU HATE, YOU CAN OF COURSE REPLACE IT.

Ovens – Timings and Temperatures
The oven times given are only approximate because every oven behaves differently. Check that the food is properly cooked before removing it from the oven. For cakes, this can be done by pressing the top lightly or inserting a wooden pick. Press meat or fish with your fingers – it will feel firm when cooked. Always allow meat to rest in a warm place before carving – for at least 5 minutes for a small amount and for up to 15 minutes for a large joint. This allows the flesh to retain its juices. Some recipes also suggest refreshing vegetables in cold water to stop them cooking so that they retain their color.

Kitchen Equipment
On page 170 there is a list of what I consider the ideal equipment for a party kitchen. Obviously you will not have everything on the list, but some of the recipes will require you to use a few special utensils such as an ice cream maker or a deep-fat fryer. Do not always feel you have to rush out and buy these – it may well be that a friend can lend you the item you need.

Plate Sizes
I recommend that the size of plates used for every course – first and dessert as well as main – should be a dinner size. Trying to arrange food on smaller plates will make the presentation over-crowded and messy. Always warm plates before using them to serve hot food, although they should not be so hot that the food continues to cook and the sauce starts to separate; you want to be able to handle the plates comfortably.

A HANDY HINT
I KEEP DISPOSABLE GLOVES IN MY KITCHEN AND FIND THEM VERY USEFUL FOR MESSY JOBS SUCH AS HANDLING FOOD THAT STAINS, OR STRONG-SMELLING INGREDIENTS SUCH AS CHILES, GARLIC AND ONIONS TO KEEP THE ODORS FROM YOUR HANDS.

Be Vegetarian Friendly

If one or more of your guests is vegetarian, whatever sort of party you are having, they must not go hungry. The buffets and cocktail food section all include vegetarian dishes and most of the dinner menus in this book can easily be adapted for vegetarians: fill the cabbage parcels on 128 with beans or lentils rather than duck confit; marinate vegetables rather than lamb or chicken in the Moroccan Buffet; and if serving the Mediterranean Dinner (page 133), you could make the risotto with a vegetable stock, garnish it with fresh herbs and offer that as the vegetarian main course. Be sensitive too to the less obvious 'meat' products used in cooking: avoid chicken stock and animal fats – use vegetable-based oils instead and check before adding gelatin. Some people do not eat red meat but will eat chicken and fish, while others may not eat any fish, meat or dairy products. The Vegetarian Dinner on page 142 is completely free of meat and dairy products to allow you to cater for vegetarians and vegans alike – in fact it's delicious enough for all to enjoy.

Well-Stocked Kitchen

Plan a well-stocked pantry and freezer so that you can always cater for unexpected visitors. The foods should be interesting and easy to prepare when it comes to cooking an impromptu meal. For example, there is a wonderful range of dried pastas and bottled sauces on the market today and Parmesan, if stored as I recommend, will keep for a long time. Other excellent staples include potato chips and crackers, ready-made tart shells, cans of Italian beans for salads, risotto rice, vegetable stock cubes, jars of marinated baby artichokes, olives and sundried tomatoes, and cans of tuna and anchovies. Always have a supply of eggs in the refrigerator, too, as a plate of scrambled eggs makes a perfect late-night snack. Whole salamis and slices of ham will keep well if stored correctly. In the freezer, keep some interesting bread, soups that freeze well, Parmesan choux puffs and ice creams. Corn and wheat tortillas are good stand-bys as well, making tasty snacks when filled with salad, sausage and cheese. Always keep a bottle of wine, beers and soft drinks in the refrigerator so that chilled drinks are readily on hand.

A Good Cook's Kitchen Guide
• Always cover food left to cool with a cloth, pierced foil or cheesecloth
• Keep jars with lids; once washed, they are useful for storing dressings, flavored oils or soaking dried fruit
• Make sure that all containers are clean and dry before use
• After a party, dispose of food that has been on a table and in the heat for a long time
• Never put food that is still warm in the refrigerator as this raises its internal temperature and bacteria may start to breed
• Cover food in the refrigerator with either a lid, plastic wrap or foil
• Wrap cheese for the refrigerator in greaseproof paper and muslin before placing it in a plastic bag or box
• Wrap a cooked ham for the refrigerator, such as honey roast, in greaseproof paper and muslin before placing in a container to prevent it from sweating
• Store salad leaves for up to a week in airtight boxes lined with tea towels, wiping the inside of the lid daily to remove any moisture
• Keep all surfaces clean and tidy, and only bring out utensils necessary for the meal you are preparing at the time

A Note on the Recipes
• Work in either imperial or metric when measuring and never mix the two.
• Amounts for chopped herbs are given in an average-sized tea cup measurement (approximately 8fl oz or 1 cup)
• Tablespoon and teaspoon measures are level unless otherwise stated – a set of measuring spoons is invaluable
• Onions, shallots and garlic are all medium size unless specified
• Eggs are large size; buy organic ones, for their flavor and color

• All the vegetables are peeled raw weight unless otherwise stated
• Immune-impaired people, children, the elderly and pregnant women should avoid eating lightly cooked or raw eggs and unpasteurized cheese due to possible salmonella exposure

Food Quantities for Large Parties
The following is a guide to estimating amounts of food required for 1 portion. The raw weights given for fish and meat allow for shrinkage.

MEAT, CHICKEN, DUCK AND GAME
Lamb, beef, veal and pork 8oz (225g) per person for roasting; 5oz (140g) meat per person for stews and casseroles; 4oz (115g) meat per person for a buffet, if serving fish and poultry
Grilled ribs 3 per person
Roasted whole duck serves 2
Roasted large chicken serves 4
Braised or roasted whole pheasant serves 2
Grouse or Cornish game hen 1 bird per person
Quail 2 per person

FISH AND SEAFOOD
Fish 7oz (220g) filleted weight per person for a main course; 4oz (115g) fish per person for a buffet; 3–4oz (85–115g) per person for a buffet, if also serving meat and poultry
Large lobster half per person
Small lobster whole per person
Scallops 2 large for a first course; 4 large cut in half for a main course
Large shrimp 3 per person for grilling

VEGETABLES AND SALAD
Vegetables (prepared) 4oz (115g) per person if served with another vegetable
Salad leaves (washed and picked) 2oz (60g) per person for a first course or buffet; 1oz (30g) for a main course.

POTATOES, RICE, PASTA AND GRAINS
Potatoes (unpeeled) 6oz (180g) per person
Potatoes (washed and scrubbed new) 4oz (115g) per person

Risotto rice 1½oz (45g) per person for a first course; 3oz (85g) per person for a main course
Rice (all other types) 1oz (30g) per person with a main course or in a salad
Dried beans, lentils or grains 2oz (60g) per person to accompany a main course or in a salad
Pasta and noodles 3oz (85g) per person for first course; 5oz (140g) per person for single main course
Pasta and noodles 1oz (30g) per person to with a main course and 2 vegetables

DAIRY PRODUCTS
Cheese 4oz (115g) per person served as a separate course; 2oz (60g) cheese per person for a buffet
Butter 2 tbsp per person for bread and biscuits with cheese
Cream or milk ¼ cup (50ml) per person for coffee or tea
Cream (pouring) ⅓ cup (85ml) per person for desserts
Ice cream ¼ cup (50ml) per person to accompany a dessert; ⅔ cup (140ml) for a single dessert
Eggs 2 per person for omelettes and scrambled eggs

BREADS, DESSERTS AND FRESH FRUIT
Small rolls 2 per person
Large rolls 1½ per person
Bread 2 slices per person
Mousses, parfaits and brûlées 4oz (115g) per person
Fresh fruit (prepared) 4oz (115g) For a buffet, a 12in (30cm) tart gives 10 portions

SAUCES AND DRESSING
Sauce ¼ cup (50ml) per person for a main course
Mayonnaise 2 tbsp per person
Salad dressing 2 tbsp per person

Key to Recipes

To prepare the recipes in advance, follow this key to when to do each step.

1 hour	(1h)	1 week	(1w)
1 day	(1d)	1 month	(1m)

Cocktail parties are the most flexible and inexpensive way of entertaining a large crowd, be they friends, family or business colleagues. By the nature of the party, guests can circulate freely, stay as long as two hours or for only half an hour. For the host, a cocktail party is a very good way of returning hospitality.

for a cocktail party

The drinks served can be as grand and sophisticated as champagne or cocktails from a cocktail bar, or simply wines and beers. Make sure you also have a good supply of soft drinks and mineral water. As a host, you should offer your guests their first drink. Make the drinks table – or bar – accessible so that later on guests can help themselves. If you have help, offer a good range of drinks from serving trays so, as guests enter, they immediately have a selection to choose from. (See page 64 for more on the Party Spirit.)

Serving Canapés in Style

There are many ways to present canapés on serving trays. We serve ours on myriad trays and dishes, from gloriously colored Vietnamese lacquer trays to simple Shaker-style trays to steamer baskets lined with banana leaves. Canapés look best arranged in lines, which offers a good selection and makes a colorful and tempting display. Alternatively, some of our canapés are offered on spoons, forks or poured into shot glasses. Arranging your canapés in a different style can become a talking point with your guests. Do not try to be too clever, however. Simple elegance is best and most dramatic.

Tempting Table Snacks

Some 'nibbles' can be left on tables so that guests can help themselves. I like to fill bowls with Parmesan Choux Sticks, Parmesan Tuiles and Vegetable Crisps (see recipes on page 92). Another idea is to make 'birds' nests' from thin pasta and fill them with quails' eggs, then make an accompanying Chinese salt dip to hand out in a broken hen's egg. Arranging baby vegetables on a bed of herbs in baskets, Shaker-style boxes, glass tanks or trays is also popular. These should be refilled whenever necessary throughout the party – if you have staff, make sure they know this.

Professional Tips
• **Check that you have enough serving dishes – they do not need to match**
• **Canapés should be a single mouthful. Start with a combination of cold canapés, then serve hot ones**
• **Offer a supply of finger napkins ready for sticky fingers**
• **Avoid over-garnishing – it is very distracting**
• **Avoid serving food on fabrics, unless they will be changed each time you replenish your trays with food**

HOW MANY CANAPES?
For a 1–1½-hour cocktail party, allow 8–9 canapes per person. For a 2–2½-hour party, allow 10–12 pieces per person.

hot canapés

Salmon Fish Cakes with Spicy Tomato Dip

This is irresistible comfort food to add warmth to a party. MAKES 30

Spicy Tomato Dip
1 red chile, seeded & chopped
vegetable oil
3 shallots, finely sliced
2 garlic cloves, finely chopped
3 plum tomatoes
2 tsp tomato paste
1¼ cups (300ml) vegetable stock
1 tsp white wine vinegar
2 tsp sugar
salt & freshly ground black pepper

Fish Cakes
1lb (500g) salmon fillet, bones removed
  & cut lengthwise into 2in- (5cm-) wide strips
1lb (500g) potatoes, peeled & quartered

½ cup (½ tea cup) dill, chopped
2 shallots, finely diced
2 tbsp ketchup
1 tbsp anchovy paste
1 tbsp Worcestershire sauce
salt & freshly ground black pepper

Fish Cake Coating
1 cup (100g) all-purpose flour
2 eggs, whisked
1 cup (100g) fine bread crumbs
⅓ cup (60g) white sesame seeds

SPECIAL EQUIPMENT **deep-fat fryer**

(3d) To prepare the dip
Sauté the chile, shallots and garlic in a little oil until soft, then add the tomatoes and tomato paste and cook for 2 minutes more. Add the stock, vinegar and sugar and continue cooking for 10–12 minutes. Let cool, pour into a blender and blend until

Salmon Fish Cakes with Spicy Tomato Dip

smooth. Pass through a fine sieve, season and pour into an airtight container. Refrigerate until needed.

(1d) To prepare the cakes
Bring a pan of salted water to a boil, then lower the heat and simmer. Poach the salmon strips in the water for 3–4 minutes. Drain and let cool. Place potatoes in a pan of cold water, bring to a boil and simmer until soft, then pass through a potato ricer or a fine sieve into a bowl. Flake the salmon into the potato, add the dill, shallots, ketchup, anchovy paste and Worcestershire sauce. Season and mix well. Line a ½in- (1.5cm-) deep, 12 x 8½in (30 x 22cm) pan with parchment paper and pat the mixture into the pan. Cover with more paper, then roll the top with a rolling pin until the mixture is level. Cover and chill.

(8h) To coat the cakes
Cut out the fish cakes using a 1¼in (3.5cm) round cutter and place on a tray. In 3 separate bowls, place the flour, the eggs, and the bread crumbs mixed with sesame seeds. Coat 1 cake with each ingredient in order and repeat for the rest. Return all the fish cakes to the tray, cover and refrigerate.

To assemble
Preheat oven to 220°F/100°C and a deep-fat fryer to 350°F/180°C. Heat the dip slowly in a saucepan. Once the oil is hot, place a few cakes at a time in the fryer to cook until golden brown. Place on a tray lined with paper towels and keep warm in the oven until ready to serve. Pour the sauce into a dipping bowl and push the fish cakes on to forks. Serve.

DUMPLING PREPARATION
THE PRAWN DUMPLINGS (RIGHT) CAN BE MADE 2 WEEKS IN ADVANCE AND FROZEN. THEN JUST DEFROST, STEAM AND SERVE.

Cheese Soufflé Tartlets

A party-food classic. MAKES 30

Pastry Bases
3 sheets phyllo pastry, 18 x 12in (46 x 30cm)
2 tbsp unsalted butter, melted

Soufflés
1¼ cups (300ml) milk
2 tbsp unsalted butter
¼ cup (30g) all-purpose flour
½ cup (60g) aged Cheddar, grated
¼ cup (30g) Parmesan, grated
¼ tsp cayenne pepper
2 tsp hot powdered mustard
salt & freshly ground black pepper
2 eggs, separated
paprika, to dust

(2d) To make the tartlets
Preheat the oven to 375°F/190°C.
Brush a sheet of phyllo pastry with
melted butter, place a second sheet
over the first, brush with butter, then
top with a third sheet and repeat. Cut
out 30 discs with a 2in (5cm) round
cutter. Lay the discs butter side down
in little tartlet molds; press the pastry
into the corners. Half-fill with baking
beans. Bake for 8–9 minutes, or until
golden. Let cool, remove the beans,
then remove the tartlets from the
molds. Store in a cool place.

(8h) To prepare the base
Bring the milk to a boil then barely
simmer. In a pan, melt the butter then
add the flour and mix to a smooth
paste. Add the milk slowly, a little at
a time, mixing until smooth. Cook over
low heat, stirring for 4–5 minutes. Add
both cheeses, cayenne and mustard,
and mix until the cheese has melted.
Remove from heat and check
seasoning. Pour into a bowl and cover
with greaseproof paper. Cool and chill.

(½h) To finish and serve the soufflés
Preheat the oven to 375°F/190°C.
Lay the tartlets on a baking tray. Mix
the egg yolks into the soufflé base. In
an electric mixer, whisk the egg whites
until they form firm peaks. Fold into
the soufflé mix, then pipe or spoon
into the tartlets. Bake in the oven for
4–5 minutes, then transfer to a serving
tray and dust with paprika. Serve.

Prawn Dumplings

These and the Chicken Dumplings
(right) were developed by our Thai
chef, Yani. MAKES 30

12½ oz (350g) fresh prawns, peeled
  (preferably tiger prawns)
3 garlic cloves, finely chopped
¼ cup (¼ tea cup) cilantro roots, washed
  & finely chopped
¼ cup (30g) bamboo shoots, finely chopped
¼ cup (30g) water chestnuts, finely chopped
1 tbsp light soy sauce
1 tbsp soy bean sauce (kecap manis)
1 tbsp sugar
1 tbsp potato flour or cornstarch
1 egg white
1 tbsp light sesame oil
salt & freshly ground black pepper
thirty 3½ in (8.5cm) white dumpling wrappers
½ red pepper, cut into small diamonds

(8h) To make the filling
Mince the prawns in a food processor
and transfer to a mixing bowl. Add the
remaining ingredients, season and mix
well. Cover and refrigerate.

(6h) To fill the dumplings
Lay the dumpling wrappers on a cool
surface. Place 1 teaspoon of the filling
in the center of each wrap. Moisten
the edges of the wrappers with water.
Pinch each wrapper into 8, then make
into rounds with a little of the filling
showing. Top with red pepper. Place on
a tray, cover and refrigerate.

To cook and serve the dumplings
Half-fill a pan with water, bring to a
boil, then reduce to a simmer. Brush a
steamer basket that fits the pan with
a little oil. Put in the dumplings, then
cover and steam for 4–5 minutes.
Remove from the heat and transfer to
a clean steamer lined with a banana
leaf or bamboo sushi mat.

Chicken Dumplings

Eternally popular! MAKES 30

1lb (450g) minced chicken breast
3 garlic cloves, puréed
¼ cup (¼ tea cup) cilantro roots, finely chopped
1 tbsp potato flour or conrstarch
4 green onions, washed, & finely chopped
1 head of bok choy, washed, & finely chopped
1oz (30g) shiitake mushrooms
3 tbsp light soy sauce
1 tbsp soy bean sauce (kecap manis)
¼ tsp white pepper
1 egg yolk
1 tbsp sugar
salt
five 8 x 7in (20.5 x 18cm) nori sheets
30 picked cilantro leaves, to garnish

Dipping Sauce
⅔ cup (150ml) light soy sauce
⅔ cup (150ml) water
1 tbsp sugar
1 tbsp rice wine vinegar

(2d) To make the filling
Mix all the main ingredients in a large
bowl, cover and refrigerate.

(2d) To make the sauce
Combine the ingredients for the sauce
in a pan and bring to a boil. Remove
from the heat when the sugar has
dissolved. Cool, and refrigerate.

(8h) To fill the dumplings
Transfer the filling into a piping bag
fixed with a 1in (2.5cm) nozzle. Lay
a sheet of nori on a sushi mat, then
carefully pipe a line of mixture along
the nearest edge. Brush the opposite
edge with water, then, using the mat,
roll up gently into a cylinder. Cover
tightly in plastic wrap. Repeat for
all the nori, then freeze for 1 hour.
Remove, trim the ends and cut into
1in (2.5cm) rounds. Cover and chill.

To cook and serve the dumplings
Cook following the instructions for
cooking Prawn Dumplings, then garnish
with cilantro, pour the sauce into a
bowl and serve with finger napkins.

cold canapés

Buckwheat Blinis with Smoked Salmon Curls

You can finish these with a little caviar for a touch of sheer luxury. MAKES 30

1lb (450g) long, sliced smoked salmon
1¾ cups (450ml) milk
1 tbsp fresh or dried yeast
pinch of sugar
scant 1 cup (100g) all-purpose flour
1¾ cups (200g) buckwheat flour
4 eggs, separated
1 tbsp unsalted butter, melted
salt & freshly ground black pepper
vegetable oil for cooking the blinis
¾ cup (150g) crème fraîche
¼ cup (60g) caviar (optional)
chives, to garnish

(1d) To prepare the curls
Cut the salmon into 4 x 1in (10 x 2.5cm) pieces, allowing 1 per portion. Line a tray with greaseproof paper. Take one end of each salmon slice between your thumb and index finger and wrap around delicately to create a rose effect. Lay all the 'roses' on a tray, cover with plastic wrap and place in the refrigerator.

(8h) To make the blinis
Heat the milk in a pan over a low heat until warm, then pour into a jug. Stir in the yeast and sugar. Sift the flours into a large metal bowl, add the egg yolks, then whisk in the warm milk until smooth. Cover with a clean, damp tea towel and let rise in a warm place for about 1 hour. Do not allow the batter to rise for any longer then this, otherwise the blinis may taste too yeasty. After rising, stir in the melted butter and season. In a clean bowl, whisk the egg whites until firm and fold into the blini mixture. Heat a little oil in a sauté or frying pan. Pour in enough batter to cover the base of the pan – about ¼in (7mm) thick. When golden brown on one side, turn and repeat for other side. Slide onto a dry cloth to cool, and continue until all the batter is cooked. When cool, cut into rounds with a 1½in (3.5cm) cutter. Store in a cool place.

(4h) To assemble
Place the blinis on a tray. Pipe crème fraîche in the center of the blinis and place the salmon rose on top. Snip the chives roughly, and garnish each blini with a couple of snips. Cover with plastic wrap and refrigerate until needed. If using caviar, top the salmon just before serving and garnish with chives.

Thai Beef Salad

My friend, Alison, had the idea for this in Antigua while we were enjoying a glass of her husband Steve's rum punch (page 69). MAKES 30

Dressing
2 tbsp Thai fish sauce
2 tbsp lime juice
1 tbsp sugar
1 small red chile, seeded & finely diced
1 garlic clove, finely diced
salt & freshly ground black pepper

12oz (320g) sirloin steak
1¼ cups (300ml) light soy sauce
2 medium cucumbers
vegetable oil
½ cup (90g) carrots, finely diced
1 large red onion, finely diced
2 plum tomatoes, peeled, seeded & finely diced
2 stems of lemon grass, finely sliced
2 lime leaves, finely chopped
salt & freshly ground black pepper

(1d) To prepare the dressing
Mix the fish sauce, lime juice, sugar, chile and garlic in a bowl. Season, pour into a small jar, seal and refrigerate.

(1d) To marinate the beef
Coat the beef liberally with soy sauce. Refrigerate in an airtight container.

(1d) To prepare the cups
Cut the cucumber into ½in (1.5cm) slices. With a 1¼in (3.5cm) fluted cutter cut into the center of each slice. Scoop out the middle with a small melon scoop. Invert the cups and lay on a tray lined with a clean cloth, cover with plastic wrap and refrigerate.

(8h) To cook the beef
Preheat the oven to 375°F/180°C. Heat a little oil in a pan. Sear the beef until golden brown on all sides, then transfer to the oven. Cook for about 10 minutes or until medium rare. Remove, let cool and cut into small dice. Refrigerate in an airtight container.

(1h) To assemble
Turn the cucumber cups hollow side up. Place the beef and the vegetables in a bowl, add the lemon grass, lime leaves and dressing. Mix and check the seasoning. With a teaspoon, fill the cups with the beef salad.

Tomato & Mozzarella Shortbreads

These delicious savory biscuits can be served on their own or with pre-dinner drinks. MAKES 30

Shortbread
⅔ cup (115g) all-purpose flour, sifted
7 tbsp unsalted butter, cubed
⅓ cup (85g) Parmesan, grated
pinch of salt
pinch of cayenne pepper
flour, to dust

Topping
8oz (250g) mozzarella, cut from a block
10 cherry tomatoes
1 tbsp Pesto Sauce (see page 169)

(3d) To prepare the shortbreads
Preheat the oven to 375°F/170°C.
Using the paddle blade in an electric mixer, beat the flour and butter on a slow speed to the consistency of bread crumbs. Stop the mixer, add the Parmesan, salt and cayenne pepper, then continue on a slow speed until the mixture begins to combine. On a floured board, pat the mixture into a round, cover with plastic wrap and refrigerate for at least 1 hour. Line a baking tray with greaseproof paper, dust a cool surface with flour and roll out the pastry to about 1/4in (5mm) thick. Cut out the discs with a 1 1/2in (3.5cm) cutter, place on the baking tray and return to the refrigerator for about 1/2 hour. Transfer to the oven and bake for 15-18 minutes, or until golden brown. Remove and let cool. Layer with greaseproof paper and place in an airtight container.

(1d) To prepare the mozzarella
Using a sharp knife, slice the mozzarella into 1/8in (2mm) slices, dipping the knife into hot water after each slice. Cut into 30 rounds with a 1 1/2in (3.5cm) cutter. Lay on a flat tray, cover with plastic wrap and refrigerate.

(6h) To prepare the tomatoes
Slice the cherry tomatoes into 30 rounds. Remove the mozzarella from the refrigerator, place a tomato round on top of each slice and cover with plastic wrap. Return to the refrigerator.

To assemble
Place the shortbreads on a tray. Using a knife, position the discs of mozzarella and tomato in the center of each biscuit, top with pesto and serve.

CELEBRATIONS
Cut these into any shape you like, perhaps to complement a theme — hearts for Valentine's Day or stars for Christmas.

Back to front: Thai Beef Salad, Buckwheat Blinis with Smoked Salmon Curls, Crostini with Asparagus & Wild Mushrooms, Tomato & Mozzarella Shortbreads

Crostini with Asparagus & Wild Mushrooms

For sophisticated party snacks, these tastily topped crostini cannot be beaten. MAKES 30

1 loaf thin French bread (ficelle)
olive oil
salt & freshly ground black pepper
1 small shallot, finely diced
2 tsp white wine vinegar
1/2 tsp sugar
60 spears of asparagus (preferably Thai)
2oz (60g) trumpet or other wild mushrooms, washed & cut into small pieces
6 tbsp mascarpone cheese
30 small shavings of Parmesan

(1d) To prepare the crostini
Preheat the oven to 400°F/200°C. Cut the bread about 1/4in (7mm) thick, on an angle. Brush with olive oil and season. Lay on a baking tray and bake for about 4–5 minutes, or until golden.

Remove from the oven and cool. Layer with greaseproof paper and place in an airtight container.

(2d) To prepare the dressing
Place the shallot, 2 tablespoons of olive oil, vinegar and sugar in a bowl. Mix well, season, pour into a clean jar or bottle and refrigerate.

(1d) To prepare the asparagus
Cut the asparagus into 1 1/4in (3cm) spears and blanch in salted boiling water for about 30 seconds, then drain and refresh in ice water. Store in an airtight container and refrigerate.

To assemble
Lay the crostini on a tray. Toss the mushrooms into the dressing and season; repeat for the asparagus. Pipe a little mascarpone in the center of the crostini. Place 2 spears of asparagus on top and garnish with the mushrooms and Parmesan shavings. Serve.

spoons

Quails' Eggs with Caviar

For sheer indulgence, this recipe cannot be beaten. MAKES 30

15 quails' eggs, hard boiled, peeled & stored
 in water in the refrigerator
½ cup (125g) Sevruga caviar
sixty 1in (2.5cm) snipped chives

To assemble

Lay 30 horn spoons or teaspoons on a tray. Remove the eggs from the refrigerator, drain and dry them with a clean tea towel. Use a sharp knife to cut the eggs in half lengthways, cutting a thin slice off the base of each so that it sits straight on the spoons. Top the eggs with a little caviar and garnish with the chives.

Spiced Indian Crab

You can serve this on spoons and it is also makes an excellent sandwich filling. MAKES 30

1 tbsp vegetable oil
1 medium onion, finely chopped
2 garlic cloves, finely chopped
3 tsp medium-hot curry powder
½ tsp brown mustard seeds
1 tsp ground cumin
½ tsp chili powder
2 tbsp chicken stock
1lb (450g) picked white crab meat, shelled
¼ cup (¼ tea cup) cleaned cilantro leaves
2 lemons, juiced
salt & freshly ground black pepper
4 tbsp yogurt
30 cilantro leaves, picked, washed & dried

(4d) To prepare the paste

Heat the oil in a saucepan, add the onion and garlic and cook until soft, without browning. Add the spices and cook for 2–3 minutes more, then pour in the stock and cook on a low heat for 10 minutes. Transfer to an airtight container. Cool and refrigerate.

(1d) To finish the paste

In a bowl mix the crab meat, cilantro and lemon juice into the spice mixture. Season with salt and pepper, place in an airtight container and chill.

To assemble

Lay teaspoons on a tray. Use a spare teaspoon to mold the crab paste onto each teaspoon. To serve, top each with a little yogurt and a cilantro leaf.

Chinese Duck with Plum Sauce

These neat parcels are a delicious treat certain to impress. MAKES 30

Marinade
4 tbsp light soy sauce
2 tbsp dry sherry
1 tbsp yellow bean paste (miso)
1 tbsp sugar
2 star anise
1 tsp 5-spice powder
2 thin slices of fresh ginger
1¼ cups (300ml) chicken stock

1 large duck breast
vegetable oil for cooking
¼ cucumber, seeded & julienned
2 green onions, julienned
4 tbsp plum sauce

(4d) To prepare the marinade
Place all the marinade ingredients in a saucepan and bring to a boil. Lower the heat and simmer for 10 minutes. Let cool then pour into a container. Cover and refrigerate.

(2d) To cook the duck
Place the marinade in a large pan, bring to a boil and lower the heat. Meanwhile, sauté and sear the duck breast in a little oil until golden brown on all sides; add to the marinade, bring this back to a boil and simmer for 1 minute. Remove from heat and cool. Place the duck breast in a container, pour on the marinade, cover and chill.

(3h) To roll the sliced duck
Cut the duck crosswise into ⅛in- (2mm-) thick slices. Place a few pieces of cucumber and green onion in the center of each duck slice, roll up the slice and place on a tray. Cover with plastic wrap and refrigerate.

To serve
Lay the teaspoons on a tray, place a duck roll in the center of each and coat with a little plum sauce. Serve.

Chinese Duck with Plum Sauce; Spiced Indian Crab

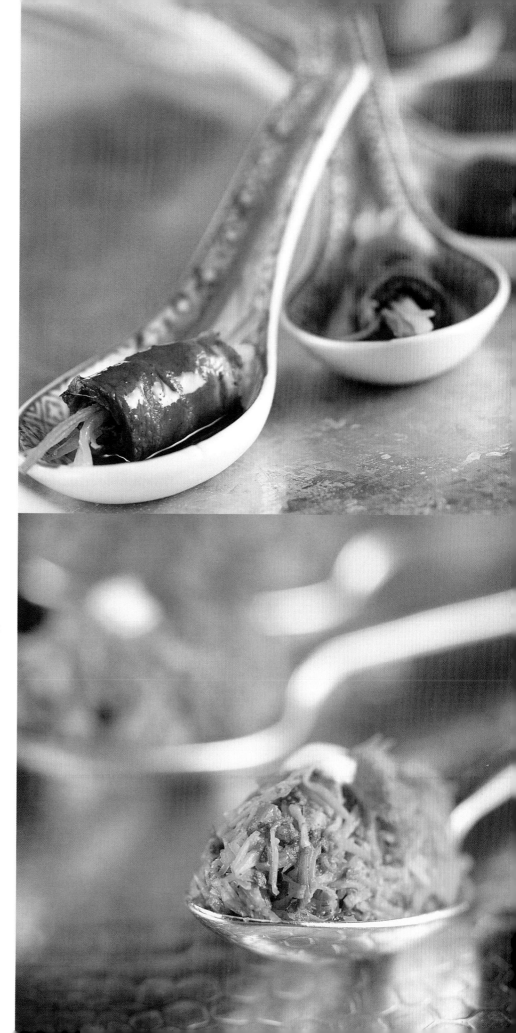

Corn Chowder Soup Sips

You can fill a thermos with this soup and serve it for a warming treat at a winter picnic. MAKES 30

3 fresh ears of corn
4 cups (1 liter) milk
2⅓ cups (600ml) chicken stock
1 tbsp sugar
¼ cup (60g) butter
½ cup (60g) all-purpose flour
1 bunch of green onions, washed and sliced
    into rounds
cayenne pepper
salt & freshly ground black pepper
1¼ cups (300ml) heavy whipping cream
snipped chives, to garnish

 To make the soup
Remove the husks from the corn, cut each of them into 3 portions and place in a medium-sized saucepan. Add the milk, chicken stock and sugar, bring to a boil, then simmer for about 1 hour. Heat the butter until melted in a pan, then add the flour to make a roux; set aside. Remove the corn from the milk, cut off the kernels and place in a bowl. Return the roux to a medium heat, add the milk slowly and mix until smooth. Lower the heat and cook for about 10 minutes, then add the green onions, corn kernels and cayenne pepper, and season. Cook for 10 minutes more, then add the cream and remove from the heat. Let cool, then pour into a blender and blend until smooth. Pass through a sieve into a container, cover and chill.

To assemble
Pour the soup into a pan and bring to a boil. Transfer to a jug, then pour into shot glasses. Garnish with snipped chives and serve.

CHANGING THE CHOWDER
YOU CAN USE THIS METHOD TO MAKE SUBSTANTIAL CHOWDERS OF ALL VARIETIES – TRY SUBSTITUTING SEAFOOD, CHEDDAR CHEESE AND SAGE, CHICKEN OR MIXED VEGETABLES FOR THE CORN.

Gazpacho Soup Sip

soup sips

Gazpacho Soup Sips

Our head chef, Richard Cubbin, brought this recipe from Spain. Unlike other recipes for gazpacho, it omits the bread and I think this makes it all the more delicious. MAKES 30

3 shallots, chopped
3 garlic cloves, chopped
½ cucumber, peeled, seeded & chopped
1 red pepper, seeded & chopped
1 yellow pepper, seeded & chopped
3 plum tomatoes, chopped
2⅓ cups (600ml) tomato juice, preferably a
    thin variety
1 cup (250ml) white wine
2 tbsp olive oil
salt & freshly ground black pepper

 To make the soup
Place the shallots, garlic, cucumber, peppers and tomatoes in a food processor and blend for about 10 seconds until finely chopped, not puréed. Pour into a bowl and stir in the tomato juice, white wine, and olive oil, and season. Cover and refrigerate.

To assemble
Pour into shot glasses and serve.

PERFECT ALL-YEAR ROUND
THESE LITTLE SOUPS CAN BE SERVED IN SHOT GLASSES AS GUESTS ARRIVE. THE HOT SOUPS ARE PARTICULARLY WELCOME ON CHILLY NIGHTS AND THE COLD ARE VERY REFRESHING. YOU CAN ALSO MAKE LARGER AMOUNTS TO SERVE AT LUNCH OR DINNER.

Green Pea Soup Sips

Try this soup very cold for a summer lunch. MAKES 30

3 shallots, finely chopped
2 garlic cloves, finely chopped
vegetable oil
2 quarts (2 liters) vegetable stock
2lb (900g) frozen peas
½ cup (½ tea cup) fresh mint leaves
1¼ cups (300ml) heavy whipping cream
1 small bag of ice cubes
salt & freshly ground black pepper
3 tomatoes, skinned, seeded & finely
  chopped, to garnish

(1d) **To make the soup**
Half fill a sink with cold water. Sauté the shallots and garlic in a little oil for about 2 minutes, without browning. Add the stock, bring to a boil, then add the peas and cook for 5 minutes or until are soft. Remove from the heat and add the mint and cream. Place the ice cubes in the sink of water, and put the pan in the sink. This will prevent the soup from cooking and retain the color of the peas. When cold, season, blend until smooth and pass through a fine sieve into a container. Chill.

To assemble
Pour a little soup into the shot glasses, garnish with the chopped tomato.

Tomato & Lemon Grass Soup Sips

This soup captures the light fresh tastes of eastern cuisine. MAKES 30

vegetable oil
3 shallots, finely chopped
2 garlic cloves, finely chopped
5 stems of lemon grass, finely chopped
1oz (30g) ginger, peeled & finely chopped
10 plum tomatoes, skinned & seeded
1 tbsp tomato paste
1 tbsp sugar
2 quarts (2 liters) vegetable stock
1 tsp tom yum (Thai curry) paste
1 stem of lemon grass, thinly sliced, to
  garnish
30 cilantro leaves, to garnish

(1m) **To make the soup**
Heat a little oil in a pan. Add the shallots, garlic, lemon grass and ginger, cook until soft; add the tomatoes, tomato paste and sugar and cook for 2 more minutes. Then add the tom yum paste and stock and simmer over low heat for 1 hour, pass through a fine sieve into a container, cool and freeze.

To assemble
Pour the defrosted soup into a pan, bring to a boil, then transfer to a jug. Pour into shot glasses, garnish with the lemon grass and cilantro

Green Pea Soup Sip

wraps

Goat Cheese & Rocket Wraps

A deliciously mouthwatering combination. MAKES 30

1 cup (200g) sour cream
3 spinach tortillas, 12in (30cm) rounds
1oz (30g) rocket (arugula), picked & washed
5 tbsp Red Onion Jam (see page 168)
7oz (200g) long log of goat cheese, cut into
   fifteen ½in (1.5cm) pieces
salt & freshly ground black pepper

(1d) **To make the wraps**
Spread the sour cream evenly over the tortillas. Cover the first quarter of the wrap with rocket and onion jam, then top with goat cheese and season. Roll up the wraps, seal with plastic wrap to stop them drying out, and chill.

To serve the wraps
Cut the wraps at an angle and serve.

Parma Ham & Avocado Wraps

Made with ripe avocado and good-quality Parma ham, this is quite sensational. MAKES 30

1 cup (200g) sour cream
3 tomato tortillas, 12in (30cm) rounds
3oz (90g) sliced Parma ham (prosciutto)
2oz (60g) spinach, picked & washed
1 avocado, peeled, pitted & cut into strips
salt & freshly ground black pepper
juice of 1 lemon

(6h) **To prepare the wraps**
Spread the sour cream over the tortillas, followed by the sliced ham, the spinach and the avocado strips. Season, then sprinkle lemon juice over the avocado. Roll up the wraps and seal with plastic wrap.

To serve
Cut the wraps at an angle and serve.

Rice Paper Wraps with a Spicy Soy Dip

These oriental-style wraps look very elegant when served. MAKES 30

Filling

5½oz (150g) fresh tuna, the tail end
½ cup (60g) sugar snap peas, julienned
½ cup (60g) carrot, julienned
½ cup (60g) daikon radish, julienned
1 bunch of watercress, trimmed from the base
1 tbsp sweet soy sauce
juice and zest of 2 limes
1 tbsp seasoned rice vinegar

Spicy Soy Dip

2 tbsp light soy sauce
1 tbsp sugar
1 tbsp seasoned rice vinegar
1 tsp ginger, peeled & finely chopped
1 garlic clove, finely chopped
2 tsp sweet chile sauce
salt & freshly ground black pepper

8 sheets of Vietnamese rice paper, 8½ in (21cm) round
black sesame seeds for garnish

TUNA ALTERNATIVES

IF YOU DO NOT LIKE TUNA, FRESH SALMON OR COOKED TIGER PRAWNS CAN BE USED INSTEAD.

(1d) To prepare the filling and dip
Line a tray with parchment paper. Slice the tuna into wafer-thin discs, place on the tray, cover with plastic wrap and refrigerate. On a separate tray, lay out the vegetables and watercress, cover with plastic wrap and refrigerate. For the marinade, combine the sweet soy sauce, zest and juice of limes, and vinegar in a bowl. Pour into a container and refrigerate. Mix together all the ingredients for the spicy soy dip, pour into a container and chill.

(8h) To make the wraps
Soak the rice paper in a bowl of cold water for 3–4 minutes until soft. Remove from the water and cut on the diagonal into triangle quarters, laying these on a tea towel so that all the points are facing the same way; season. Dip the tuna in the marinade and place on the rice-paper triangles at the opposite side to the points. Place 3 pieces of each vegetable on the tuna and top with cress. Roll up the rice paper, then place each wrap on a tray lined with a cloth. Cover the wraps with plastic wrap to prevent them drying out. Refrigerate until needed.

Rice Paper Wraps with Spicy Soy Dip

To serve

Place the wraps on a tray and sprinkle liberally with sesame seeds. Transfer the dip into a small bowl and serve.

WRAP IT UP

I DISCOVERED WRAPS AS ON A RECENT TRIP TO SAN FRANCISCO AND HAVE ADAPTED THEM FOR CANAPÉS. MADE LARGER THEY ARE FABULOUS FOR PICNICS.

easy snacks

Parmesan Choux Sticks

Eat with a glass of wine. MAKES 30

Egg Wash
2 eggs
water
pinch of salt

pinch of cayenne pepper
3 cups (350g) Parmesan, grated
1¾ cups (450ml) water
1 tbsp salt
1 tbsp sugar
14 tbsp (200g) unsalted butter, cubed
3½ cups (400g) all-purpose flour, sifted
10 eggs

WHEN FRIENDS DROP BY
CHOUX STICKS FREEZE WELL AFTER BAKING.
FOR A READY-MADE COCKTAIL SNACK, COOK
STRAIGHT FROM FREEZER IN A PREHEATED
OVEN FOR 10 MINUTES.

Parmesan Choux Sticks

To prepare the egg wash
Whisk together all the ingredients.
Cover and keep in a cool place.

(8h) **To prepare the sticks**
Preheat the oven to 350°F/180°C.
Line a baking tray with a sheet of
parchment paper. Mix the cayenne
pepper into the Parmesan, and place
in a bowl. In a saucepan, mix the
water, salt, sugar and butter, and
bring to a boil. Add the flour and
beat vigorously until the mixture
comes away from the sides of the
pan. Transfer to an electric mixer with
a paddle beater and beat on a slow
speed until the mixture cools. Add
the eggs 1 at a time. When they are
all incorporated, add 2 cups (250g)
of the Parmesan and cayenne mixture;
mix well. Put a ½in (12mm) nozzle
on a piping bag, fill the bag with ⅔
of the mixture and twist the end. Pipe
along the length of the parchment
paper lining the baking tray. Continue
piping, leaving a 1in (2.5cm) gap
between each row. Brush the top of
each stick with the egg wash and
sprinkle with the remaining Parmesan
and cayenne mixture.

To cook the sticks after making
Preheat the oven to 350°F/180°C.
Place in the oven and cook for 10
minutes, then turn the sticks and cook
for a further 15–20 minutes, or until
the sticks are golden brown and will
stand up when held. Let cool and
place in an airtight container lined
with kitchen paper.

CRISP AND CRUNCHY
IF, WHEN YOU ARE READY TO SERVE THEM,
THE VEGETABLE CRISPS (RIGHT) ARE A
LITTLE SOGGY, PREHEAT THE OVEN TO
275°F/140°C, SPREAD THE CRISPS ON
A BAKING TRAY AND COOK FOR A FEW
MINUTES UNTIL CRISP.

Vegetable Crisps

For a change, toss these in herbs
and spices. SERVES 30

vegetable oil for frying
6 green plantains
2lb (900g) long parsnips
2lb (900g) white sweet potatoes
2lb (900g) orange sweet potatoes
2lb (900g) salsify or white potato,
  washed and peeled
3 medium uncooked beets
sea salt flakes

SPECIAL EQUIPMENT deep-fat fryer

(8h) **To make the vegetable crisps**
Preheat the deep-fat fryer to
325°F/160°C. Slice the vegetables
lengthways as thinly as possible. Make
sure that each slice remains intact
and is uniform in thickness. Place the
slices on a tray, then deep-fry in small
batches until golden brown and crisp.
Drain on paper towels and sprinkle
with sea salt. Cool and store covered.

Parmesan Tuiles

Make these snacks in different
shapes and sizes – they are also
delicious with soup. MAKES 30

3 cups (300g) Parmesan, very finely grated

(8h) **To make the tuiles**
Preheat the oven to 375°F/190°C. Line
a tray with parchment paper or, better
still, a silicon mat. Sprinkle Parmesan
evenly inside several ring cutters.
Remove the cutters and bake for 4
minutes. The tuiles are ready when
slightly bubbly and golden. Remove
from the oven and use a knife to
transfer the discs onto a wire cooling
rack. Let cool and store layered in
parchment paper in an airtight container.

Vegetable Crisps

Buffet parties, like cocktail parties, are usually planned for entertaining a large number of guests in an informal atmosphere for special occasions such as an open house, a christening, or a New Year's Eve party. They are also ideal for brunch occasions such as before important sporting events.

for a buffet party

Buffet parties offer a great opportunity to be expressive in the way that you combine flavors, textures and colors, and lend themselves to themes. We have served fantastic buffets with Indian, Moroccan, Chinese, Thai, Italian, French, American, West Indian and Japanese themes, for example, and there are many more possibilities. One option is to serve canapés followed by beautiful desserts and a cheese buffet. You can be expansive and serve lots of dishes, or decide that simplicity is best and serve only a few. For formal buffets, set an arrangement of a few small tables with fine china and silver. If you are organizing a stand-up buffet, eaten with a fork or chopsticks, you can ensure that guests move around and mingle by serving the dessert in another area or room.

Arranging Tables

Plan ahead, deciding where to place the bar and buffet table so that they are not too near each other, which will create a bottleneck. Calculate how your space and whether you will need to use other rooms or areas – in summer, the yard or deck can become another room. If possible, position the food tables near the kitchen so that you do not have to carry hot dishes too far. For formal, seated buffets, a first course can be placed on the tables just before guests are seated. The main course should be a self-service buffet, but then serve a plated dessert. While adding a touch of formality to an occasion, this also allows guests to move around and chat with each other.

Estimating Food Quantities

Most people tend to over-cater for a buffet. This is fine, as you can always eat what is left the next day (see page 79 for a guide to food quantities). Plan your menu, allowing for each guest to have a little of everything – most of the recipes on the following pages will give 20 portions. From the menus, choose about 6 items for a small gathering and 8 for a larger party, plus desserts and coffee.

Professional Tips

- Arrange food and place china, cutlery and napkins at both ends of each table
- Set aside a separate table for desserts
- Invite guests to serve themselves in small groups
- Present hot food in small dishes that can be replenished frequently
- Always offer guests the opportunity for 'seconds'
- At any sort of buffet, there will be a considerable amount of movement from the guests, so ensure there is enough space around the chairs and tables
- Set up a separate table for coffee and tea – guests can help themselves when they wish

CLEARLY BEAUTIFUL

IF GUESTS ARE STANDING UP TO EAT, SERVE FOOD THAT IS NOT MESSY OR EASY TO SPILL – AVOID THIN SOUPS, OR CASSEROLES OR DESSERTS WITH THIN SAUCES.

street food buffet

Apart from the clam chowder, this menu is designed to be eaten with your fingers, and is therefore ideal for eating while moving around. Perfect for teenage social gatherings and for street parties, the recipes are easy to prepare and offer plenty of interesting flavors, colors and textures.

Manhattan Clam Chowder

Serve this soup from big galvanized containers, ladling it into either disposable cups or sturdy bowls. The clam shells are a vibrant decoration. SERVES 20

vegetable oil
5 medium onions, peeled cut into large dice
8 garlic cloves, finely chopped
1 head of celery, washed, peeled & diced
4oz (120g) smoked bacon, diced

10lb (4.5kg) fresh clams, washed and rinsed of sand and grit
2¹/₃ cups (600ml) dry white wine
7 cups (1.8 liters) thick tomato juice
3¹/₂ quarts (3.6 liters) fish stock
2 tsp Tabasco sauce
2 bay leaves
salt & freshly ground black pepper
5 ears of corn, cooked & kernels removed
2¹/₄lb (1kg) potatoes, diced & cooked
12 plum tomatoes, peeled, seeded & diced
1 tbsp sugar
¹/₂ cup (¹/₂ tea cup) flat-leaf parsley, washed, dried & chopped, to garnish

Manhattan Clam Chowder, Pan Bagnat

(1d) **To make the soup**
Heat a little oil in a saucepan that is large enough to cook the clams. Add the onions, garlic, celery and bacon, then sauté until soft. Turn up the heat and add the clams and white wine. Cover with a lid and cook for about 4–5 minutes until the clams open. Remove the clams from the shells, discarding any that have not opened; reserve 12 for garnishing. Let cool, cover and refrigerate. Return the pan to the heat with the cooking liquid. Add the tomato juice, fish stock, Tabasco and bay leaves and bring to the boil; simmer for 20 minutes. Season, remove from heat and let cool, then place in an airtight container in the refrigerator.

To serve
Bring the soup to a boil, then add the corn, potatoes, clams, tomatoes and sugar. Check the seasoning, pour into a bowl, sprinkle with parsley and garnish with the clams in their shells.

Pan Bagnat

These sandwiches are ideal for a large group and bring back memories of eating on the beach. SERVES 20

two 7oz (200g) chicken breast halves
vegetable oil
4 large ciabatta loaves
6 tbsp Pesto (see page 168)
²/₃ cup (150ml) extra-virgin olive oil
salt & freshly ground black pepper
8 shallots, finely sliced
10 plum tomatoes, sliced
7oz (200g) baby spinach leaves, washed & dried
4 tbsp balsamic vinegar

(1d) **To prepare the pan bagnat**
Preheat the oven to 350°F/180°C. Heat a grill pan. Brush the chicken with a little oil, season and cook until good grill marks are visible. Transfer to a metal tray and cook in the oven for about 10 minutes. Let cool, then cut into slices about ¹/₄in (6mm) thick and

cover. Cut the loaves in half lengthwise, spread each half with pesto, brush with oil and season. To assemble the filling, place a layer of chicken followed by the shallots, tomatoes and spinach; season between each layer and drizzle on the vinegar. Put on the tops of the loaves and wrap each bagnat in plastic wrap. Press with cans or weights for 24 hours in the refrigerator.

To serve
Remove from refrigerator 1 hour before needed, slice into individual servings and arrange in rough piles on large plates.

Chopped Steak with Chunky Tomato Sauce

This tasty alternative to a traditional hamburger cannot be beaten. The sauce works well with sausage and hash too. SERVES 20

MADE TO ORDER
THESE STEAKS DO REQUIRE A BIT OF LAST-MINUTE ATTENTION, SO BE PREPARED.

Chunky Tomato Sauce
vegetable oil
8 shallots, thinly sliced
6 garlic cloves, finely diced
3½ cups (900ml) tomato juice
1 tbsp white wine vinegar
4 tbsp sugar
5 plum tomatoes, skinned, seeded, diced
salt & freshly ground black pepper
1 tsp West Indian pepper sauce (optional)

Chopped Steak
vegetable oil
3 onions, thinly diced
8 garlic cloves, finely diced
7½lb (3.6kg) beef rump roast, coarsely minced
5 tbsp tomato paste
5 tbsp Worcestershire sauce
1 tsp Tabasco sauce
5 egg yolks
2 cups (2 tea cups) flat-leaf parsley, washed, dried & chopped
salt & freshly ground black pepper

20 sesame-seed buns

Garnish
20 slices of tomato
2 Romaine lettuce heads, washed, dried & shredded into large pieces
20 slices of Spanish onion

(2d) **To make the sauce**
Heat a little oil in a saucepan. Add the shallots and garlic, sauté until soft, then add the tomato juice, vinegar and sugar; simmer for about 20 minutes. Add the tomatoes and season. Let cool, cover and place in the refrigerator.

(1d) **To prepare the steak**
Line a tray with greaseproof paper. Heat a little oil in a sauté pan and cook the onions and garlic until soft, without browning; let cool. Place the remaining ingredients, including the cooled onion and garlic, in a large mixing bowl and mix well; season. Mold the mixture into twenty 6oz (180g) steaks and place on a metal tray, layering with greaseproof paper. Cover with plastic wrap and refrigerate.

(½h) **To grill the steak** Heat a grill or grill pan. Brush the steaks with a little oil and grill for 5 minutes on each side or until medium done. Keep warm.

To serve
Pour the tomato sauce into a bowl, then add the pepper sauce if using; stir. Halve the buns, grill and serve with the steak, tomato sauce and garnishes.

Quesadillas with Tomatillo Salsa

Quesadillas are delicious with this salsa; serve with a green salad for supper. SERVES 20

Tomatillo Salsa
3½lb (1.5kg) tomatillos, husks removed
1 onion, finely chopped
½ cup (½ tea cup) cilantro, finely chopped
4 Serrano chiles, chopped
a few drops of lime juice
a few drops of nut oil
salt & freshly ground black pepper

a few avocado slices or crumbly, white cheese such as feta (optional)

Quesadillas
vegetable oil
10 green onions, washed & finely sliced
3 garlic cloves, finely chopped
1¾ lb (800g) refried beans
salt & freshly ground black pepper
½ cup (½ tea cup) cilantro, washed, dried & chopped
eight 10in (25cm) round flour tortillas
2 cups (250g) Monterey Jack cheese, grated
8 plum tomatoes, skinned, seeded & diced
½ cup (100g) jalapeños, chopped (optional)
2 egg whites, beaten
sour cream, to garnish

(8h) **To prepare the salsa**
Grind the tomatillos in a mortar and pestle then transfer to a bowl. Add the remaining ingredients, season and stir well. Cover and place in the refrigerator.

(2h) **To make the quesadillas**
Heat a little oil in a sauté pan, then add the onions and garlic and sauté until soft. Add the beans and cook for about 5 minutes; stir, season and then stir in the cilantro. Let cool. Place 4 tortillas on a work surface and spread with the beans. Sprinkle on the cheese, then top with the tomatoes and jalapeños and season. Brush the edges with the egg whites, place the remaining tortillas on top; seal and place on a baking sheet. Cover and refrigerate.

To serve
Preheat the oven to 350°F/180°C. Warm up the quesadillas for about 10 minutes, then cut into triangles and serve with bowls of sour cream and the tomatillo salsa.

SPECTACULAR SALSA
REMEMBER THAT FOR TACOS AND QUESADILLAS IT IS BEST TO SERVE SALSA VERDE RAW OR MIXED WITH AVOCADO TO MAKE A GUACAMOLE MIXTURE. COOKED SALSA IS FOR ENCHILADAS OR FOR BRAISING MEAT OR CHICKEN.

Chicken Satay Sticks

It is worth taking the time to make these. SERVES 20

Chicken Marinade
3 heaped tbsp coriander seeds
3 heaped tbsp cumin powder
4 whole star anise
2 tbsp mild curry powder
1 tbsp ground turmeric
3 mild red chiles, seeded & chopped
1/2 cup (1/2 tea cup) cilantro leaves, chopped
3 tbsp palm sugar or coarse raw sugar
2/3 cup (150ml) chili sauce
2/3 cup (150ml)) light soy sauce
1¾ cups (450ml) coconut milk
4 garlic cloves, finely chopped
1 tbsp fresh ginger, chopped

Peanut Dipping Sauce
2 tbsp smooth peanut butter
1/3 cup (60g) unsalted roasted peanuts, chopped

five 7oz (200g) chicken breast halves, skin removed & cut into 1½ in (4cm) pieces
vegetable oil
salt & freshly ground black pepper

(3d) To make the marinade and sauce
Dry-fry the spices for 2–3 minutes in a sauté pan, without browning. Remove from heat and let cool. Grind in a food processor and place in a bowl. Add the remaining marinade ingredients and mix well. Pour 2/3 cup (150ml) of this marinade into a separate bowl, mix with the peanut butter and peanuts, cover and chill. Coat the chicken with the rest of the marinade. Cover and refrigerate.

(8h) To skewer the satay
Soak wooden skewers in water for at least 30 minutes. This prevents the sticks from burning during cooking. Place 2 pieces of chicken on each stick, cover and return to the refrigerator.

(½h) To cook the satay
Preheat a grill pan or grill. Brush the chicken lightly with oil, season and grill on each side until golden and firm to the touch. Pour the dipping sauce into a pan and heat.

To serve
Line bamboo steamers or trays with banana leaves, arrange the satay, pour the peanut sauce into a serving bowl and serve. The satay can be served hot or cold.

Marinated Tiger Prawns

This is a great favorite of mine – the sauce can also be served with grilled sea bass or tuna. SERVES 20

Mango Dipping Sauce
2 ripe mangoes, peeled & flesh removed
1 red chile, seeded & finely chopped
1/4 cup (1/4 tea cup) cilantro, chopped
1/4 cup (1/4 tea cup) mint, chopped
2 garlic cloves, finely chopped
juice of 3 limes
salt & freshly ground black pepper

Prawn Marinade
5 tbsp thin, light honey
2 tbsp red Thai curry paste
2 tbsp ginger, finely chopped
juice & zest of 3 limes
60 tiger prawns, shells left on
vegetable oil
salt & freshly ground black pepper

(1d) To make the sauce
Blend the mango flesh in a food processor until smooth. Remove and place in a bowl with the remaining ingredients; season and stir. Cover and place in the refrigerator.

(6h) To marinate the prawns
Mix together all the marinade ingredients in a bowl, then add the prawns. Cover and refrigerate.

(½h) To skewer and cook the prawns
Soak wooden skewers as for the satay. Preheat a grill pan or grill. Skewer the prawns and brush with a little oil; season and grill on both sides until firm to the touch. Keep warm.

To serve the prawns
Pour the dipping sauce into a bowl, arrange the skewers on a serving dish with the sauce and serve.

Focaccia Bruschetta

Experiment with other interesting breads or invent your own toppings. This recipe is enough for 10 of each topping. MAKES 20

Flavored Oil & Bread
2/3 cup (150ml) olive oil
2 garlic cloves, sliced
5 sprigs of thyme
20 slices of focaccia, cut into 4in- (10cm-) long pieces

Mozzarella & Red Pepper Topping
3 garlic cloves
2 shallots, thinly sliced
olive oil
2 tbsp white wine vinegar
4 tbsp Demerara raw sugar
4 red peppers, skinned, seeded, veins removed & cut into strips
2 plum tomatoes, skinned, seeded & diced
salt & freshly ground black pepper
4 fresh mozzarella balls, cut into 20 slices
2 tsp rosemary, roughly chopped
10 Coppa or Parma ham (prosciutto) slices
10 basil leaves, to garnish

Mushroom, Tomato & Rocket Topping
9oz (250g) flat mushrooms, cut into 20 slices
olive oil for grilling
salt & freshly ground black pepper
1 tbsp extra-virgin olive oil
1 tbsp aged balsamic vinegar
2 shallots, thinly sliced
2 garlic cloves, finely chopped
20 baby plum tomatoes
1 tsp sugar
1oz (30g) rocket (arugula), washed & dried
shavings of Parmesan

(2d) To flavor the oil
In a pan, warm the oil and the garlic for about 5 minutes. Remove from heat and let cool. Pour into a jar with a lid, add the thyme and store in a cool place.

(2d) To make the red pepper topping
Finely chop 2 of the garlic cloves. Sauté the shallots and garlic in a little olive oil for about 5 minutes without browning. Add the vinegar and sugar and reduce until syrupy. Add the peppers and

tomatoes, season and cook for 5 more minutes. Let cool then refrigerate in an airtight container. Place the mozzarella in an airtight container. Finely slice the remaining garlic clove, and mix with the rosemary and 3 tablespoons of olive oil, season and pour over the cheese. Cover and refrigerate.

(1h) To prepare the mushroom topping

Preheat a grill pan. Brush the mushrooms with olive oil and season. Grill for 2 minutes on each side or until grill marks are visible; let cool. Pour the olive oil and balsamic vinegar into a bowl, add the shallots and garlic, season, add the mushrooms and toss well. Cover and chill. In a sauté pan, cook the tomatoes in a little olive oil with the sugar until soft. Remove from the heat and cool. Cover and refrigerate.

(8h) To grill the focaccia

Preheat the oven to 350°F/180°C. Heat a grill pan and brush the focaccia lightly with flavored oil. Season and grill on both sides until grill marks are visible. Bake in the oven for 3–4 minutes. Let cool and store in an airtight container in a cool place.

To assemble

Lay out the bruschetta on a dish. On 10 of the breads arrange 2 mushroom slices, 2 tomatoes and a rocket leaf; top with a shaving of Parmesan. Top the other bruschetta with the mozzarella, ham and red pepper topping; garnish with basil leaves and serve.

Marinated Tiger Prawns, Focaccia Bruschetta (Mozarella & Red Pepper Topping; Mushroom, Tomato & Rocket Topping)

moroccan buffet

We are very lucky to have Moroccan chef Djery, and apart from the rosewater cream which one of our pastry chefs developed, these are his family's recipes. Other typical desserts include fresh fruits and sweet pastries purchased from a specialist baker. The only thing you should ever drink is of course mint tea, so Djery's recipe is an essential.

Moroccan Lamb

This popular buffet dish looks great in a traditional tagine. SERVES 20

Harissa Sauce
¼ cup (60g) hot red chile, chopped
4 garlic cloves, chopped
4 tsp cumin seeds, toasted
½ tsp coriander seeds, toasted
salt & freshly ground black pepper
4 red peppers, roasted, skins & seeds removed
2 tbsp olive oil
lemon juice to taste

Lamb Marinade
olive oil to cover
8lb (3.7kg) middle neck of lamb fillet, cubed
2 tbsp ground turmeric
6 tbsp ground cumin
1 cup (1 tea cup) cilantro, chopped
4 medium onions, thinly sliced
⅔ cup (150ml) extra-virgin olive oil
8 garlic cloves, chopped
4 cinnamon sticks
salt & freshly ground black pepper
3½ quarts (3.5 liters) chicken stock
7oz (200g) dried prunes
3 tbsp brown sugar
picked cilantro, to garnish

(1w) To make the harissa sauce
Grind or blend the dry ingredients in a mortar or food processor until smooth, then add the peppers, olive oil

Chicken with Lemon & Olives,
Carrot & Orange Salad (see following page)

and lemon juice and blend for a further 10 seconds. Transfer the paste to a sterilized jar and cover with a layer of olive oil. Seal and refrigerate.

(1d) To marinate the lamb
Put the lamb in an airtight container. Place the dry spices, cilantro, onions, olive oil, garlic, cinnamon sticks, salt and black pepper in a bowl and mix. Rub the mixture into the meat until it is completely coated. Cover with plastic wrap and marinate for 24 hours.

(1d) To cook the lamb
Heat a little olive oil in a large pan. When it starts to smoke, add the lamb (in batches if necessary) and cook until browned (about 8 minutes). Add the stock, prunes and sugar; cover. Cook on low heat for about 45 minutes or until the lamb is tender. Remove the meat from the pan with a slotted spoon, place in an airtight container and set aside. Turn up the heat to reduce the remaining sauce by half. It is ready when shiny and it coats the back of a spoon. Pour the sauce over the lamb and let cool. Cover and refrigerate.

To assemble
Preheat the oven to 250°F/130°C. Warm the tagine or serving bowl. In a large pan, bring the lamb to a boil then reduce the heat to low. Check the seasoning and transfer the lamb to the tagine or bowl. Garnish with cilantro.

Chicken with Lemon & Olives

This is great for serving chicken to a large group, especially since it is so easy to prepare. SERVES 20

Chicken Marinade
20 skinless chicken breast halves
2 tsp saffron strands
2 tbsp ground cumin
4 garlic cloves, chopped
1/2 cup (1/2 tea cup) chopped cilantro
2/3 cup (150 ml) olive oil
4 large onions, finely diced
3 quarts (3 liters) chicken stock
2 lemons
1lb (450g) pitted green olives
salt & freshly ground black pepper
2 tbsp shelled, unsalted pistachio nuts
picked cilantro or mint, to garnish

(2d) To marinate the chicken
Cut the chicken into 1 1/2in (4cm) cubes, or leave whole; place in a bowl. Add the saffron, cumin, garlic, cilantro and olive oil. Cover and place in the refrigerator for 24 hours.

(1h) To cook the chicken
Heat a little olive oil in a large saucepan. When it starts to smoke, add the chicken and onions and cook until lightly golden. Add the chicken stock, bring to a boil then simmer for about 10 minutes. Remove the chicken from the sauce using a slotted spoon and place in an airtight container. Increase the heat and reduce the sauce by about half. Pour over the chicken and let cool. When cold, cover and place in the refrigerator. Peel and slice the lemons, about 1/8in (4mm) thick. Place in an airtight container and refrigerate.

To assemble
Preheat the oven to 250°F/130°C. Heat the serving dish. Place the chicken in a large saucepan and bring to a boil. Add the green olives and sliced lemons; reduce to a low heat and check the seasoning. Transfer to the serving dish and scatter on the pistachio nuts. Garnish with picked cilantro or mint.

Chermoula Marinated Sea Bass

Djery recommends daurade (bream) or large red mullet as excellent alternatives to sea bass. SERVES 20

Sea Bass Marinade
1 3/4 cups (450ml) extra-virgin olive oil
4 medium onions, peeled & finely chopped
6 garlic cloves, finely chopped
2 tbsp ground cumin
2 tsp paprika
1 tsp cayenne pepper
juice of 4 lemons
2 large sea bass (total weight of 8lb/3.6kg), whole, scaled & fins removed
salt & freshly ground black pepper
1 1/4 cups (300ml) water

Garnish
1 cup (1 tea cup) cilantro, washed, dried & chopped
1 cup (1 tea cup) flat-leaf parsely, washed, dried & chopped
15 plum tomatoes, skinned, seeded & diced

(8h) To prepare the marinade
Heat a large sauté pan and when hot, add the olive oil, onions, garlic, spices and lemon juice. Sauté for about 3–5 minutes, without browning. Remove from the heat, place in a bowl and let cool. Place the fish on a baking pan that will fit in the oven. Make 6 slashes on each side; season with salt and freshly ground black pepper. When the marinade is cold, rub it into the fish on both sides. Cover and place in the refrigerator for at least 6 hours.

(1h) To cook the sea bass
Remove the fish from the refrigerator at least 20 minutes before baking. Preheat the oven to 375°F/190°C. Pour the water into the baking pan, place the fish in as well, cover tightly with foil and bake for 45 minutes to 1 hour. Remove and keep warm.

To serve
Remove the foil and place the fish on a warm serving platter. Scatter on the herbs and tomatoes and serve.

Carrot & Orange Salad

A refreshing foil to the highly flavored main dishes. SERVES 20

4lb (1.8kg) carrots, coarsely grated
8 large oranges, preferably Valencia, peeled, segmented & seeds removed
zest of 2 oranges
1 3/4 cups (250g) large raisins

Dressing
2 tsp ground cumin
1 tsp ground cinnamon
1 tsp sugar
juice of 2 lemons
2 tbsp orange flower water (optional)
1 1/4 cups (300ml) olive oil
salt & freshly ground black pepper
1 1/2 cups (1 1/2 tea cups) flat-leaf parsley, washed, dried & chopped
2 tbsp toasted sesame seeds

(8h) To prepare the salad
Place the carrots, oranges, orange zest and raisins in an airtight container; cover and refrigerate.

(8h) To prepare the dressing
Place the cumin, cinnamon and sugar in a bowl. Add the lemon juice and orange flower water; mix. Pour in the oil and mix. Season and pour into a jar with a lid. Store in a cool place.

To assemble
Remove the salad from the refrigerator. Pour the dressing over it, add the parsley, toasted sesame seeds and toss well. Check the seasoning and arrange in a salad bowl.

DJERY'S MINT TEA
TO MAKE 10 MOROCCAN GLASSES OF TEA, POUR 7 CUPS (1.8 LITERS) BOILING WATER INTO A TEAPOT CONTAINING 4 TEASPOONS JAPANESE GREEN TEA AND 2 CUPS (2 TEA CUPS) CHOPPED FRESH MINT. ADD SUGAR TO TASTE. POURING THE WATER FROM A GOOD HEIGHT HELPS TO OXYGENATE THE TEA. LET STAND FOR 5 MINUTES THEN POUR INTO TEA GLASSES. SERVE WITH EXTRA SUGAR.

Couscous

If you are having vegetarians to dinner, this can make an interesting salad for a first course. SERVES 20

6 cups (1.5 liters) vegetable stock
2/3 cup (150ml) olive oil
2lb (900g) couscous
2 cups (2 tea cups) chopped cilantro
2 cups (2 tea cups) chopped parsley
2 cups (300g) dried apricots, cut into thirds
juice of 4 limes
3 cups (350g) whole roasted almonds, skins removed
salt & freshly ground black pepper
picked cilantro to garnish

(1d) To prepare the couscous

In a pan, bring the vegetable stock and olive oil to a boil. Place the couscous in a large bowl and pour in the boiling vegetable stock and olive oil. Cover with plastic wrap for 10 minutes; remove the plastic wrap and break up the grains with your hands. When completely separate, re-cover and then refrigerate when cool.

(6h) To prepare the herbs and fruit

Place the herbs, apricots, lime juice and two thirds of the almonds in an airtight container; mix. Cover and chill.

To assemble

Preheat the oven to 250°F/130°C. Heat the serving bowl. Warm the couscous in a microwave for about 4 minutes. Alternatively, place the couscous in a fine sieve over a pan of simmering water. When hot, transfer to the serving bowl and add the prepared herbs, apricots, lime juice and almonds. Season and mix well. Garnish with cilantro and remaining almonds.

USING GOLD LEAF

USE ONLY 22 CARAT GOLD LEAF TO DECORATE THE MOROCCAN ROSEWATER CREAM (RIGHT). THE BEST METHOD IS TO PICK THE LEAF UP WITH A GILDERS BRUSH MADE FROM SQUIRREL HAIR AND LET IT FLUTTER ONTO THE DESSERT (CHECKING FIRST THAT YOUR ROOM IS DRAFT-FREE!)

Rosewater Cream and Moroccan pastries

Rosewater Cream

Make this delicious cream in individual molds or in one 7 cup (1.9 liter) mold as here. SERVES 20

9 gelatin leaves (or 2 pkgs. granulated gelatin)
4½ cups (1.2 liters) whole milk
3 vanilla beans, split
10 egg yolks
¾ cup (180g) superfine sugar
3 tbsp rosewater
2 tsp lemon juice
2⅓ cups (600ml) heavy whipping cream

Garnish

edible gold leaf (optional)
rose petals
pistachio nuts, shelled & unsalted

(2d) To make the cream

Cover the gelatin with cold water and set aside. Pour the milk into a heavy-bottomed saucepan. Scrape out the vanilla seeds from the pods, then add the seeds and pods to the milk and bring to a boil. Remove the pods. In an electric mixer, whisk the egg yolks and sugar until smooth. Turn down the speed and pour the boiling milk in a steady stream onto the egg mixture; whisk until smooth. Pour the mixture back into the pan, add the rosewater and lemon juice and return to the heat. Continue to whisk until the mixture coats the back of a spoon. Remove from the heat. Drain the gelatin, squeeze out the excess water and stir into the hot mixture. Pass through a fine sieve into a large bowl; let cool then whisk until the cream just holds its shape. When the rosewater cream is cold, fold in the cream; pour into the mold and place on a tray. Cover and refrigerate.

To assemble

Fill a large bowl or sink with hot water and dip the mold into the water to about ½in (1.5mm) from the top. Remove when the mold feels warm and place the serving platter on top; turn over quickly. Leave for about 2 minutes then remove the mold. Decorate the top with gold leaf if using and scatter on the rose petals and nuts. Serve with Moroccan pastries or fresh fruit.

east-west buffet

The people I work with all, like me, love oriental food. Our executive chef, Steve Bailey, has a particular flair and this is the menu that he has developed over the years. Take time to search out the unusual ingredients – nowadays the majority can be found in supermarkets and most towns have a good ethnic shop for the rest. Chilled dry white wines and Asian lagers are the perfect drinks to serve.

Warm Beef Salad with Orange Dressing

This recipe epitomizes East meets West cuisine. It is easy to prepare, too – just remember to marinatde the beef for at least a day. SERVES 20

Beef Marinade
1¼ cups (300ml) light soy sauce
1¼ cups (300ml) mushroom soy sauce
2 tbsp cornstarch
5 tbsp light brown sugar
4 tbsp chili oil
4 red chiles, seeded & finely chopped
5½lb (2.5kg) rump roast, any fat removed, cut into finger-size pieces.

Orange Dressing
1 tbsp sugar
juice & zest of 3 small (ideally blood) oranges
juice & zest of 1 lemon
3 tbsp peanut oil
2 tbsp chili oil
½ tsp cayenne pepper
4 garlic cloves, chopped
⅔ cup (150ml) aged balsamic vinegar
4 tbsp light soy sauce

Salad
11oz (300g) baby spinach, picked, washed & dried
1lb (450g) mixed salad greens, washed, dried & torn into small pieces
10 green onions, washed & thinly sliced
2 cups (2 tea cups) mint leaves, washed & dried
1 cup (1 tea cup) snipped chives
½ cup (½ tea cup) cilantro leaves, washed & dried
deep-fried rice sticks, to garnish (optional)

(1d) To marinate the beef
Place the marinade ingredients in a large bowl, mix well and add the beef. Cover and place in the refrigerator.

(1d) To make the orange dressing
Combine all the ingredients in a jar with a lid, shake well, cover and refrigerate.

To assemble the salad
Place the leafy salad ingredients in a serving bowl and put to one side. Drain the beef. Heat a little vegetable oil in a large wok or sauté pan and add the beef a few handfuls at a time; sauté until medium-done and place in a metal bowl. Dress the salad, add the beef and mix; garnish with the deep-fried rice sticks, if using, and serve.

TO SEED CHILES
IT IS BEST TO WEAR DISPOSABLE GLOVES WHEN HANDLING CHILES. CUT THE CHILE IN HALF LENGTHWISE AND THEN EITHER (WEARING GLOVES) REMOVE THE SEEDS WITH THE POINT OF THE KNIFE; OR REMOVE THE SEEDS UNDER RUNNING WATER. IF YOU ARE NOT USING GLOVES, DO NOT RUB YOUR EYES OR MOUTH — THEY WILL BURN!

Massaman Chicken

Serve this with a bowl of steamed jasmine rice. SERVES 20

Chicken Marinade
1 tbsp cornstarch
6 tbsp Massaman curry paste dissolved in 2 tbsp boiling water
8 garlic cloves, finely chopped
3 red chiles, seeded & finely chopped
1 cup (1 tea cup) cilantro leaves & roots, washed & chopped
twenty 7oz (200g) chicken breast halves, skinned, wing bone removed, in 1½in (4cm) cubes

Curried Sauce
vegetable oil
6 medium onions, diced
3 tbsp tamarind pulp
3 tbsp palm sugar or coarse raw sugar
⅔ cup (150ml) Thai fish sauce
5 quarts (4.8 liters) coconut milk
2 cups (450ml) reduced white chicken stock
2¼lb (1kg) cooked sweet potatoes, cut into large dice

Garnish
1 cup (1 tea cup) cilantro leaves, washed & dried
2 medium chiles, cut into strips
⅓ cup (60g) toasted, unsalted cashew nuts

(2d) To marinate the chicken
In a large bowl, mix together all the ingredients for the marinade, add the chicken and coat well. Cover and chill.

(1d) To make the curried sauce
Cook the onions in a little oil until soft but not colored. Add the chicken to the pan and sauté for about 5 minutes. Add the remaining sauce ingredients, omitting the potatoes, and bring to a boil. Simmer for 30 minutes, then remove from the heat and let cool. Cover and chill.

To serve
Bring to a simmer slowly, add the potatoes, stir and leave for 5 minutes. Pour into a warmed bowl and garnish with cilantro, chile strips and nuts.

Front to back: *Warm Beef Salad, Massaman Chicken*

Pickled Cucumber & Pawpaw Salad

The sweet and spicy Thai-inspired combination is irresistibly uplifting. SERVES 20.

Salad

4 cucumbers, cut in half lengthwise, seeded & sliced

4 ripe pawpaws or paypayas, peeled, seeded & cut into thin wedges

2 red onions, thinly sliced

1 cup (1 tea cup) cilantro leaves, washed & dried

Pickling liquid

3²/₃ cups (900ml) rice wine vinegar

1¼ cups (300g) sugar

1¼ cups (300ml) water

3 garlic cloves, finely chopped

2 red chiles, seeded & cut into thin strips

½ tsp turmeric

salt & freshly ground black pepper

(8h) To prepare the salad

Place the cucumbers, pawpaws and onions in an airtight container. Mix the pickling ingredients in a stainless steel saucepan, bring to a boil, season, then simmer for about 5 minutes. Cool slightly. Pour over the salad ingredients and let cool; cover and place in the refrigerator.

To serve

Drain the salad, check the seasoning and mix in the cilantro. Arrange in a serving bowl.

Front to back *Spicy, Hot and Sour Prawns, Pickled Cucumber & Pawpaw Salad*

Spicy, Hot & Sour Prawns

As other recipes, these are easy to do. They are perfect for a picnic eaten straight from the container with chopsticks. SERVES 20.

Prawn Marinade

1 cup (1 tea cup) cilantro, washed, dried & chopped

6 garlic cloves, finely chopped

4 small hot red chiles, seeded & finely chopped

5 stems of lemon grass, finely sliced

10 green onions, finely sliced

¼ cup (60g) peeled fresh ginger, finely chopped

2¼lb (1kg) shelled tiger prawns

Hot & Sour Dressing

juice of 5 limes

²/₃ cup (150ml) Thai fish sauce

²/₃ cup (150ml) light soy sauce

2 tsp sugar

5 choy sum (Chinese cabbage) (about 1lb/500g)

lemon grass to garnish

(1d) To marinate the prawns

Place the cilantro, garlic, chiles, lemon grass, green onions and ginger in a large bowl, then mix well. Add the prawns and mix. Cover and place in the refrigerator.

(1d) To make the dressing

In a bowl, mix the lime juice, fish sauce, soy sauce and sugar, stirring until the sugar is dissolved. Pour into a jar with a good lid and store in the refrigerator.

(8h) To cook the prawns and choy sum

Heat a little oil in a wok or sauté pan. Sauté the prawns, a handful at a time, and place in a bowl. Wilt the choy sum in the wok or sauté pan and place in the bowl with the prawns. Cover and chill.

To serve

Remove the prawns from the refrigerator at least 30 minutes before serving. Pour the dressing over the prawns and choy sum; toss well. Arrange on serving dishes and garnish with lemon grass.

Spicy Red Mullet on a Bed of Asian Greens

Red mullet is a very under-rated fish which, when cooked properly, is very tasty. Buy this fish ready-filleted, checking that all the bones have been removed. Do not over-cook, otherwise the fish will be very dry. SERVES 20

Asian Greens
peanut oil
3 garlic cloves, finely sliced
¼ cup (60g) pickled ginger, finely shredded
10 baby bok choy, washed, dried & leaves separated
⅔ cup (150ml) sweet soy sauce
salt & freshly ground black pepper

Topping for the Red Mullet
5 shallots, finely diced
3 kaffir lime leaves finely shredded
3 red chiles, seeded, cut into fine strips
2 tbsp fresh ginger, cut into thin strips
4 garlic cloves, finely chopped
½ cup (½ tea cup) cilantro, washed, dried & chopped
4 tbsp Thai fish sauce
juice of 2 limes
salt & freshly ground black pepper
1½lb (800g) red mullet fillets, pin boned, cut into 20 pieces (if unavailable, replace with red snapper)

(8h) **To cook the greens**
Heat a little peanut oil in a wok or sauté pan, then add the garlic and pickled ginger and cook for about 1 minute. Add the greens and soy sauce, cooking until the greens are wilted, then remove and season. Let cool, cover and place in the refrigerator.

(2h) **To cook the red mullet**
Preheat the to oven 350°F/180°F. Line a baking pan with parchment paper. Mix all the ingredients for the topping (apart from the fish) in a bowl. Place the fish on the pan, spoon the mixture over the fillets and bake in the oven for about 5–6 minutes. Remove from the oven and let cool. Pour the cooking juices into a container, cover and place in the refrigerator.

To serve
Remove the red mullet from the refrigerator at least 30 minutes before serving. Line a wooden board with banana leaves. Pour a little of the red mullet cooking juices into the greens and mix. Place the greens on the banana leaves, top with the red mullet and serve.

Baby Pork Ribs

There is something very convivial about eating food without a knife and fork, so encourage it with these pork ribs, but supply lots of napkins for sticky fingers. SERVES 20

6 garlic cloves, finely chopped
1¼ cups (300ml) sweet soy sauce
⅔ cup (150ml) soy sauce
3 tbsp sweet chili sauce
1 tsp shrimp paste or fish sauce
1 tbsp cornstarch
1 cup (1 tea cup) Thai basil leaves, shredded
20 baby ribs (about 4½lb/2kg)
Thai basil leaves, to garnish

(1d) **To marinate the ribs**
Mix the main ingredients in a large bowl, adding the ribs at the end so they can be evenly coated. Cover and place in the refrigerator.

To cook the ribs
Preheat the oven to 350°F/180°C. Place the ribs on a metal baking pan, pouring any remaining marinade over them. Cook for about 1 hour. If the ribs begin to dry out or start to burn, cover them with foil. Transfer to a serving tray and garnish with Thai basil.

UNUSUAL INGREDIENTS
IF YOU CANNOT FIND EXACTLY THE INGREDIENT YOU ARE LOOKING FOR IN THE SUPERMARKET THERE IS USUALLY SOMETHING YOU CAN REPLACE IT WITH. FOR EXAMPLE, THE SLIGHTLY PURPLISH THAI BASIL USED IN AUTHENTIC ASIAN COOKING CAN EASILY BE SUBSTITUTED WITH SPRIGS OF FRESH COMMON BASIL.

Two-bean Salad with Sesame Dressing

We try to use different vegetables for salads, but if you find that some are not easy to obtain then replace them with the suggested alternatives – the salad will taste just as good. As with any salad do not dress this until just before serving or it will lose its crunch. SERVES 20

Sesame Dressing
2 tbsp light sesame oil
2 tbsp sugar
2 tbsp rice wine vinegar
2 tbsp light soy sauce
2 tbsp toasted sesame seeds
freshly ground Szechwan pepper

Salad
1lb (500g) winged beans, sliced into 3in (7.5cm) slices (if unavailable, use whole, thin asparagus stems)
1¼lb (600g) long beans, cut into 4in (10cm) slices (if unavailable, use extra-fine, whole French beans)
11oz (300g) Chinese chives, cut into 3in (7.5cm) lengths (if unavailable, use green onions)
chive flowers

(8h) **To make the dressing**
Combine all the dressing ingredients in a jar with a lid, mix and store in a cool place.

(8h) **To blanch the beans**
Fill a large bowl or sink with iced water and bring a large saucepan of salted water to a boil. Blanch the winged beans and then the long beans each for a couple of minutes in the boiling water, refreshing each batch in the iced water. Drain and shake to dry. Mix the beans together then place in an airtight container lined with a tea towel. Put in the refrigerator.

To serve
Mix the beans and chives with the dressing in a large bowl; toss well and season. Arrange in a serving bowl and garnish with chive flowers.

brunch buffet

Weekends are brunch time, starting as early as 11:30am or as late as 2:00pm. What could be better than a lazy day spent reading the papers, relaxing with family and friends and enjoying this truly delicious selection of light meals and refreshing drinks? The menu has every essential for a classic brunch, but when entertaining, I will also have lots of fresh fruit on hand – or perhaps you could make a fruit salad.

BRUNCH-TIME DRINKS
BELLINI (PAGE 68)
BLOODY MARY (PAGE 68)
MELON, APPLE & LIME COOLADE (PAGE 74)
PAWPAW & PINEAPPLE COOLER (PAGE 75)
FRESHLY SQEEZED BLOOD ORANGE JUICE
GALLONS OF FRESH COFFEE

New York Waffles with a Selection of Toppings

These waffles bring back happy memories of brunch in New York City 30 years ago. SERVES 20

Spiced Apple Topping
½ cup (120g) unsalted butter
4 cinnamon sticks
3 vanilla beans, spilt
1½ tsp freshly ground nutmeg
10 large tart apples, peeled, cored
  & sliced
1 cup (150g) golden raisins, soaked in
  rum or brandy for 24 hours
zest of 1 lemon
zest of 1 orange
¼ cup (60g) Demerara raw sugar

Apricot & Pumpkin Seed Topping
1 lb (500g) dried apricots, sliced
¼ medium-sized pineapple, peeled, cored,
  cut into small slices
1 tbsp fresh ginger, peeled & sliced
½ cup (100g) blanched almond slivers
Demerara raw sugar to taste

Waffle Mixture
1¼ cups (300ml) whole milk
¼ cup (60g) unsalted butter, melted
2 egg yolks
2¼ cups (250g) all-purpose flour
3 tsp baking powder
pinch of salt
4 egg whites

Garnish
2½ cups (500g) crème fraîche or
  whipped cream
1 cup (150g) toasted pumpkin seeds
sprigs of mint
2 cups (560ml) good-quality maple syrup
½ cup (250g) unsalted butter

SPECIAL EQUIPMENT **waffle iron or
sandwich maker**

(1d) **To make the apple topping**
Melt the butter in a pan, when hot add the cinnamon, vanilla and nutmeg; stir. Add the apple slices, raisins and citrus zest, and simmer until soft; do not cover. Add the sugar, stir well and remove from the heat. Cool, then remove the vanilla beans and cinnamon sticks. Cover and refrigerate.

BEST APPLESAUCE
DO NOT ALLOW THE APPLES TO OVER-COOK, OTHERWISE THEY WILL BE LIKE APPLESAUCE. THE AIM IS TO PRODUCE A CHUNKY TOPPING.

New York Waffles with a Selection of Toppings

1d) To make the apricot topping

Bring a pan of water to a boil. Place the apricots in a bowl and pour in the boiling water to cover the fruit. Leave for about 1 hour. Pour the apricots and water into a large saucepan, bring to a boil and simmer for about 1 hour or until the apricots are almost turning to a pulp (during the poaching you may need to add more water). Add the pineapple, ginger and almonds; continue to cook for 15 minutes more or until the pineapple is just soft. If you wish to add sugar to taste, remove from the heat and stir in the sugar. Let cool, cover and place in the refrigerator.

1h) To prepare the batter

In a large bowl, add the milk, butter and egg yolks; mix until smooth. Sift the flour with the baking powder into a separate bowl. Add the milk mixture to the flour slowly and mix until smooth; add salt. Cover and refrigerate.

To cook the waffles

Preheat the oven to 275°F/140°C. Heat the waffle iron. Beat the egg whites until stiff and fold into the batter. Pour some batter onto the iron and cook until golden. Repeat for the rest of the mixture. Keep warm in the oven.

To serve

Place the toppings and crème fraîche in serving bowls, sprinkle pumpkin seeds on the apricot topping, offer leftover seeds on the side and garnish with fresh mint. Pour the maple syrup into a small pitcher and put the butter on a serving dish. Pile up the waffles and let everyone help themselves.

SMOKED SALMON SPECIAL

AS WELL AS SERVING THE WAFFLES, YOU MAY ALSO LIKE TO TOAST SOME HALVED BAGELS FOR DELUXE SMOKED SALMON SANDWICHES. WHIP UP CREAM CHEESE AND CHIVES, SPREAD THICKLY ON THE BAGELS, THEN JUST ADD A GENEROUS SLICE OF SMOKED SALMON, A SQUIRT OF LIME AND A TWIST OF BLACK PEPPER. THE PERFECT SANDWICH!

Hot Salt Beef & Pickles

Salt beef (corned beef) with creamed carrots and split peas is also a wonderful winter supper dish. SERVES 20

7½lb (3.5kg) salt beef (corned beef)
3 large carrots, cut into chunks
2 large onions, halved & each studded with
  6 whole cloves
3 garlic cloves, crushed
2 bay leaves
10 sprigs of thyme
6 whole black peppercorns
selection of mustards
6 medium pickled cucumbers
2 loaves of New York rye bread

(1d) **To soak the beef**
Place the beef in a large airtight container, cover with water and store in the refrigerator.

(4h) **To cook the beef**
Remove the beef from the container and place in a large saucepan, cover with cold water and add the vegetables, herbs and peppercorns. Place on the heat, bring to a boil and simmer for about 3–3½ hours. Remove from heat, but leave in the water.

To serve
Place a selection of mustards and pickled cucumbers in serving dishes. Slice the bread and arrange in boxes or baskets. Drain the beef, place it on a large wooden board and carve into thin slices to serve with bread and garnishes.

Blueberry Muffins

These delicious muffins are courtesy of Annie Waite, head chef at Nicole's in London. MAKES 10

7 tbsp (100g) unsalted butter, melted
all-purpose flour to dust
10 tbsp (150g) unsalted butter, softened
10 tbsp (150g) sugar
3 eggs
1¾ cups (200g) sifted whole wheat flour
1 tsp baking powder

1 tbsp mixed spices or pumpkin pie spice
⅓ cup (85ml) milk
11oz (300g) fresh blueberries

(1d) **To make the blueberry muffins**
Brush the muffin cups with melted butter; dust with flour and set aside. Preheat the oven to 375°F/190°C. In an electric mixer, cream the butter and sugar until light and fluffy, then add the eggs one at a time, beating well. Remove the bowl from the mixer to fold in the flour, baking powder and mixed spices. Mix well, then pour in the milk and mix again; gently fold in the blueberries. Spoon the mixture into the muffin cups and bake for 25–30 minutes, until golden brown and springy to touch. Let the muffins cool, remove from the pan and place in an airtight container in a cool place.

To serve
Preheat the oven to 325°F/160°C. Place the muffins on a baking pan and warm for about 6 minutes before arranging in a bowl or basket lined with a napkin to serve.

Savory Muffins

The basic mixture is enough for 10 muffins, then just choose which of the flavors you want to add. Why not double the basic mixture and make 10 of each? MAKES 10

Basic Savory Muffin Mixture
¼ cup (60g) unsalted butter, melted
all-purpose flour
scant 1 cup (100g) fine cornmeal
1¼ cups (140g) all-purpose flour
1½ tsp salt
1½ tsp ground white pepper
4 eggs
10 tbsp (140g) unsalted butter, melted
scant 1 cup (200g) sour cream
1 cup (1 tea cup) finely grated Parmesan
  cheese
1½ tsp baking powder

Goat Cheese & Basil Muffins
9oz (250g) goat cheese
12 basil leaves, shredded

Cheddar & Mustard Muffins
1 tbsp grain mustard
1 cup (100g) grated aged Cheddar

(1d) **To make the goat cheese muffins**
Preheat the oven to 375°F/190°C. Brush the muffin cups with the butter, dust with flour and set aside. Place all the ingredients for the basic savory mixture in a large mixing bowl and mix until well combined. Crumble in the goat cheese and add the basil. Spoon the mixture into the cups and bake for 20–25 minutes or until golden. Let cool, then place in an airtight container in a cool place.

(1d) **To make the Cheddar muffins**
Preheat the oven to 375°F/190°C. Brush the muffin cups with the butter, dust with flour and set aside. Mix the mustard with all the ingredients for the basic savory mixture in a large mixing bowl. Spoon the mixture into the cups, sprinkle with the cheese and bake for 20–25 minutes or until golden. Let cool, then place in an airtight container in a cool place.

To serve
Preheat the oven to 325°F/160°C. Place the muffins on a baking pan and warm for about 6 minutes, then arrange them in a bowl or basket lined with a napkin to serve.

MUFFIN MOLDS
IF YOU DON'T HAVE A MUFFIN PAN, YOU CAN BUY PAPER CASES FROM KITCHEN SHOPS. IF USING ANOTHER MOLD, ADJUST THE COOKING TIME ACCORDINGLY.

Hash Brown Potatoes

Hash browns with bacon and eggs was one of the first breakfasts I ever ate in Florida. SERVES 20

vegetable oil
2 medium onions, finely diced
7oz (200g) Parma ham (prosciutto), finely diced
4½lb (2kg) potatoes, parboiled
sea salt & freshly ground black pepper

(6h) To prepare the hash browns

Heat a little oil in a sauté pan, then add the onions and cook for about 4–5 minutes. Add the ham and cook for 2 minutes more without coloring; set aside. Grate the potatoes coarsely and place in a bowl, then add the onions and ham; season and mix well. Roll out the potato mixture and cut into twenty 3½in (9cm) squares. Heat a little oil in a sauté pan and fry the squares, a few at a time, until golden brown on both sides. Place on a baking pan to cool, then cover and refrigerate.

To serve

Preheat the oven to 400°F/200°C. Cook for about 10–12 minutes until crisp. Transfer to a warm serving platter.

Huevos Rancheros

My friends, Gab and Lynn, have cooked these scrumptious eggs for me on many occasions. MAKES 10

Mexican Sauce

2lb (900g) tomatillos, husks removed
1 large onion, finely chopped
3 garlic cloves, chopped
vegetable oil
4 Serrano chiles or green chiles
juice of 2 limes
1 tsp nut oil
salt & freshly ground black pepper
½ cup (½ tea cup) of picked & chopped
 cilantro

Refried Beans

vegetable oil
1 bunch of green onions, washed & sliced
4 garlic cloves, finely chopped (optional)
2¼lb (1kg) refried beans
salt & ground black pepper
½ cup (½ tea cup) chopped cilantro
juice of 2 limes

20 corn tortillas, 6in (15cm) in diameter
20 eggs

TIMING

ALLOCATE YOURSELF ENOUGH TIME TO COOK THE TORTILLAS AND EGGS BEFORE SERVING.

Huevos Rancheros

(1d) To prepare the Mexican sauce

Heat a grill pan. Place the tomatillos on the hot grill to singe the skin, then chop in a food processor for about 10 seconds. Sauté the onion and garlic in a little oil until transparent, without browning. Add the tomatillos and chiles, bring to a boil, reduce the heat and cook for about 5 minutes. Remove from the heat, pour into a container. Add the lime juice, nut oil, then season and let cool. When cold, stir in the cilantro. Cover and place in the refrigerator.

(½h) To prepare the beans

Sauté the onions and garlic in oil until soft. Add the beans and cook for about 5 minutes; stir and season. Add the cilantro and lime juice, stir and cool.

(½h) To cook the tortillas

Heat a little oil in a frying pan and fry the tortillas on each side for about 10–15 seconds – holding them down with a pair of tongs makes this easier. Remove and keep warm. Heat a little oil in a sauté pan and fry the eggs; transfer them to paper towels and keep warm.

To serve

Place the tortillas in a basket lined with a napkin. Place the refried beans and Mexican green sauce in bowls and serve with the eggs. The best way to eat Huevos Rancheros is to spread the tortilla with beans, place the egg on top and drizzle on the sauce. If the occasion calls for it, offer iced Mexican beers and frozen margaritas to accompany the dish.

desserts buffet

Creating a spectacular dessert buffet in a separate room or area lifts a buffet party out of the ordinary, giving guests a real sense of occasion. Fill tall glass vases with mousses, fruits and sauces and use Moroccan tea glasses to hold vanilla brûlée creams topped with melted sugar. For an impressive effect, serve chocolate, lemon or fruit tarts and meringues layered with fruits and whipped cream on glass cake stands.

Three-Chocolate Mousse with Chocolate Shapes

Three-Chocolate Mousse with Chocolate Shapes

This recipe for a triple-layered chocolate mousse makes about 4 quarts (4 liters) in total. Serve it in glass vases so you can appreciate the swirls of the different mousses. To decorate the dessert, have fun creating your own abstract marbled patterns with the tempered chocolate. SERVES 20

Sugar Syrup
4½ cups (1kg) sugar
3 cups (750ml) water

Bitter Chocolate Mousse
9oz (275g) bittersweet chocolate, chopped into small pieces
8 egg yolks
2⅓ cups (600ml) heavy whipping cream

White Chocolate Mousse
2 leaves of gelatin, or ½ pkg. granualted gelatin
12oz (350g) white chocolate, broken into small pieces
8 egg yolks
2⅓ cups (600ml) heavy whipping cream

Milk Chocolate Mousse
9oz (275g) milk chocolate, chopped into small pieces
8 egg yolks
2⅓ cups (600ml) heavy whipping cream

Chocolate Shapes
7oz (200g) bittersweet chocolate, 70% cocoa, chopped into small pieces
5oz (150g) white chocolate, chopped into small pieces
cocoa powder to dust

(1d) **To make the sugar syrup**
Place the sugar and water in a large pan and leave for about 5 minutes. Bring to a boil, then turn down the heat and whisk; let simmer for 5 minutes. Divide into three 1 cup (250ml) amounts.

(1d) **To make the bitter chocolate mousse**
Place the chocolate in a bowl that will fit over a saucepan. Fill the saucepan almost halfway with water and bring to a

boil; reduce the heat to simmer. Place the bowl over the heat and melt the chocolate, stirring occasionally until smooth. Reheat the sugar syrup. In an electric mixer, beat the egg yolks until doubled in volume. With the mixer on a slow speed, pour the hot sugar syrup in a steady stream into the egg mixture. Continue beating until the mixture is cool and thick. Whip the cream until it just holds its shape and put to one side. Once all the chocolate has melted, remove it from the heat and fold into the egg mixture. Mix until smooth, then fold in the cream. Pour the mousse into the base of the vases or containers, taking care not to dirty the sides.

BLOWING AWAY AIR BUBBLES

IF YOU SEE ANY AIR BUBBLES AS YOU POUR THE MOUSSE INTO THE VASE, KNOCK THEM OUT BY STIRRING GENTLY WITH THE HANDLE OF A WOODEN SPOON.

To make the white chocolate mousse,

Cover the gelatin in cold water and let soak. Place the chocolate in a bowl that will fit over a saucepan. Fill the saucepan almost halfway with water and bring to a boil, then reduce the heat to simmer. Place the bowl over the heat and melt the chocolate, stirring occasionally until smooth. Heat the sugar syrup. Beat the egg yolks in an electric mixer until doubled in volume. With the mixer on a slow speed, pour the hot sugar syrup in a steady stream into the egg mixture. Continue beating until the mixture is cool and thick. Drain the gelatin and squeeze out any excess water, if necessary. Melt the gelatin over a low heat, stirring continuously and taking care not to let it boil. Pass through a fine sieve, pour into the egg mixture and whisk for about 30 seconds. Whip the cream until it just holds its shape, then put to one side. Fold the chocolate into the egg mixture, then fold in the cream. Pour into the vases and let set.

To make the milk chocolate mousse

Make just as the bitter chocolate mousse and pour into the vase.

1d To make the chocolate shapes

To make the chocolate malleable enough to create shapes, you will need to temper it. By following this method you will also be able to make cylinders, long cigarettes, or any shapes you wish for this dessert or any other. The important part is making sure that the correct temperature is achieved. Line 2 pans with parchment paper. Choose 2 mixing bowls that will hold the chocolate and fit over 2 saucepans. Half-fill the saucepans with water, bring to a boil, then reduce the heat to simmer. Put 2/3 of the bittersweet chocolate in the first bowl and place over one saucepan. Put all the white chocolate in the second bowl and place over the other saucepan. Stir continuously and use a thermometer to take the temperature of the chocolates – it should be no higher than 113°F (45°C). Remove the pans from the heat and add the remaining bittersweet chocolate, stirring continuously until all the chocolate is melted. Take the temperature of the chocolates again – it should be 88°F (31°C). If it is lower, return to the heat until the correct temperature is obtained. This makes the chocolate much easier to use. When both types of chocolate are the desired temperature, use a spoon or spatula to make spiral patterns with each chocolate at at time on parchment paper on the first pan. With a large palette knife, spread the chocolate until it covers the whole sheet on the second pan, then place in the refrigerator. Once set, peel off the paper and break the chocolate into the desired shapes.

To serve

Dust the tops of the mousses with cocoa powder, arrange the chocolate shapes on top and serve.

MULTIPLE MOUSSES

FOR VARIATION, ALTERNATE WHICH ORDER YOU LAYER THE DARK, WHITE AND MILK CHOCOLATE MOUSSES IN EACH OF THE VASES. OR, IF YOU HAVE A BIG ENOUGH CONTAINER, MAKE ONE HUGE MOUSSE.

Brioche & Butter Pudding

The puddings can be assembled the day before but are best cooked and eaten on the day of the party. Serve warm in delicate (6 fl oz/180ml) Chinese tea cups. MAKES 10

8 baby brioches
2 cups (600ml) heavy whipping cream
5 eggs
1/2 cup (100g) sugar
1/2 cup (125g) unsalted butter, softened
1 tsp grated nutmeg
2/3 cup (100g) raisins, soaked in rum or
   brandy for 24 hours or more
2 oranges, zested
2 lemons, zested
powdered sugar, to dust
sprigs of mint to garnish

4h To prepare the pudding

Slice the brioche into 30 slices (allowing 3 slices per tea cup) and place in an airtight container. Bring the cream to a boil and whisk the eggs and sugar in an electric mixer until pale. When the cream boils, remove from the heat and pour into the egg mixture in a steady stream, whisking until combined; pass the custard mix through a fine sieve, then let cool, cover and refrigerate.

1-2h To assemble the puddings

Preheat the oven to 325°F/160°C. Warm the custard. Butter the brioche and sprinkle each slice with the nutmeg; place one piece in the base of each cup. Add a few raisins, sprinkle with the citrus zest and pour on enough custard to cover the brioche. Repeat the process for 2 more slices in each cup, finishing with the custard. Let soak for 1/2 hour, then top with custard.

To cook and serve the puddings

Put the puddings in a deep roasting pan, then pour in boiling water to halfway up the cups. Do this while the pan is in the oven so that you do not have to carry it too far. Cook for about 15–20 minutes until the puddings are almost set. Serve dusted with powdered sugar and garnish with mint.

Glazed Lemon Tart

This recipe is simply delicious and very easy to make.
MAKES TWO 10IN (26CM) TARTS

Pastry Shells

1lb (450g) unsalted butter
1½ cups (180g) powdered sugar
5 egg yolks
5 cups (650g) all-purpose flour
¼ cup (60ml) water

Lemon Filling

1¾ cups (450ml) heavy whipping cream
24 eggs
4 cups (900g) superfine sugar
juice & zest of 8 lemons
powdered sugar
bunches of red currants, to garnish

SPECIAL EQUIPMENT **blow torch**

(1d) **To make the pastry**

For the pastry shells, beat the butter and powdered sugar in an electric mixer until pale. Add the egg yolks one at a time, whisking well and making sure that each yolk is mixed in before adding the next one. If the mixture begins to curdle, add ½ tablespoon flour. When all the egg yolks are mixed in, add ½ the flour and, when this is incorporated, add the water and mix. Add the remaining flour and mix until the dough just comes together. Transfer to a cold work surface. Divide the dough in 2, wrap in plastic wrap and let rest in the refrigerator for at least 2 hours. Now make the filling.

(1d) **To make the filling**

In a pan, bring the cream to a boil. Meanwhile in an electric mixer, whisk the eggs and sugar until smooth; add the lemon juice and whisk. Remove the cream from the heat and pour into the egg mixture in a steady steam. Whisk until smooth, then pass through a fine sieve; add the lemon zest.

(1d) **To bake the tarts**

Preheat the oven to 325°F/170°C. Remove the pastry from the refrigerator. On a floured board, roll the dough

halves into circles about 14in (36cm) in diameter by ⅛in (3mm) thick. Line the tart pan carefully and trim the pastry. Make sure that the pastry does not have any holes in it, otherwise the filling will leak out. Line the pastry shells with foil and fill with ceramic baking beans. Bake for about 20 minutes until the edges are golden. Remove from the oven and lift out the foil and beans. Return to the oven and bake for about 30–35 minutes until golden brown. Now reduce the oven heat to 225°F/110°C. Pour the filling into the pastry shells and return to the oven. Cook for about 1 hour and 15 minutes or until the filling is set. Remove and let cool. Place in airtight containers in a cool place.

To serve

Dust the top of the tarts liberally with powdered sugar, and with a blow torch, glaze the sugar to obtain a light caramel. Garnish with red currants and serve.

Brûlée Cream

To vary the flavor add orange zest or mocha, or infuse the cream with cinnamon or cardamom. MAKES 10

6 vanilla beans
2½ cups (1.2 liters) heavy whipping cream
16 egg yolks
½ cup (100g) superfine sugar
½ cup (120g) Demerara raw sugar

SPECIAL EQUIPMENT **blow torch**

(1d) **To make the brûlees**

Split the vanilla beans lengthwise, scrape out the seeds and add all to the cream. Bring the cream to a boil over medium heat. In an electric mixer, whisk together the egg yolks and superfine sugar. Pour the egg mixture in a steady stream into the cream as it boils; whisk until combined. Remove the vanilla beans. Bring a pan of water to a boil and remove from the heat. Pour the mixture into a flat-bottomed bowl that will fit over the pan. Place

the pan over the heat and return to a boil, then turn down the heat to a simmer and whisk continuously until the mixture coats the back of a spoon (about 20–30 minutes). Remove the bowl from the heat and pass the mixture through a fine sieve. Pour into the glasses and let cool. Cover and refrigerate.

FRUIT SURPRISE
AS A VARIATION, LINE THE TEA GLASSES WITH APRICOTS OR RASPBERRIES BEFORE POURING IN THE BRÛLÉE MIXTURE.

To serve

About 30 minutes before serving, sprinkle the tops of the brulees with raw sugar and burn lightly with a blow torch to caramelize. Alternatively, decorate with Macadamia Nut Brittle (page 169).

Summer Fruits with Raspberry Sauce

The sauce can be made with any soft fruit. The amounts are enough for a 3-quart (3-liter) vase. SERVES 20

Soft Fruits

2¼lb (1kg) strawberries, hulled, washed & dried
2¼lb (1kg) of raspberries
2¼lb (1kg) of blackberries
2¼lb (1kg) of blueberries
1lb (500g) of red currants
1lb (500g) of loganberries or tayberries
1lb (500g) of white currants
1lb (500g) of golden raspberries
1lb (500g) of wild strawberries
mint & edible flowers, to garnish

Raspberry Sauce

2¼lb (1kg) raspberries (fresh or frozen)
4 cups (500g) powdered sugar
juice of 1 lemon

(1d) **To make the sauce**

Purée the berries for the sauce, sugar and lemon juice until smooth, then pass through a fine sieve. Pour into an airtight container and store in the refrigerator.

To serve

Layer the berries in a vase, garnishing with mint and flowers. Pour the sauce into a small jug. If serving with biscuits these can be placed on glass cake stands and dusted with powdered sugar.

Passion Fruit Pyramid

This dessert can also be made with soft summer fruits. SERVES 20

Meringue
12 egg whites
2¼ cups (500g) superfine sugar

Passion Fruit Cream
30 whole passion fruit, halved, juices & pits scooped out, sieved to yield 1 scant cup (200ml) purée
1 cup (250ml) water
3¼ cups (800ml) heavy whipping cream
1 cup (250g) sugar
⅓ cup (50g) cornstarch
10 egg yolks
¾ cup (170g) unsalted butter, cut into cubes
3 passion fruit
8 mangos, peeled & sliced

Garnish
powdered sugar
oven-dried mango slices (page 169), optional
6 passion fruit
edible flowers, fresh or crystallized

1w **To make the meringue**

Preheat the oven to 225°F/110°C. Taking 4 sheets of parchment paper, draw a 12in (30.5cm) circle on the first, on the second a 10in (25.5cm) circle, on the third an 8in (20cm) circle and on the fourth a 6in (15cm) circle. Place these sheets on baking pans. Whisk the egg whites with ½ cup (100g) of the sugar until it forms stiff peaks. Continue to whisk, adding the sugar gradually. Once all the sugar is added, the egg whites should be stiff and glossy. Fill a piping bag with this mixture and pipe to fill each of the paper circles. Bake for about 10–12 hours until the meringue is dry and hard to the touch. Let cool, then layer with waxed paper and store in airtight containers.

1d **To make the fruit cream**

In a heavy-based pan, bring the passion fruit purée, the water, 3 tablespoons cream and the sugar to the boil, stirring continuously. Mix the cornstarch with a little cold water then add to the boiling mixture, stirring. Reduce the heat and cook for 5 minutes, stirring to prevent it from burning. Remove from heat and let cool for about 2 minutes. Beat in the egg yolks then the butter. Cover with waxed paper and let cool. Cut the 3 passion fruit in half, squeeze out the juice and pits and add these to the mixture. Whisk the remaining cream until it holds its shape and fold into the passion fruit. Cover and chill.

Passion Fruit Pyramid

2h **To assemble**

Pipe a blob of cream in the center of a glass cake stand to prevent the meringue from sliding around. Place the largest disc of meringue on the stand and spread with cream, leaving a 1in (2.5cm) rim of meringue. Top with a layer of mango, then the next meringue disc. Repeat the process twice to finish with the smallest disc of meringue.

To garnish

Dust with powdered sugar and arrange remaining slices of fresh or oven-dried mango on the top, squeezing over the juice of the passion fruits. Decorate the sides with fresh or crystallized flowers.

Giving a dinner party at home is generally the most popular form of entertaining. Large or small, formal or informal, it is offering your guests the warmest welcome. Dinners I give tend to be simple affairs. I like to serve champagne and wine before dinner with savory biscuits if I've made them.

for a dinner party

Ten or 15 minutes after the last guests have arrived and have had time to collect their thoughts and a drink, I start seating everyone. It is generally best not to be too clever with your plans – for example, I hate being moved from my place for dessert. If you do not know many guests, by the time dessert is served you are relaxed and to be moved and have to start the process of getting to know the people around you again is a great dampener.

An Affair to Remember

Planning a menu is not only very important, but fun to do. I always like to serve food that is in season, from wonderful asparagus and fresh berries in the summer, to juicy apples and pears in the autumn. Giving a dinner is very rewarding; you can set the table in a dramatic way, arrange flowers and decorations, serve wonderful food and wines, and enjoy the evening in the knowledge that your guests will have a memorable time. Dinner parties can last from 2½ to 4 hours; as a host you will then be able to judge when to start moving guests to serve coffee. If there is space, move to an adjoining room or area – in summer, this could be a garden or terrace. This will move the guests around and prevent the party from carrying on too late into the night.

Panic-Free Parties

The following menus are designed to make giving dinners easy and panic-free – because nearly all the dishes can be prepared ahead of time. I would advise never to cook any recipe for guests that you have not attempted beforehand. Trying out dishes for the first time on close friends or family will give you confidence on the night of the party. There is nothing worse than worrying – you should be relaxed to enjoy your party. Take plenty of time to plan the menu, and enjoy preparing each dish. It is very satisfying when you see your guests' plates empty. If any of your guests are vegetarian, you will find that most of the menus are easy to adapt.

Professional Tips

- Make sure your table linen (including the napkins) is clean
- Organize an area for clearing dirty plates and glasses to and make sure the dishwasher is empty before dinner
- Serve pre-dinner drinks but not for longer than 1 hour
- Allow 10 minutes for latecomers but then stick to your plan – they will understand
- Every once in a while you'll get a 'no-show' – bear this light-heartedly and no one will mind
- Choose wines that complement the food – suggestions are given for each dinner

CLEAN AND TIDY

Do not give way to the temptation to wash up between courses – guests do not want to hear the clatter of plates while they are still eating.

Roasted Vegetable Terrine

spring dinner

This menu makes the most of the produce available at this time of year – lamb, asparagus, strawberries and rhubarb. All the courses are easy to prepare ahead of time, allowing you to relax and enjoy the company of your guests. SERVES 10

Roasted Vegetable Terrine

Vegetable Terrine
6 red peppers, seeded & quartered
olive oil
2 large eggplants
6 large zucchini
12oz (340g) goat cheese log
salt & freshly ground black pepper
6 tbsp Pesto (see page 168)
¾ cup (80g) Parmesan, grated
SPECIAL EQUIPMENT **electric carving knife**

Red Pepper Sauce
1 garlic clove, chopped
1 shallot, chopped

olive oil
2 red peppers, roasted, skinned, seeded
  & chopped (roast these at the same time
  as the peppers for the terrine)
2 plum tomatoes, chopped
1 tsp tomato paste
1¼ cups (300ml) vegetable stock
salt & freshly ground black pepper

Glaze
1 cup (250ml) aged balsamic vinegar
WINE Crisp Sancerre

(2d) To make the terrine
Preheat the oven to 375°F/190°C.
Brush the red peppers with oil, salt them and bake for 15–20 minutes.

Let cool, remove skins and set aside. Slice all the vegetables as straight as possible into ¼in- (7mm-) thick strips. Score the strips, salt them, and leave for ½ hour. Cut the goat cheese into ¼in- (7mm-) thick slices. Dry the eggplant and zucchini. Heat a grill pan, brush the eggplant and zucchini with olive oil, season with pepper and grill until bar marks are visible. Transfer to a tray and set aside.

(2d) To build the terrine
Preheat the oven to 350°F/180°C. Cut thick cardboard to fit the top of a terrine mold, 12in (30cm) long by 4in (10cm) wide, and cover with foil. Brush the mold with olive oil and line with parchment paper. Cover the base with red pepper and season. Layer in the following way: eggplant, zucchini, goat cheese, red pepper, then eggplant, zucchini, goat cheese, zucchini, eggplant, finishing with the red pepper. Spread pesto and sprinkle Parmesan over each layer. Cover the terrine with foil and cook for 25 minutes. Let cool, then place the covered cardboard on top and press with weights or cans. Refrigerate.

(2d) To prepare the glaze
Reduce the balsamic vinegar by half in a pan over medium heat. Let cool to a thick, syrupy consistency. Store in a squeeze bottle and refrigerate.

(1d) To make the sauce
Sauté the garlic and shallot in a little olive oil for 2 minutes. Add the 2 peppers, tomatoes and tomato paste, and sauté for 2 minutes more. Add stock and seasoning. Cover and simmer for 20 minutes. Cool, then purée and sieve. Pour into a squeeze bottle and chill.

To serve the terrine
Turn out the terrine onto a board. Mop up any juices. Slice the terrine with an electric carving knife into ¾in- (2cm-) wide portions. Place in the center of the plates (up to 1 hour before serving), drizzle on the pesto, balsamic glaze and pepper sauce. Serve.

Lamb with Potato Cake & Thyme Sauce

Thyme Sauce
3 shallots, chopped
10 sprigs of thyme
vegetable oil
1 glass red wine
7 cups (1.8 liters) reduced chicken stock

5 short loins of lamb
salt & freshly ground black pepper

Potato Cake
2 shallots, finely chopped
2 garlic cloves, finely chopped
vegetable oil
1lb (500g) mixed wild mushrooms
4 1/2lb (2kg) yellow potatoes, peeled
3 sprigs of thyme, chopped
1 tbsp unsalted butter

3 carrots, cut into 1in (2cm) cubes
30 asparagus spears, peeled & cut into
  3in (8cm) lengths

WINE *Savigny-les-Beaune or Californian Pinot Noir*

(2d) **To prepare the sauce**
Sauté the shallots and thyme in a little oil in a sauté pan until golden. Pour in the wine and reduce by half. Add stock, reducing to a syrupy consistency and allowing approximately 2 1/2 cups (600ml) for 10 portions. Strain the sauce and let cool. Cover and refrigerate.

(8h) **To sear the lamb**
Heat a little vegetable oil in a sauté pan. When the pan starts to smoke, add two loins and season. Sear on all sides until brown, then place on an oiled pan. Repeat for all the lamb. Cover and chill.

(6h) **To make the potato cake**
Preheat the oven to 375°F/190°C. Sauté the shallots and garlic in a little oil in a sauté pan until soft. Add the mushrooms, season and sauté for 3–4 minutes. Set aside in a colander. Julienne the potatoes, place in a bowl, season and mix in the thyme. Heat the butter with a little oil in an ovenproof sauté pan about 12 x 2 3/4in (30 x 7cm).

When hot, add half the potatoes, spreading them evenly. Cook for 5 minutes or until golden at the edges. Add the mushrooms, spreading them from the middle of the pan outwards to leave a gap of about 1in (2.5cm) from the rim. Put in the remaining potatoes, spreading them evenly. Brush with a little oil and place in the oven for 20 minutes. Remove from the oven and turn it over onto a plate. Slide the cake back into the pan, then return to the oven for 10 minutes, or until the other side is golden. Slide the potato cake onto a board, slice into portions (flattening off the rounded edges if serving as in the photograph) and place on a baking tray. Cool, cover with plastic wrap and chill.

(6h) **To prepare the carrots**
Sauté the carrots in a little oil until slightly brown, season and place on a

baking pan. Let cool, cover with plastic wrap and refrigerate.

To assemble
Preheat the oven to 400°F/200°C. Bring the sauce to a boil then simmer slowly, checking the seasoning. Place the potato cake portions and carrots in the oven for about 15 minutes. After 5 minutes, put in the lamb and cook for 8–10 minutes. Remove and rest, but keep warm. Bring a pan of salted water to a boil. Add the asparagus and cook for 3–4 minutes. Drain and season. Place a potato-cake portion (upright if desired) in the center of each plate and lean asparagus next to it. Halve the short loins, then slice each half at a 45° angle. Place next to the cake with the points in opposite directions. Drizzle sauce around the plate, scatter on 1 or more carrots and serve.

Lamb with Potato Cake & Thyme Sauce

Strawberry Tart with Rhubarb Ice Cream

Rhubarb Ice Cream

1lb (500g) rhubarb, peeled & cut into 1in
  (2.5cm) lengths
3 cardamom pods
1 cup (250g) sugar
2⅓ cups (600ml) heavy whipping cream
SPECIAL EQUIPMENT ice cream maker

Tart Base

1¾ cups (200g) powdered sugar for rolling
1lb (500g) frozen puff pastry, thawed
butter for greasing baking tray

Strawberry Sauce

9oz (250g) strawberries
½ cup (60g) powdered sugar
juice of 1 lemon

Topping

Diplomat Cream (see page 169)
Sugar Cobwebs (see page 169)
1lb (500g) strawberries, hulled, washed & dried

WINE Sauternes or Australian Botrytis
Riesling

(4d) To make the ice cream

Tip the rhubarb into a saucepan and
cover with 2 tablespoons of water; add
the cardamom pods and sugar, then
cover, bring to a boil and simmer to a
purée for about 5–8 minutes. Pour into
a bowl and remove the cardamom. Let
cool, then stir in the cream. Pour into
an ice cream maker and churn for about
30 minutes. Remove, place in an
airtight container and freeze.

(4d) To prepare the pastry

Sprinkle a cold work surface with powdered sugar and roll out the puff pastry
into an oblong 13 x 9in (33 x 23cm).
Dust with sugar. Take the longest side
and roll up the pastry like a jelly roll.
To seal the roll, dampen the edge with
water and press gently in place along its
length. Wrap the cylinder of pastry in
plastic wrap. It can now be frozen.

Strawberry Tart with Rhubarb Ice Cream

(2d) To make the sauce

Put all the ingredients in a pan and
bring to a boil. Now simmer until the
berries are soft. Remove from the heat
and let cool. Blend until smooth, then
pass through a fine sieve. Pour into a
squeeze bottle and refrigerate.

(1d) To prepare the pastry

Preheat the oven to 400°F/200°C.
Butter a baking pan. Remove the pastry
from the freezer and sprinkle a cool
work surface with powdered sugar.
Cut the pastry into ¾in- (2cm-) thick
slices. Let defrost for 10 minutes.
Sprinkle more powdered sugar on the
work surface and roll the pastry out
very thinly. Cut out the discs with a 5in-
(12.5cm-) round pastry cutter.
If the frozen pastry starts to crack
around the edges, let defrost a little
longer. Place the discs on the tray and
refrigerate for ½ hour. Place in the
oven for 10 minutes. Remove the tray,
turn the discs and bake for 5 minutes
more or until golden brown and glazed.
Cool on a wire rack. Place the discs in
an airtight container, layering with
greaseproof paper.

(8h) To ball the ice cream

Follow the instructions for balling
Ginger Ice Cream on page 126.

(8h) To prepare the topping

Make the Diplomat Cream and Sugar
Cobwebs. Halve the strawberries, and
refrigerate in an airtight container.

To assemble

Fill a piping bag with the Diplomat
Cream and pipe a small blob of cream
onto the center of each plate to prevent
the tart from sliding around. Place a
pastry disc on top. Pipe a large blob of
cream onto the tart and arrange the
strawberry halves around the cream.
Drizzle the sauce around the plate.
Place a ball of ice cream on top of the
tart, followed by a cobweb. Serve. (The
tarts can be assembled 2 hours in
advance, then kept in a cool place and
topped with an ice cream ball just
before serving.)

summer menu

I used to grow vegetables on a plot of land with my friend, Bruce. In summer, one of our great joys was collecting bunches of asparagus, herbs and artichokes for a simple, fresh salad. To follow this, the sea bass recipe is from holidays spent in Southwold, where I would grill fish fresh from the local fishermen for a delicious, healthy meal. SERVES 10

Asparagus & Artichoke Salad

12½ oz (350g) mixed prepared salad greens

Salsa Verde
2 cups (2 tea cups) parsley, washed & dried
½ cup (½ tea cup) marjoram, washed & dried
1 tbsp mini capers
5 tbsp olive oil
2 limes, zested & juiced
2 garlic cloves, finely chopped
2 shallots, finely chopped
2 tsp whole-grain mustard
1 tbsp sugar
salt & freshly ground black pepper

Asparagus & Artichoke
10 medium globe artichokes, cooked, with
  leaves & chokes removed to leave hearts
3 tbsp olive oil
salt & freshly ground black pepper
2 garlic cloves, crushed
5 sprigs fresh thyme
30 white asparagus spears, peeled & cut
  into 4in (10cm) lengths
30 green asparagus spears, peeled & cut
  into 10cm (4in) lengths
1 cup (1 tea cup) chives, cut into 1½in
  (4cm) lengths
WINE Californian Sauvignon or Pouilly Fumé

(3d) **To prepare the salad greens**
Salad greens keep best in an airtight container lined with a clean tea towel. Wash the leaves and dry well; refrigerate.

(3d) **To prepare the salsa verde**
Finely chop the herbs and place in a bowl. Add the remaining ingredients, season, mix well and refrigerate in an airtight container.

Asparagus & Artichoke Salad

(1d) **To grill artichokes**
Trim the hearts around the artichoke base with a sharp knife, ensuring that none of the choke has been left on. Slice each in half crosswise to give a total of 20 discs. Heat a grill pan. Brush the discs with olive oil, season and grill for about 45 seconds until the grill marks are defined. Turn the discs and repeat. Place the discs in an airtight container, drizzle with a little olive oil and cover with the garlic and thyme. When cool, cover and refrigerate.

ARTICHOKE PREPARATION
THE DELICIOUSLY MELT-IN-THE-MOUTH FLAVOR OF GLOBE ARTICHOKES IS WORTH PURSUING. COOK FOR ABOUT 30–45 MINUTES IN BOILING WATER FLAVORED WITH SHALLOTS, GARLIC, HERBS AND PEPPERCORNS. ADD LEMON JUICE TO STOP DISCOLORATION AND POUR A LAYER OF OLIVE OIL ON TOP. WHEN READY, PULL OFF ALL THE LEAVES AND THEN PULL OFF THE HAIRY CENTRAL CHOKE OR REMOVE IT WITH A SPOON TO LEAVE THE FLESHY HEART.

Sea Bass with Sweet Potato Mash & Fennel

To grill asparagus
(1d)

Bring a pan of salted water to a boil. Blanch the asparagus for 1 minute, drain and refresh. Dry and brush with olive oil, season and grill until the grill marks are defined. Cool, then toss with a little olive oil. Cover and chill.

To assemble

Place a small handful of salad greens in the center of each plate, add an artichoke disc, then continue to build up layers with another small handful of greens followed by 3 asparagus spears. Add a second artichoke disc, then the remaining salad leaves followed by 3 asparagus spears. Top with chives. Drizzle salsa verde around the plate. Serve with Parmesan Tuiles if desired (see page 92). (The salad can be assembled 20 minutes before serving.)

COOKING WITH WINE

WHEN WINE IS A MAIN COMPONENT OF A DISH AS WITH THE RED WINE SAUCE (SEE RIGHT), MAKE SURE IT IS GOOD QUALITY.

Sea Bass with Sweet Potato Mash & Fennel

Red Wine Sauce
vegetable oil
4 shallots, chopped
1 cup (1 glass) red wine
7 cups (1.8 liters) reduced brown chicken stock

Sweet Potato Mash
3lb (1.35kg) orange sweet potatoes, cut into large chunks.
2¼lb (1kg) yellow potatoes, cut into chunks
3 garlic cloves, finely chopped
⅔ cup (150ml) olive oil
salt & ground white pepper

ten 7oz (200g) fillets sea bass, with skin, pin boned
20 baby fennel, roots trimmed, shoots cut at the top at an angle
7oz (200g) chanterelle mushrooms, cleaned, brushed & sautéed in a little vegetable oil (optional)
14oz (400g) baby broad (fava) beans, blanched & shelled
freshly ground black pepper

WINE Australian Dry Riesling or Fleurie

To make the sauce
(2d)

Sauté the shallots in a little oil until golden brown. Pour in the red wine and reduce by half. Add the stock and reduce until the mixture has a smooth, velvet consistency. Pass through a sieve. Allow 2½ cups (600ml) for 10 portions.

To prepare the sweet potato mash
(6h)

Simmer all the potatoes with the garlic in salted water until the potatoes are soft. Drain and pass through a potato ricer or sieve. In a bowl, add the olive oil and mix to a creamy consistency. Season with salt and white pepper. Cool and place in a container. Cover and chill.

To sear the sea bass
(6h)

Heat a little oil until smoking in a sauté pan, lay the fish skin side down and season. Sauté until the edges are golden and the skin is crispy. Turn and sauté for 10 seconds more then place on a greased metal pan, skin side up. Let cool, cover and refrigerate.

To prepare the fennel
(6h)

Blanch the fennel in boiling salted water for 4–5 minutes, drain and refresh in ice water. Dry, then brush with oil and season. Heat a gill pan and grill the fennel until marks are defined. Remove and let cool. Place on a greased metal pan. Cover and refrigerate.

To assemble

Preheat the oven to 400°F/200°C. Bring the sauce to a simmer and season. Bring a pan of salted water to a boil. Stir the potato mash in a pan over low heat until bubbling. Season and keep warm. Place the fish and fennel in the oven for 7–8 minutes and heat up the mushrooms, if using. The sea bass is ready when firm. Cook the beans in the boiling water for 1 minute, drain and set aside. Dip a spoon into a jug of hot water and scoop an oval of potato mash onto the center of each plate. Place 2 pieces of fennel over the mash, then top with the sea bass. Scatter on the beans and mushrooms, drizzle on the sauce and serve.

Champagne Berry Jelly with Summer Fruits

Pistachio Biscotti

3 eggs
scant 1 cup (200g) superfine sugar
4 cups (450g) all-purpose flour
1/2 tsp baking powder
3 cups (320g) shelled pistachio nuts

Champagne Jelly

vegetable oil
9oz (250g) strawberries
9oz (250g) red currants
9oz (250g) white currants
9oz (250g) golden raspberries
9oz (250g) blueberries
9oz (250g) loganberies
10 leaves of gelatin (or 2½ pkg.
  granulated gelatin)
2/3 cup (150g) sugar
2/3 cup (150ml) water
1 bottle (750ml) pink champagne

Berry Compote

1/2 cup (100g) sugar
3/4 cup (200ml) water
9oz (250g) blueberries
9oz (250g) strawberries
9oz (250g) red currants
9oz (250g) white currants
9oz (250g) golden raspberries
9oz (250g) loganberries
CHAMPAGNE *Pink Champagne*

(1w) To prepare the biscotti dough

In an electric mixer, beat the eggs and sugar until white. Add the flour, baking powder and nuts, mixing to a smooth dough. On a floured board, roll the mixture into a 4in- (10cm-) thick roll. Cover with plastic film and freeze.

(2d) To cook the biscotti

Preheat the oven to 375°F/190°C. Defrost the biscotti roll and place on a greased baking pan. Bake for 30 minutes or until golden brown. Remove and cool on a wire rack. Cut into 1/4in (7mm) slices, angling these at 45°, and place on a baking pan. Return to the oven and bake for 5 minutes. Remove, let cool and place in an airtight container.

(1d) To make the jelly

Brush 10 tall jelly molds (holding about 2/3 cup/150ml) with a little vegetable oil. To remove excess oil, turn the molds upside down and place on paper towels. Pick over the fruit, wash and dry well. Place the gelatin leaves in a bowl and add cold water to cover; let the leaves soften. In a pan, bring the sugar and water to a boil. Reduce the heat and simmer for about 5 minutes to form a clear syrup. Remove from the heat. Squeeze out excess water from the gelatin then dissolve it in the syrup. Add the champagne, stir and strain through a fine sieve into a large jug. Place the jelly molds onto a tray that will fit inside your refrigerator. Pour in enough jelly to coat the base of the molds – about 1/4in (7mm). Let set in the refrigerator. When set, remove from the refrigerator and half-fill the molds with fruit. Pour in enough jelly

Champagne Berry Jelly with Summer Fruits

to cover three quarters of the fruit (any more and the fruit will float). Let set in the refrigerator then fill to the top with the remaining jelly to encase the fruit entirely. Let set in the refrigerator.

(1d) To make the compote

Place the sugar and blueberries in a stainless-steel pan, add the water and bring to a boil. Add the remaining fruit and return to a boil. Once boiling, remove from the heat immediately. Pour into a container and let cool. Cover and refrigerate.

To assemble

Dip the jelly molds in warm water; remove and shake to loosen the jelly. Place a jelly in the center of each plate and spoon a little compote around it. (This can be done 2 hours in advance.) When ready to serve, add the biscotti.

autumn menu

In the autumn I love to serve squash soup inside baby pumpkins. The French black-legged challans chicken has a melting texture which combines perfectly with the spring rolls, but you could use a good free-range variety. SERVES 10

Butternut Squash Soup

Soup Base
3 tbsp butter
2 tbsp vegetable oil
3½lb (1.5kg) butternut squash, seeded
 & diced
3½ cups (430g) carrots, chopped
5 shallots, chopped
4 garlic cloves, chopped
7 cups (1.8 liters) vegetable stock
10 baby pumpkins
2⅓ cups (600ml) heavy whipping cream

Chile Cream
1 cup (250ml) heavy whipping cream
2 large red chiles, seeded & finely diced
2 tbsp cilantro
salt & freshly ground black pepper

WINE *Australian unoaked Chardonnay*

(1d) **To make the soup**
Heat the butter and vegetable oil in a large pan. Add the squash, carrots, shallots and garlic, and sweat for 5 minutes. Pour in the stock, bring to a boil, then simmer for 1 hour. Cool, purée until smooth, then store in an airtight container and chill.

(1d) **To prepare the pumpkins**
Cut a slice off the base of the pumpkins so that they will sit flat on the plates. Do not cut off too much – you do not want to make a hole in the base. Cut off the top to remove all the seeds. Cover in plastic wrap and refrigerate.

(8h) **To make the chile cream**
Whisk the cream until it just holds its shape. Fold in the chopped chiles and cilantro, then season. Place in an airtight container and refrigerate.

To assemble
Preheat the oven to 300°F/150°C. Arrange leaves on the dinner plates if using (see below). Place the pumpkins on a pan to warm in the oven for about 20 minutes. Bring the soup to a boil, then add the cream. Stir, check the seasoning, lower the heat and simmer. If serving with fresh bread, warm it in the oven, then wrap in a linen napkin. Wipe the insides of the warmed pumpkins with paper towels to remove any moisture. Place a pumpkin in the center of each plate. Fill it with soup and top with chile cream. Serve.

AUTUMN LEAVES
TO PRESENT THIS SOUP IN AN ORIGINALLY BEAUTIFUL WAY, LINE THE PLATES WITH A SELECTION OF WASHED, DRIED LEAVES.

Black Challans Chicken with Spring Rolls

vegetable oil
10 breast halves of black challans, trimmed
 with skin on; or free-range, corn-fed chicken
1¼lb (620g) carrots
10 baby bok choy
peanut oil
1 tbsp white sesame seeds
1 tbsp ginger, chopped
salt & freshly ground black pepper
5 cups (1.2 liters) reduced chicken stock
⅔ cup (150ml) sweet soy sauce

Butternut Squash Soup

Spring Roll

1 tbsp all-purpose flour

2 tbsp water

3½oz (100g) glass (cellophane) noodles

peanut oil

3 garlic cloves, puréed

14oz (400g) carrots, thinly sliced

11oz (300g) Chinese cabbage, thinly sliced

7oz (200g) shiitake mushrooms, sliced

14oz (400g) sugar snap peas, thinly sliced

5 tsp sugar

10 tbsp light soy sauce

salt & freshly ground black pepper

10 spring roll pastry sheets, each 10in² (25cm²)

SPECIAL EQUIPMENT deep-fat fryer

WINE *Spanish Chardonnay or Chilean oaked Chardonnay*

(8h) **To sear the chicken**

Heat a little oil in a sauté pan. When the pan starts to smoke, add the breasts of chicken, 2 at a time, skin side down, and season. Turn when golden brown to sear the other side. Place on a metal pan to cool, then cover and refrigerate.

(8h) **To prepare the vegetables**

Bring a pan of salted water to a boil. Cut the carrots so that they have 4 flat sides. Using a mandolin, slice each carrot into ⅛in- (3mm-) thick ribbons. Fill a bowl with iced water. Blanch the ribbons, a handful at a time, for about 1 minute, then refresh in the iced water. Dry, cover and put aside. Separate the bok choy leaves and wash. Heat a little peanut oil in a sauté pan. Add half the sesame seeds, the ginger and a handful of bok choy. Season and continue to sauté until the leaves wilt. Place in a large bowl. Repeat, using the remaining sesame seeds. Cool, mix with the carrot ribbons and divide into 10 portions on a greased metal pan. Sprinkle with water, seal with foil, then refrigerate.

(8h) **To prepare the chicken and sauce**

In a pan, bring the (preferably brown) chicken stock to a boil then reduce to about 2½ cups (600ml), which is enough for 10 portions. Add the sweet soy sauce and simmer for 5 minutes. Let cool, then cover and refrigerate.

Black Challans Chickens with Spring Rolls

(8h) **To prepare the spring roll filling**

Mix the flour and water into a smooth paste for the glue; cover. Bring a pan of salted water to a boil and blanch the noodles for 1 minute, or until soft, then drain. Cut into 1in (2.5cm) lengths and set aside. Heat a little peanut oil in a wok or sauté pan. Add the garlic, carrots, cabbage and shiitake mushrooms, and sauté for 2 minutes. Add the peas, sugar, soy sauce and noodles. Cook for 2 minutes more and season. Let cool, then cover and refrigerate.

(2h) **To prepare the spring roll wrapping**

Line a metal tray with a clean tea towel. Place a spring roll wrapper on a work surface to form a diamond shape. Put a heaped tablespoon of vegetable filling in the center of the first third. Brush the corners with the glue. Fold the bottom corner over the filling (quite tightly so that it is 1½in/4cm round). Fold the sides into the center, then roll up. Each roll should be 5in (12.5cm) long. When all the rolls are made up, place them on a tray, cover and chill.

To assemble

Preheat the oven to 400°F/200°C; heat the deep-fat fryer to 375°F/190°C. In a pan, bring the sauce to a boil, lower the heat and simmer. Cook the spring rolls in the deep-fat fryer until golden. Drain on paper towels and keep warm until needed. Place the chicken, carrots and bok choy in the oven for about 10–12 minutes. The chicken is ready when it is firm to the touch. Remove from the oven and keep warm. Trim off the ends of the spring rolls and cut in half on an angle. On each plate, place 2 spring roll halves, bok choy and carrots. Slice each chicken breast half into 3 and place against the bok choy. Pour a little sauce around the plate. Serve.

COOKING REFRIGERATED FOOD

WHEN ROASTING ANY MEAT OR FISH, OR REHEATING VEGETABLES, ALWAYS REMOVE FROM THE REFRIGERATOR 15 MINUTES BEFORE COOKING. OTHERWISE THE INITIAL COOKING PROCESS WILL BE LESS EFFECTIVE.

Ginger Ice Cream with Glazed Pineapple

Ice Cream
12 egg yolks
2 cups (250g) sugar
2⅓ cups (600ml) milk
2⅓ cups (600ml) heavy whipping cream
7 tbsp (100g) chopped ginger
SPECIAL EQUIPMENT **ice cream maker**

1 large coconut, for the coconut curls

Glazed Pineapple
2 large pineapples, peeled, cut into ten 1¼in
  (3cm) rounds, cored, & cut into fingers
freshly ground black pepper
vegetable oil
⅔ cup (150g) soft brown sugar
WINE *Australian Botrytis Riesling*

(7d) **To make the ice cream**
Place the egg yolks and sugar in an electric mixer, and whisk until pale and creamy. In a heavy-based saucepan, bring the milk and cream to a boil. Remove from the heat. On a slow speed, pour into the egg mixture in a steady stream, then scrape down the sides. Return the mixture to the pan and heat, stirring until the custard coats the back of the spoon. Do not allow the mixture to boil. Sieve into a bowl and add the ginger, then let cool. Pour into an ice cream maker and churn. Store the ice cream in a container and freeze.

(2d) **To prepare the coconut curls**
Preheat the oven to 325°F/160°C. Break open the coconut and remove the flesh. (Reserve the liquid since it makes a lovely cold drink.) Peel the flesh into long strips and place on a tray in the oven until golden. When cool they will be crispy. Store in an airtight container.

(8h) **To ball the ice cream**
Line a metal pan with nonstick paper and place in the freezer for 30 minutes. Fill a jug with hot water. Dip a scoop into the water then into the ice cream. Make a ball, place it on the tray and repeat for all the ice cream. Return the tray to the freezer.

Ginger Ice Cream with Glazed Pineapple

PEELING PINEAPPLES
Place the pineapple on a board and cut off its top and base using a sharp knife with a serrated edge. Stand the pineapple upright and slice around it, about ¼in (6mm) deep, to remove the rind and eyes.

(8h) **To glaze the pineapple**
Place the pineapple fingers on a tray and grind black pepper over them. Heat a little oil in a sauté pan and, when it begins to smoke, add a few pineapple fingers. Sauté until golden, then turn. Repeat for all the pineapple, and place on a tray, leaving the juices in the pan.

Add the brown sugar to the pan juices and caramelize. If the sugar starts to become too dark, add a little water and continue to cook. Pour the caramelized sugar over the pineapple fingers. Let cool, then cover and refrigerate.

To assemble
Preheat the oven to 300°F/150°C. Place the pineapple fingers in the preheated oven for about 6 minutes, then drain the juices into a jug. Place 4 fingers of pineapple in the center of each plate. Top with ice cream and arrange the coconut curls. Drizzle a little juice on the plates, and serve.

winter menu

To brighten winter's long, grey days and dark nights, I always think that salmon gives a welcome splash of color at the dinner table. Its fresh flavor seems particularly piquant in this season, and marinated and mixed with smoked salmon, it is always popular with guests. The exquisite chocolate tart (one of our most requested desserts) marries delightfully with the seasonal and unusual tamarillo or tree tomato. Serves 10

Fresh Salmon Wrapped in Smoked Salmon

2¼lb (1kg) fresh salmon fillet, skin removed
2 shallots, finely diced
3 tbsp virgin olive oil
1 tbsp sea salt flakes
½ tsp ground black pepper
10 lime segments
10 orange segments
10 pink grapefruit segments
1lb (500g) long, sliced smoked salmon
1 bunch of chives
½ cup (½ tea cup) picked dill, washed
  & refrigerated

Whole-Grain Mustard Dressing
2 tsp whole-grain mustard
1 tbsp white wine vinegar
1 tsp sugar
1 tbsp virgin olive oil
salt & freshly ground black pepper
WINE *Pink Sancerre or Chablis Grand Cru*

(1d) **To marinate the salmon**
Cut the salmon into 1in- (2.5cm-) wide strips, then slice each strip as thinly as possible widthwise. Place in a bowl. Add the shallots, olive oil, salt and black pepper, then mix thoroughly. Place in an airtight container and chill for 12 hours.

(1d) **To make the dressing**
Mix together all the ingredients and season. Pour into a jar and refrigerate.

(8h) **To prepare the fruits**
Cut the lime, orange and grapefruit segments into ¼in (7mm) pieces. Place in an airtight container and refrigerate.

(8h) **To prepare the smoked salmon**
Cut the smoked salmon into 10 strips, 10 x 2in (25.5 x 5cm). Layer in greaseproof paper and chill. Cut 20 of the chives into 6in (15cm) lengths, then snip the rest up for the garnish. Place in an airtight container and chill.

REMOVING SMALL BONES FROM FISH
A PAIR OF ARTERY FORCEPS (AVAILABLE FROM SURGICAL INSTRUMENT SHOPS OR A GOOD DRUGSTORE) ARE THE BEST UTENSILS FOR REMOVING THE SMALLEST BONES.

Fresh Salmon Wrapped in Smoked Salmon

To serve
Thirty minutes before serving time, mix half the citrus segments and dill with the fresh salmon. Place a 2¾in-wide x 1¼in-deep (7 x 3cm) ring mold in the center of each plate (10 in all). Wrap a piece of smoked salmon around the inside of each mold, making sure it reaches the base of the mold and flaps over the top. Fill with marinated salmon, then remove the mold. Place the long chives vertically in the center. Drizzle over dressing and scatter on the remaining segments and chives. Serve.

Port Wine Duck with Cabbage Parcels

Duck Confit

3 duck legs, weighing 1½lb (700g)

2 garlic cloves, crushed

5 sprigs of thyme

3 tbsp sea salt flakes

6 peppercorns

1 quart (1 liter) goose or duck fat

Cabbage Parcels

2 medium savoy cabbages

2 tbsp unsalted butter

2 medium onions, thinly sliced

1 cup (250ml) white chicken stock

salt & freshly ground black pepper

vegetable oil

Potato & Turnip Gratin

2 tbsp unsalted butter

3 cups (750ml) heavy whipping cream

3 garlic cloves, finely chopped

3lb (1.3kg) yellow potatoes, very thinly sliced

2lb (900g) turnips, very thinly sliced

a generous pinch of grated nutmeg

salt & ground white pepper

10 female barbary (Muscovy) duck breasts

Port Wine Sauce

4 shallots, chopped

olive oil

1 glass port wine

7 cups (1.8 liters) reduced brown chicken stock

WINE *Nuit St Georges or Chilean Cabernet*

(2½d) To prepare the confit

Place all the ingredients except for the fat in a large bowl and mix, covering the legs with the herbs and seasoning. Cover and refrigerate for 12 hours.

(2d) To make the confit

Heat the fat in a large pan. Wash the marinade from the duck legs and dry. Add them to the fat and cook on a very low heat for about 2 hours, then place on a tray. Let cool, then remove the skin and shred the meat. Place in an airtight container and refrigerate.

(1d) To prepare the parcels

Bring a pan of salted water to a boil. Select 5 leaves from each cabbage and blanch them, 2 at a time, in the pan of boiling water for 30 seconds, remove and refresh in iced water. Dry, place in an airtight container and chill. Remove

Port Wine Duck with Cabbage Parcels

the core of 1 cabbage and shred the leaves finely. Heat the butter in a pan and sauté the onions until soft. Add the stock and cabbage and cook for 8–10 minutes. Drain and let cool. Add to the duck confit, season and mix well.

(1d) To make the parcels

Place the leaves on a cloth and season with salt and pepper. Put 1 tablespoon confit and cabbage in the center of each leaf and fold up into a round. Wrap in a cloth and twist to form a tight ball. Put onto a buttered metal pan and sprinkle with water. Seal with foil and chill.

(1d) To make the sauce

Sauté the shallots in olive oil until golden. Add the port and reduce by half. Pour in the stock and reduce to a velvety consistency (1 pint/600ml for 10 portions). Strain, cool and chill.

(8h) To sear the duck

Heat a little oil in a sauté pan. When the pan starts to smoke, add 2 duck breasts, skin side down, and season. When golden, turn and sear until the second side is golden. Place on a greased metal pan. Repeat for all the duck breasts. Cover and refrigerate.

(8h) To prepare the gratin

Preheat the oven to 350°F/180°C. Butter an ovenproof dish. In a pan, bring the cream to a simmer and add the garlic. Sprinkle the potatoes and turnips with salt and leave for 5 minutes, then squeeze to remove water and starch. Add the potatoes, turnips and nutmeg to the cream and return to a boil for 5 minutes. Stir, check seasoning, then pour into the ovenproof dish, smoothing the top. Cook in the oven for 1 hour, or until soft and golden. Let cool, then divide into 10 portions. Do not refrigerate, but store in a cool place.

To serve

Preheat the oven to 400°F/200°C. Bring the sauce to a boil, season and lower the heat. Place the gratin in the oven. After about 10 minutes, add the cabbage parcels and duck, cooking for

10–12 minutes. Remove the gratin, cabbage parcels and duck. Cover the duck loosely with foil and let rest for 5 minutes before slicing into 3 portions. Place the gratin and cabbage in the center of the plates. Arrange the duck against the cabbage and gratin, then pour on the sauce. Serve.

Bitter Chocolate Tart

Pastry
10 tbsp (140g) unsalted butter
scant 1 cup (100g) powdered sugar
1 egg
2¼ cups (250g) all-purpose flour, sifted
¼ cup (30g) ground almonds
melted butter
flour for rolling the pastry

Tamarillos & Sauce
10 tamarillos
2 star anise
1 vanilla bean, split
3 cloves
3¼ cups (750g) superfine sugar
1 bottle (750ml) red wine
1 cup (250ml) water

Chocolate Ganache
11oz (310g) unsweetened chocolate, about 70% cocoa butter, broken into small pieces
2¾ cups (675ml) heavy whipping cream
13 egg yolks
1 cup (110g) superfine sugar
cocoa powder, to dust
1⅓ cups (250g) crème fraîche or sour cream, to garnish
WINE *Nuit St Georges or Chilean Cabernet*

Bitter Chocolate Tart

(2d) To prepare the tart crust
Preheat the oven to 350°F/180°C. In a mixer, beat the butter and sugar until pale and creamy. On a slow speed, add the egg, then the flour and almonds. Transfer the mixture to a floured board and knead until smooth. Cover with plastic wrap and refrigerate for 2 hours. Place a flan ring on a baking sheet and brush with melted butter. Dust a cool work surface with flour and roll out the pastry to a thickness of ¼in (7mm). Use the pastry sheet to line the flan ring, allowing 1in

(2.5cm) overlap. Line the pastry with foil, fill with baking beans and refrigerate for 1 hour. Transfer to the oven to bake for about 30 minutes until golden brown. Remove the beans and foil and return to the oven for 30–35 minutes. Let cool and cut off the overlap. Store in an airtight container.

(2d) To poach the tamarillos
Clean the stalk of the tamarillos. Put the spices, sugar, wine and water into a large pan. Bring to a boil. Reduce the heat, then add the tamarillos and simmer for about 5 minutes. Let cool in the liquor then strain 1¼ cups (300ml) into a pan. Peel the tamarillos, place in an airtight container and pour the remaining liquor over them. Refrigerate. Bring the reserved liquor to a boil and reduce by half. Let cool, place in a jar and keep this sauce refrigerated.

(8h) To make the ganache
Put the chocolate in a large bowl. In a pan, bring the cream to a boil. Whisk together the egg yolks and sugar until

pale and creamy. Pour the cream onto the chocolate and whisk smooth. Add the egg mixture gradually and whisk for 1 minute. Sieve into a jug.

(8h) To bake the tart
Preheat the oven to 250°F/120°C. Place the tart crust on a baking pan. Pour the chocolate mixture into it and bake for 45–50 minutes or until the tart is set. Remove and let cool. Store in an airtight container in a cool place.

(2h) To cut the tart and tamarillos
Cut the tart into slices then reassemble, leaving small gaps between each slice. Cover and store in a cool place. Drain the tamarillos and cut a small slice off the base of each fruit so that it stands up. Return to the container and chill.

To serve
Dust the top of the tart with cocoa powder. Place a slice in the center of each plate with a tamarillo and a blob of crème fraîche next to it. Drizzle the sauce over the tamarillo and serve.

do-ahead dinner

This menu is easy to prepare ahead of time, and each delicious course is sure to impress your guests. The hot chocolate mousse, in particular, is always extremely popular. I once served it, still hot, for 400 guests in a tent in the middle of a field! SERVES 10

Mussel & Saffron Broth

Mussel & Saffron Broth

vegetable oil
4 shallots, thinly sliced
3 garlic cloves, finely chopped
1 medium-sized fennel bulb, thinly sliced
2 large leeks, washed & thinly sliced
9lb (4kg) fresh mussels in their shells
1 cup (1 glass) dry white wine
10 cups (2.4 liters) fish stock
1 tsp saffron dissolved in 1 tbsp boiling water
1¼ cups (300ml) heavy whipping cream
salt & freshly ground black pepper
10 plum tomatoes, skinned, seeded & cut
  into large dice
½ cup (½ tea cup) flat-leaf parsley, chopped
Wine *Muscadet or a young, unoaked Chardonnay*

(5h) **To prepare the broth**
Scrub the mussels thoroughly to remove all barnacles and any trace of grit or sand. Remove the beard from the side of each mussel by pulling it sharply. Heat a little oil in a large pan and sauté the shallots, garlic, fennel and leeks for 2 minutes. Turn up the heat, then add the mussels and white wine. Cover and, after 1 minute, shake the pan well, then continue cooking for 2–3 minutes more. The mussels are cooked when the shells are open. Drain the mussels into a clean pan, keeping the cooking liquid and vegetables. Discard any unopened mussels, and reserve 60 mussels in their shells to garnish. Remove the remaining mussels from their shells. Place in a bowl, cool, cover and chill. Bring the liquid back to a boil, add the fish stock, saffron and cream and simmer for 5 minutes. Take off the heat and season. Let cool, place in an airtight container and chill.

To serve
Place the serving bowls in a warm oven. Remove the mussels from the refrigerator. Bring the broth to a boil slowly, then add the tomatoes and parsley. Remove from the heat and pour into a jug. Divide the mussels between the serving bowls and pour the broth over them. Decorate with the reserved mussels and serve.

Pheasant Breast with Crispy Potato

Pheasant Breast with Crispy Potato

Red Wine Sauce

vegetable oil

3 shallots, roughly chopped

4 sprigs of thyme

1 cup (1 glass) red wine

2 tbsp quince jelly

7 cups (1.8 liters) reduced brown
   chicken stock

Pheasant & Vegetables

vegetable oil

salt & freshly ground black pepper

10 pheasant breast halves, thigh bone
   trimmed

6–8 carrots, cut into forty 2in- (5cm-) strips

4–6 leeks, cut into forty ¾in (2cm) slices

40 shallots, peeled

3 tbsp sugar

Crispy Potato

2¼lb (1kg) yellow potatoes, julienned

10 strips cooked back bacon (Canadian
   bacon), cut into strips

salt & freshly ground black pepper

vegetable oil

¼ cup (60g) unsalted butter

Wine *Gevrey Chambertin*

2d To make the sauce

Sauté the chopped shallots and thyme in
a little oil until the shallots are soft and
transparent. Add the wine and jelly and
reduce by half. Pour in the stock and
reduce to about 2½ cups (600ml). Remove
from heat and sieve finely. Cool. Place in
an airtight container and refrigerate.

8h To sear the pheasant & vegetables

Heat a little oil in a large pan. Season
the pheasant on both sides and place
skin side down in the hot pan. Sear
until golden, turn and repeat. Transfer
to a pan. Cool, then cover and chill.
Clean the pan, return it to the heat and
pour in a little oil; season the leeks and
carrots. Sauté them separately until
golden; remove and place on a metal
tray. Let cool, then cover and chill.
Clean the pan again, return to the heat
with a little oil and cook the shallots
slowly until golden. Then season, add

the sugar and continue cooking until
caramelized and soft. Remove, place on
a pan. Cool, then cover and chill.

4h To make the crispy potato

In a bowl, mix the potato and bacon
strips and add seasoning. Heat a little
oil in a pan. Add half the butter and
place 5 small handfuls of potato in the
pan. Using the back of a large spoon,
press each handful into 4¾in (12cm)
round. Cook until crisp and golden on
both sides, then place on a pan. Repeat
for all the potato. Cool, cover and chill.

To assemble

Preheat the oven to 400°F/200°C. Bring
the sauce to a boil, then reduce the
heat and simmer. Season. Cook the
pheasant, vegetables and potato cakes
in the oven for 10 minutes. Remove the
pheasant and let rest for 5 minutes
covered with foil. Slice each breast half
into 3. Pour the sauce into a jug. Place
a potato cake on each plate with the
pheasant on top. Scatter the vegetables
over, drizzle on the sauce and serve.

Hot Chocolate Mousse

Hot Chocolate Mousse

Serve in Chinese tea cups about 2½ x 2½in/6 x 6cm, or 6fl oz/180ml.

70% PROOF CHOCOLATE

ALTHOUGH SOME RECIPES WILL WORK WITH 50% COCOA CHOCOLATE YOU MUST SEEK OUT THE DARKEST YOU CAN FIND FOR THIS MOUSSE — OTHERWISE YOU WILL LOSE THE ESSENTIAL RICH FLAVOR.

¼ cup (60g) butter, melted

5 tbsp superfine sugar

9oz (250g) extra-bitter chocolate (70% cocoa butter)

9 tbsp (125g) butter

8 eggs, separated

¾ cup (180g) superfine sugar

½ cup (60g) all-purpose flour, sifted

3oz (90g) extra-bitter chocolate, chopped into small pieces

powdered sugar, to dust

1 cup (250g) clotted cream or whipped cream

WINE Australian Botrytis Riesling

(9h) To prepare the tea cups

Brush the insides with melted butter and coat with superfine sugar. Refrigerate.

(8h) To make the mousses

Cut the chocolate and butter into 1in (2.5cm) pieces, then place in a metal bowl over a pan of barely simmering water to melt. Do not allow the chocolate to get too hot as this will make it difficult to combine with the other ingredients. In an electric mixer, whisk the egg whites on a high speed until foamy. Add the superfine sugar gradually, continuing to whisk until the consistency is smooth, glossy and stiff. Remove the chocolate from the heat, add the egg yolks and mix thoroughly. Fold in the egg whites and add the sifted flour. Continue to fold until all the ingredients are well combined. Remove the cups from the refrigerator. Divide the extra chopped chocolate pieces between them. Spoon the mousse mixture into the cups until each is three-quarters full. Return to the refrigerator.

To cook the mousses

Preheat the oven to 325°F/160°C. Boil a kettle of water. Put the mousses into a deep roasting pan, then pour boiling water into the pan to halfway up the cups. I suggest that you do this while the roasting pan is in the oven, so that you do not have to carry it. Cook the mousses for about 20 minutes or until well risen above the edge of the cups.

To serve

Carefully remove the tea cups from the water – remembering they will be hot. Place them on a clean tea towel to drain away any excess water. Dust with powdered sugar and serve with a spoonful of clotted cream on the side.

A LIGHT TOUCH

TAKE CARE NOT TO BE HEAVY-HANDED WHEN FOLDING IN THE INGREDIENTS. YOU DO NOT WANT TO KNOCK TOO MUCH AIR OUT OF THE MIXTURE.

mediterranean dinner

This menu is an interesting variation on some classic Mediterranean dishes. The first course was developed by head chef Richard Cubbin, in the South of France. With the enviable task of shopping in the local market, he one day prepared this tart whose flavors marry delightfully – the richness of the goat cheese enhanced by the sweetness of the figs. All the courses are easy to prepare, and you will be amply rewarded by the risotto! The tiramisu is best served in small glasses. SERVES 10

Goat Cheese, Fig & Red Onion Jam Tart

Pastry Discs
all-purpose flour for dusting
1½lb (675g) frozen puff pastry, thawed
3 egg yolks
1 tbsp milk
pinch of salt

Topping
10 fresh figs
2 tbsp sugar
8oz (225g) log of goat cheese
10 tbsp Red Onion Jam (see page 168)
1 cup (1 tea cup) picked chervil, washed & dried
1 cup (1 tea cup) picked flat-leaf parsley, washed & dried
1 cup (1 tea cup) chives, snipped into 1½in (4cm) lengths, washed & dried
Red Wine Vinaigrette (see page 168)
salt & freshly ground black pepper

SPECIAL EQUIPMENT **blow torch**

WINE *Chilled Chinon*

1d **To prepare the pastry**
Dust a cool surface with flour and roll the pastry to a thickness of ⅛in (3mm). Cut from it ten 4in (10cm) discs and place on a floured baking pan. Prick the pastry discs with a fork and chill for 1 hour. Preheat oven to 400°F/200°C. Beat the egg yolks, milk and salt in a small bowl. Brush the pastry with this glaze. Cook in the

Goat Cheese, Fig & Red Onion Jam Tart

oven for 10 minutes or until golden. Remove; let cool. Layer in greaseproof paper and store in an airtight container in a cool place.

(4h) To prepare the topping

Cut each fig into 12 segments, place on a metal pan and dust with sugar. Caramelize the figs with a blow torch. Let cool, but do not refrigerate. Cut the goat cheese crosswise into 5 equal slices. Quarter each slice.

(1h) To assemble

Place the pastry discs on a metal pan and spread half the Onion Jam over them. Arrange the figs and goat cheese alternately, then top with the remaining jam. Leave in a cool place.

To serve

Preheat the oven to 300°F/150°C. Warm the tarts for 6–8 minutes. Toss the herbs in a bowl with 1 tablespoon of vinaigrette; season. Place a tart in the center of each plate and drizzle on the vinaigrette. Top each with herb salad.

Loin of Veal with Lemon Risotto & Spinach

Mustard Sauce
3 shallots, finely diced
2 garlic cloves, finely chopped
vegetable oil
1 cup (1 glass) dry white wine
3²/₃ cups (900ml) reduced brown
   chicken stock
1¼ cups (300ml) heavy whipping cream
1 tbsp strong-flavored mustard

Veal, Spinach & Mushrooms
vegetable oil
ten 7oz (200g) loin of veal portions
salt & freshly ground black pepper
1lb (500g) spinach, washed 3 times,
   drained, dried & placed in an airight
   container lined with a clean tea towel
2 tbsp unsalted butter
7oz (200g) prepared oyster mushrooms

Lemon Risotto
10 cups (2.4 liters) vegetable stock
¼ cup (60g) unsalted butter
4 shallots, finely chopped

Loin of Veal with Lemon Risotto & Spinach

3 garlic cloves, finely chopped
5 sprigs of thyme, finely chopped
1¼lb (560g) Arborio rice
1 cup (1 glass) dry white wine
¼ cup (60g) unsalted butter
1 cup (100g) Parmesan cheese, grated
zest & juice of 4 lemons
¼ cup (¼ tea cup) flat-leaf parsley, chopped
salt & freshly ground black pepper
WINE *Chianti Classico Riserva*

(1d) To prepare the sauce

Sauté the shallots and garlic in a little vegetable oil until soft, then add the white wine and reduce until syrupy. Add the chicken stock and cream, then reduce by half. Allow 2½ cups (600ml) for 10 portions. Pour into an airtight container. Cool, then refrigerate.

(6h) To sear the veal

Heat a little oil in a large pan. When the oil begins to smoke, add the portions of veal a few at a time. Season, then sauté until golden brown on each side. Remove from the pan and place on a baking pan. Let cool, cover and refrigerate.

(6h) To prepare the spinach

Butter a metal pan. Blanch the spinach in boiling water for 10 seconds. Refresh, drain, then squeeze to remove excess water. Season in a large bowl then separate into 10 portions and set on pan. Seal with foil and chill.

(6h) To sauté the mushrooms

Heat butter in a pan, and sauté the mushrooms until soft. Drain, place on a metal pan and let cool. Seal with foil and refrigerate.

(½h) To cook the risotto

Bring the vegetable stock to a boil, turn down the heat to simmer. In a large pan, melt the butter, add the shallots and cook for 2 minutes. Add the garlic and thyme, cook for 2 minutes more without browning, then add the rice. Stir to make sure that the rice is coated with butter. Pour in the wine and when it is absorbed, add a little stock, a ladleful at a time. When almost absorbed, repeat until all the stock is used. If required, add extra boiling water. The rice should now be 'al dente' and creamy, not runny or dry. Stir, taking care not to break the grains. Add the butter and cheese, stir gently, then add the lemon zest and juice with the parsley. Stir, season and serve within 5 minutes. (See Perfect Creamy Risotto page 150.)

To assemble

Preheat the oven to 400°F/200°C. Pour the sauce into a pan and bring to a simmer. Cook the veal for 10–12 minutes and the spinach and mushrooms for 2 minutes less. Let the veal rest for about 5 minutes before serving. Whisk the mustard into the sauce and check seasoning. Spoon the risotto into the center of each plate, place the spinach, mushrooms and veal to the side. Drizzle on the sauce. Serve.

Ginger Tiramisu

Genoise Sponge

10 large eggs, separated
1lb (500g) superfine sugar
10 tbsp boiling water
1½ cups (350g) all-purpose flour
5 tsp baking powder
pinch of salt

Jasmine Tea Soaking Liquid

2 tbsp jasmine tea
1¼ cups (300ml) boiling water
1 tbsp sugar
½ cup (120ml) ginger wine
1 tbsp syrup from the crystallized ginger
1 orange, rind finely grated

Mascarpone Cream

1¼lb (625g) mascarpone cheese
6 egg yolks
½ cup (105g) superfine sugar
¼ cup (60ml) orange juice, strained
¼ cup (60ml) ginger wine
3 tbsp crystallized ginger in syrup, cut into small dice
6 egg whites
1¼ cups (300ml) heavy whipping cream
WINE Californian Orange Muscat

Ginger Tiramisu

(1d) **To make the sponge**

Preheat the oven to 350°F/180°C. Grease and line two 11 x 14in (28 x 35cm) jelly roll pans with parchment paper. Whisk the egg yolks and sugar in a mixer on a high speed until light and creamy. Add the boiling water slowly and continue to whisk for 5 minutes more. In a bowl, whisk the egg whites until they form soft peaks. Sift together the flour, baking powder and salt. With a metal spoon, gently fold in the egg yolks then the egg whites, ½ at a time until well incorporated. Divide the mixture between the 2 pans. Cook for 20 minutes or until golden brown and springy to the touch. Remove from the oven and cool on a wire rack. When cool, cut the sponge in half lengthwise, then cut 30 discs from it using a cutter slightly smaller than the molds. The discs should be about ¼in (7mm) thick.

(1d) **To make the soaking liquid**

Infuse the jasmine tea in the boiling water for about 30 minutes. Add the sugar, ginger wine, ginger syrup and orange zest, then put aside.

(1d) **To make the mascarpone cream**

Remove the mascarpone from the refrigerator ½ hour before you need to use it. Whisk the egg yolks in a mixer with ⅓ cup (75g) of sugar, until light in color and a thick consistency. Add the mascarpone, orange juice, ginger wine and pieces of crystallized ginger. Whisk until creamy and smooth. Whisk the egg whites with the remaining sugar until they form stiff glossy peaks. Whip the cream gently. With a large metal spoon, gently fold the egg whites, then the cream, into the mascarpone mixture. Mix in well, making sure that there are no lumps. Set aside.

(8h) **To assemble**

Place 1 disc in the base of each mold, brush with soaking liquid then put 1 tablespoon mascarpone mixture on top of each. Repeat for all the sponge discs, finishing with the mascarpone mixture on top. Level off the tops with a palette knife. Cover and refrigerate.

To serve

Dust ½ with cocoa and ½ with powdered sugar.

effortless dinner

I like to plan menus that do not require too much time in the kitchen, allowing you more time to spend with your guests. This menu is a perfect example of this practice. If preferred, the cherries for the clafoutis can be replaced with fresh or dried apricots, or plums. I like to serve it in individual oval dishes. SERVES 10

Tian of Crab

Dressing
2 tbsp white wine vinegar
1 tsp sugar
4 tbsp extra-virgin olive oil
2 tbsp chopped dill
salt & freshly ground black pepper

Tian
2 Hass avocados, skinned, pits removed
  & cut into small dice
juice of 1 lime
1lb (450g) cooked white crabmeat, shell
  removed
10 plum tomatoes, skinned, seeded & cut
  into small dice
2 shallots, finely diced
¼ cup (¼ tea cup) chopped chives
3 tbsp lemon-flavored olive oil
salt & freshly ground black pepper
WINE New Zealand Sauvignon Blanc

(1d) **To prepare the dressing**
Mix all the ingredients for the dressing.
Season, pour into a jar, cover and chill.

(1h) **To make the tian**
Line a flat pan with plastic wrap. Place
10 ring molds, 2¾ x 1¼in (7 x 3cm)
deep, on the pan. Mix the avocados with
the lime juice, season and divide into
10 equal amounts. Spoon into the base
of each mold and smooth with the back
of a teaspoon. Repeat with the white
crab meat. Mix the tomatoes, shallots,
chives and olive oil, season, then layer
as before. Cover lightly with plastic wrap
and refrigerate.

To serve
With a palette knife or fish slicer, place
the tians in the center of each plate.
Remove the molds carefully. Drizzle the
dressing around the plate and serve.

SKINNING A TOMATO
To remove the skin from a tomato, cut
a cross on the top and then drop it
into boiling water for 10 seconds.
Remove with a slotted spoon and
plunge directly into cold water. The
skin should now fall off easily.

Venison with Celeriac Purée & Juniper Sauce

Venison in Juniper Sauce

Juniper Berry Sauce
vegetable oil
3 shallots, thinly sliced
1 tbsp crushed juniper berries
1 cup (1 glass) dry white wine
7 cups (1.8 liters) reduced chicken stock

Venison Marinade
4lb (1.8kg) loin of venison
3 garlic cloves, crushed
3 shallots, sliced
5 sprigs of thyme
1 bay leaf
zest of 1 orange
2½ cups (600ml) good red wine
⅔ cup (150ml) olive oil
freshly ground black pepper

Spiced Red Cabbage
7 tbsp (100g) unsalted butter
1½lb (750g) finely shredded red cabbage
2 red onions, thinly sliced
3 garlic cloves, finely chopped
1¾ cups (450ml) red wine
2 tbsp Demerara raw sugar
2 tsp allspice
2 tbsp red currant jelly

1 apple, peeled & finely grated
salt & freshly ground black pepper

Celeriac Purée
1lb (500g) celeriac, diced
2¼lb (1kg) yellow potatoes, diced
⅔ cup (150ml) heavy whipping cream
¼ cup (60g) unsalted butter
celery salt & freshly ground black pepper

7oz (200g) chanterelle mushrooms, cleaned,
  brushed & sautéed in vegetable oil
70-80 broad (fava) beans, blanched & shelled
WINE Gigondas or a mature red Bordeaux

(2d) **To make the sauce**
Cook the shallots and juniper berries in
a little oil until the shallots are soft.
Pour in the wine and reduce by half.
Add the chicken stock, return to a boil,
then simmer to reduce to about 2½ cups
(600ml). Remove from the heat. Pass
through a fine sieve and let cool. Pour
into an airtight container and chill.

(2d) **To marinate the venison**
Put the venison in a bowl. Mix the
marinade ingredients together and pour
over the venison. Cover and refrigerate.

Cherry Clafoutis

Cherry Clafoutis

Cherry Compote
¼ cup (60g) sugar
2lb (900g) fresh cherries, pitted
3 tbsp kirsch

Clafoutis Batter
¼ cup (60g) butter, melted
¼ cup (60g) superfine sugar to coat molds
6 large eggs
1¼ cups (300g) superfine sugar
1½ cups (170g) all-purpose flour, sifted
1¼ cups (300ml) crème fraîche or heavy
   whipping cream
1¼ cups (300ml) whole milk
2 tbsp kirsch
powdered sugar, to dust
WINE Muscat Beaume de Venise

(1d) To prepare the compote
In a pan gently heat the sugar in
1 tablespoon of water until dissolved.
Add the cherries and kirsch, and cook
on low heat for 15 minutes, or until the
cherries are soft but still whole. Remove
from the heat. Drain half the cherries,
leaving the rest in the liquid. Let both
cool then chill in two covered containers.

(8h) To make the clafoutis
Preheat the oven to 350°F/180°C.
Brush the insides of the molds with
melted butter and sugar, then put aside.
In a mixer, whisk the eggs until frothy,
add sugar; then whisk for 2 minutes
more. Add the flour, crème fraîche or
cream, milk and kirsch, then whisk
until well blended. Divide the drained,
cooked cherries among the molds, pour
over the batter and place on a baking
sheet. Bake for 15 minutes then remove
the clafoutis from the oven and top up
the molds with any remaining batter.
Return to the oven for 15 minutes until
the clafoutis are golden in color and
firm to touch. Let cool and refrigerate.

To serve
Preheat the oven to 300°F/150°C. Place
the clafoutis on a baking pan and heat
for 10 minutes. Remove, dust with
powdered sugar and place on the plates
with a spoonful of compote. Serve.

(1d) To prepare the cabbage
Heat the butter in a large pan. When
sizzling, add the cabbage, onions and
garlic, stir, reduce the heat, cover, and
cook for 10 minutes. Add the wine, sugar,
allspice and red currant jelly. Cover and
cook, stirring occasionally, on low heat
for 1 hour. Uncover and continue to cook
until wine has almost evaporated. Add
the apple, cook for 10 minutes then
season, let cool, cover and chill.

(6h) To sear the venison
Remove the venison from the marinade,
pat dry and season. Heat a little oil in a
frying pan until smoking, add the
venison and brown on all sides. Place
on a roasting pan to cool, then cover
and return to the refrigerator.

(2h) To prepare the purée
Boil the celeriac and potatoes in salted
water until soft. Drain and pass through
a potato ricer or fine sieve into a bowl.
Clean the pan then return the purée to

it. Add the cream and butter. Return to
the heat and beat with a wooden spoon.
Season with celery salt and pepper.
Remove from the heat, cover and cool.

To assemble and serve
Preheat the oven to 400°F/200°C.
Remove the meat from the refrigerator
15 minutes before cooking. Roast in
the oven for 12–15 minutes, adding
the mushrooms on a separate pan after
5 minutes. Boil the sauce in a pan
then simmer. Heat the red cabbage and
celeriac purée in 2 covered saucepans,
stirring occasionally. Remove the venison
(and the mushrooms) from the oven and
leave for 5 minutes. Meanwhile, cook
the beans in boiling water for 1 minute,
drain and keep warm. Pour the sauce
into a jug and slice the venison. On each
plate, place a spoonful of celeriac purée
and red cabbage. Arrange the venison
over the purée. Scatter the beans and
mushrooms and drizzle the sauce around
the plate and serve.

oriental dinner

These recipes have been developed over the years to offer a range of particularly exciting oriental flavors, textures and colors. If, like me, you enjoy experimenting with different serving dishes and containers, try presenting the coconut brulée and mango sorbet in small glass candleholders – the effect is stunning. SERVES 10

Spiced Duck with Lemon Grass

Duck Marinade
2 tsp chili flakes
¼ cup (60g) chopped ginger
3 garlic cloves, chopped
⅔ cup (150ml) light soy sauce
4 tbsp sweet soy sauce
5 duck breasts
vegetable oil

Lemon Grass Dressing
juice of 3 lemons
2 tbsp water
1 level tbsp coarse raw sugar
1 tbsp fish sauce
1 tbsp sweet chili sauce
2 stems lemon grass, thinly sliced
2 garlic cloves, finely chopped
2 mild red chiles, seeded & cut into
   thin strips
4 tbsp olive oil
salt & freshly ground black pepper

Slaw
2½ cups (300g) carrots, finely shredded
2½ cups (300g) red radish, finely shredded
2½ cups (300g) sugar snap peas, finely
   shredded
1 cup (1 tea cup) picked cilantro, washed
   & dried
salt & freshly ground black pepper

10 wonton skins, finely shredded & deep
   fried till crispy (keep covered before frying
   to prevent them drying out)
WINE Alsace or Oregon Pinot Noir

(1d) **To marinate the duck**
Mix together the marinade ingredients. Place the duck breasts in an airtight container, pour over the marinade, then cover and refrigerate.

(1d) **To make the dressing**
In a saucepan, bring the lemon juice, water, sugar, fish and chili sauces

Spiced Duck with Lemon Grass

to a boil, then lower the heat and simmer for 1 minute or until slightly syrupy. Add the lemon grass, chopped garlic and red chiles and simmer for a minute more. Let cool, then whisk in the oil and season. Pour into a jar and refrigerate.

(6h) **To cook the duck**
Preheat the oven to 375°F/190°C. Drain the duck, then heat a little oil in a sauté pan and sauté the duck until golden brown on both sides. Place on a metal pan in the oven and roast for 8–10 minutes – the duck should be pink. Let cool, then refrigerate.

To serve
Slice the duck widthwise and set aside. Mix the slaw in a bowl, pour over half the dressing, mix well and season. Then mix the duck into the slaw, distributing the meat evenly. Arrange in the center of each plate, top with wontons, drizzle on the remaining dressing and serve.

Grilled Tuna with Chile Noodles & Leeks

Chile Noodles

salt

8oz (225g) fresh fine egg noodles

vegetable oil

1 red chile, seeded & thinly sliced

1 green chile, seeded & thinly sliced

7oz (200g) fresh shiitake mushrooms, sliced

¾ cup (100g) water chestnuts, thinly sliced

7oz (200g) Chinese cabbage, finely shredded

3 tbsp light soy sauce

3 tsp sugar

Tomato & Lime Sauce

3²⁄₃ cups (900ml) reduced brown chicken
 stock

¼ cup (60g) ginger, peeled & chopped

2 lime leaves, finely shredded

juice of 2 limes

1 tbsp coarse raw sugar

5 green onions, thinly sliced

5 plum tomatoes, skinned, seeded & cut into
 large dice

30 baby leeks

vegetable oil

freshly ground black pepper

ten 6oz (175g) tuna steaks, preferably from
 the tail end

WINE *White Rhône or Californian Viognier*

(8h) To prepare the noodles

Bring a large pan of salted water to a boil. Add the noodles, bring back to a boil, then simmer for 4–5 minutes until soft. Rinse under running cold water to cool. Let drain. Place in a bowl and toss with a little oil, then cover. Heat a little oil in a pan, then add chiles, mushrooms, water chestnuts, cabbage, soy sauce and sugar. Cook until the cabbage is soft. Remove from the heat, place on a tray and let cool. Mix with the noodles and season. To give 10 portions, lift a section of noodles with a carving fork, and twist around to form a nest. Place on a lightly oiled baking pan, spray with a little water and seal with foil. Chill.

Grilled Tuna with Chile Noodles & Leeks

(6h) To blanch and grill the leeks

Heat a grill pan. Fill a large saucepan with salted water and bring to a boil. Blanch the leeks for 2–3 minutes, then drain and refresh. Dry with a clean tea towel, brush with a little oil and season. Place the leeks on the grill pan and remove when grill marks are visible. Transfer to a pan, forming portions of 3 leeks tied in a knot. Cover and refrigerate.

(6h) To sear the tuna

Heat the grill pan. Brush the tuna with a little oil and season. Place on the grill pan and grill until marks are visible. Transfer to a pan, cover and refrigerate.

(6h) To prepare the sauce

Bring the stock to a boil in a saucepan, then lower the heat and simmer. Add the ginger, lime leaves, lime juice and sugar. Bring back to a boil and reduce by half. Remove from the heat and let cool. Store in an airtight container and refrigerate.

To assemble

Preheat the oven to 400°F/200°C. Pour the sauce into a pan and bring to a boil, then lower the heat and simmer. Place the noodles in the oven but do not remove the foil. After 4 minutes, add the leeks and tuna. Cook for 6–8 minutes. Add the remaining ingredients to the sauce and check the seasoning. Remove the tuna, noodles and leeks from the oven. On each plate, place a nest of noodles, leeks and tuna. Pour the sauce into a jug and spoon liberally around the noodles and over the tuna. Serve.

CUTS OF FISH AND MEAT

SEVERAL RECIPES, LIKE THIS ONE, SPECIFY THE CUT OF FISH OR MEAT TO USE. TO ENSURE YOU HAVE EXACTLY WHAT YOU NEED ASK YOUR THE FISHMONGER OR BUTCHER TO PREPARE IT FOR YOU. IF YOU ARE ORGANIZED IN TIME, CALL IN ADVANCE TO ORDER IT. A GOOD FISHMONGER OR BUTCHER WILL ALSO OFFER ALTERNATIVES IF YOUR CUT IS NOT AVAILABLE.

Coconut Brulée with Mango Sorbet

Coconut Brulée with Mango Sorbet

Mango Sorbet

3lb (1.35kg) ripe mangoes
2/3 cup (150g) superfine sugar
2/3 cup (150ml) water
3 limes, juiced
30 slices of Oven-Dried Mango (see
  page 169), to garnish
SPECIAL EQUIPMENT **ice cream maker**

Coconut Brulée

5 cups (1.2 liters) heavy whipping cream
2 vanilla beans, split
1/2 cup (90g) dried coconut
10 egg yolks
6 tbsp superfine sugar
Macadamia Nut Brittle (see page 169),
  to garnish
WINE Coteaux du Layon

MACADAMIA NUT BRITTLE

THIS CAN BE PREPARED UP TO A WEEK IN
ADVANCE, BUT THE FINAL CREATION SHOULD
BE LEFT UNTIL THE DAY. EAT THE BRÛLÉES
SOON AFTER GARNISHING.

(2d) **To prepare the sorbet**

Peel the mangoes, removing as much
flesh as possible from the pit. Purée
in a food processor or blender and
put to one side. Place the sugar and
water in a saucepan and bring slowly
to a boil. Simmer for about 2 minutes
until all the sugar has dissolved. Let
cool, then add the purée and lime juice
and refrigerate.

(1d) **To make the sorbet**

Place 10 candleholders in the freezer.
Pour the mixture into an ice cream
maker and churn. Pipe the sorbet into
the holders, smooth the tops and return
to the freezer.

(1d) **To make the brûlée**

Preheat the oven to 300°F/150°C. Place
the cream, vanilla beans and coconut
in a heavy-bottomed saucepan. Bring
to a boil slowly, stirring occasionally.
Remove from the heat and leave to
infuse for 30 minutes. With an electric
mixer, whisk the egg yolks and sugar
together. In the meantime, bring the
cream back to a boil and add the egg
yolks gradually, whisking continuously.

Pass through a fine sieve into a jug,
discarding the coconut and vanilla.
Pour into the remaining molds (candleholders) and place in a deep roasting
pan. Pour boiling water into the tray
to reach halfway up the molds. Cook
for 20 minutes, or until set – the
brulée should be quite firm to touch.
Remove from the bath of water, let
cool and then refrigerate until ready
to serve.

BOILING MILK OR CREAM

USING A HEAVY-BOTTOMED SUACEPAN IS
BEST FOR BOILING MILK OR CREAM AS IT
DISTRIBUTES THE HEAT EVENLY OVER THE
BASE OF THE PAN.

To serve

Remove the sorbets from the freezer,
and let stand for 10 minutes.
Alternatively place in the refrigerator
for 30 minutes. When ready to serve
decorate each sorbet with 3 slices
of oven-dried mangoes and stand a
triangle of Macadamia Nut Brittle
on each brulée. Offer each guest 1
candleholder of each dessert – they
will not want to miss out on either.

vegetarian dinner

Richard Cubbin is our master vegetarian menu planner and these are two of his most requested dishes. Portobello mushrooms are full of flavor and very filling, but if you cannot find them, use field mushrooms instead. SERVES 10

Mille Feuilles of Portobello Mushrooms & Lentils

French Lentil Salad

4oz (150g) French lentils, soaked for
  12 hours & drained
2½ cups (600ml) vegetable stock
salt & freshly ground black pepper
1 cup (150g) carrots, finely diced
1 shallot, finely diced
¼ cup (¼ tea cup) snipped chives

Mustard Oil

3 tbsp mustard seeds
¼ tsp turmeric
½ cup (125ml) grapeseed oil

Parsley Oil

1 cup (1 tea cup) flat-leaf parsley, washed,
  dried & chopped
½ cup (125ml) grapeseed oil

Mille Feuilles of Mushrooms

20 large Portobello mushrooms, or large
  flat field mushrooms
salt & freshly ground black pepper
olive oil to brush the mushrooms & leeks
4 large shallots, sliced into rings
1 garlic clove, finely chopped
¼ cup (¼ tea cup) fresh thyme, chopped
1¼ cups (300ml) extra-virgin olive oil
40 baby leeks, washed & roots trimmed
5 large red peppers, roasted & skinned,
  seeds removed
WINE Bergerac or Languedoc Rosé

(1d) **To make the lentil salad**
Place the lentils and vegetable stock in a medium saucepan, add the salt and bring to a boil; reduce the heat to simmer for about 15–20 minutes. Refresh, drain and set aside. At the same time, cook the carrots in salted water for 2–3 minutes; drain and refresh in cold water. In a bowl, mix together the lentils, carrots, shallot and chives; season to taste. Cover with plastic wrap and place in the refrigerator.

(1d) **To make the mustard oil**
Preheat the oven to 400°F/200°C. Place the mustard seeds on a tray and roast for about 5 minutes; let cool. Blend the mustard seeds, turmeric and oil in a blender for 2–3 minutes; strain through a fine sieve. Pour into a jar with a lid and place in the refrigerator.

(1d) **To make the parsley oil**
Bring a saucepan of water to a boil; fill a large bowl with iced water. Blanch the parsley for about 3–4 minutes. Remove and refresh in the ice-cold water, then dry on a tea towel or in a salad spinner. Chop the parsley coarsely and place in a blender with the oil. Blend for about 2 minutes, then strain through a fine sieve into a jar with a lid. Place in the refrigerator.

(8h) **To prepare the mille feuilles**
Preheat a grill pan. Remove the center stalks from the mushrooms and score lightly across the top of each mushroom. Sprinkle with salt and leave for 5 minutes. Brush the mushrooms with olive oil and grill on each side until soft; let cool. When cold, place the mushrooms in an airtight container, covering with the shallots, garlic, thyme and oil. Season and place in the refrigerator. Bring a pan of salted water to a boil; fill a large bowl with iced water. Blanch the leeks for about 3–4 minutes. Refresh, drain and dry. Heat a grill pan, brush the leeks with a little olive oil and grill on all sides. Allow the leeks to cool then add to the mushrooms.

To assemble
Place a mushroom in the center of each plate. Place 2 leeks on top, add a little of the shallot and garlic mixture and a slice of red pepper, seasoning between each layer; repeat, finishing with a slice of red pepper on top. Sprinkle the lentil mix around the mushrooms, dress with the oils and serve. The mushrooms can be assembled up to 1 hour before; dress just before serving.

Baked Onion with Carrot & Cumin Sauce

ten 10oz (300g) round white onions
vegetable oil
salt & freshly ground black pepper
5½ cups (1.4 liters) vegetable stock
4 cups (500g) cracked wheat
2 tbsp olive oil
4 cups (500g) corn kernels, cooked
1½ cups (200g) pine nuts
8 plum tomatoes, blanched, peeled,
  seeded & cut into ¼in (6mm) dice
¼ cup (¼ tea cup) flat-leaf parsley,
  washed, picked, dried & chopped
¼ cup (¼ tea cup) fresh mint, washed,
  dried & chopped
juice of 1 lime

Carrot & Cumin Sauce

vegetable oil
3 shallots, sliced
1½ tsp cumin seeds
5 cups (650g) carrots, chopped
1 garlic clove, chopped
1¼ cups (300ml) white wine
4 cups (1 liter) vegetable stock
salt & freshly ground black pepper
WINE Cru Beaujolais

THE PERFECT ONION

I CANNOT RECOMMEND VIDALIA ONIONS TOO HIGHLY FOR THIS RECIPE – THEY ARE SO SWEET AND DELICIOUS.

(1d) To prepare and cook the onions

Preheat the oven 350°F/180°C. Line
baking pans with parchment paper.
Remove the outer skins of the onions,
leaving the root and stalk intact. Cut
the top off the onion to create a lid.
Scoop out the middle using a spoon or
melon baller. Brush the insides with
vegetable oil and season. Place on the
pans in the oven and bake for about
20–25 minutes. Remove and let cool.
Pour the stock into a large saucepan
and bring to a boil. Reduce the heat,
then add the cracked wheat and simmer
for about 15–20 minutes, or until all
the stock is absorbed. Add the olive oil
and stir. Add the corn kernels, pine
nuts, tomatoes, herbs and lime juice;
stir well and season. Let cool, then fill
the prepared onions with the mixture
and replace the onion lids. Cover and
place in the refrigerator.

(1d) To prepare the sauce

Heat a little vegetable oil in a
saucepan. Add the shallots, cumin,
carrots and garlic; sauté for 3–4
minutes. Pour in the white wine and
reduce by half. Add the vegetable stock,
bring to a boil and simmer for 20–25
minutes. Season, remove from the heat
and let cool. Blend until smooth, pass
through a fine sieve into a container
and place in the refrigerator.

To serve

Preheat the oven to 350°F/180°C. Cover
the onions loosely with foil and place in
the oven for 8–10 minutes. Heat the
sauce, checking the seasoning. Place an
onion in the center of each plate, pour
on the sauce and serve.

VEGETARIAN-FRIENDLY DESSERTS

IF YOU ARE COOKING A VEGETARIAN DINNER
YOU CAN SELECT ANY OF THE DESSERTS
FROM THE OTHER DINNERS — OR EVEN TRY
ONE FROM THE DESSERT BUFFET ON PAGES
112–15. MY FAVORITE FOR THIS MENU
WOULD BE THE GINGER ICE CREAM WITH
GLAZED PINEAPPLE ON PAGE 126.

*Mille Feuilles of Portobello Mushrooms & Lentils;
Baked Onion with Carrot & Cumin Sauce*

Often we like to entertain, not on a grand scale such as a dinner party, but informally around a kitchen table or in the garden. Perhaps we want to organize a light supper after a trip to the theater or a concert, or a club or association meeting at home requires some informal hospitality.

for a supper party

About twice a year, I give a post-theater supper party for a group of friends and they always request my fish pie. I set the table and place the pie in the oven, set on a timer. When we arrive home, there is time for a glass of wine and then the pie is ready. The supper is easy to serve with little fuss, friends are on hand to help with serving drinks and everyone can seat themselves. After serving this pie, keep it warm as there will always be requests for more.

Enjoying the Evening

The way to enjoy being a host is to plan simple but interesting menus that can be cooked ahead of time. Alternatively, some dishes can be prepared while guests are chatting over a glass of wine – a delicious risotto, for example. Few people can resist the warmth of the kitchen while food is being prepared so the cook is likely to have conversation and help on hand. The menus on the following pages are uncomplicated and easy to prepare. The best and simplest rule when planning menus is to cook with seasonal ingredients.

Cheating with a Chinese Supper

If, like me, you love Chinese food but don't like serving it because it demands lots of last-minute cooking when you would prefer to be socializing with your guests, why not arrange an easy supper the cheat's way? Set the table with matt-black lacquer tablemats and celedon colored bowls, plates and serving dishes, tie the chopsticks together with chives and order your food from your favorite Chinese restaurant. When it arrives, place the food into warmed bowls and serve for a hassle-free supper.

Professional Tips

• **When you know that you're going to want something to eat when you come home, set your oven on timer delay – it can be a life-saver**

• **Before you go out, or before your guests arrive, set the table, or if eating from laps with a fork, arrange the serving area**

• **Wines can be refrigerated to chill and glasses and coffee cups arranged at the beginning of the day**

• **Remember, the best rule is to keep your supper simple – the recipes in this chapter will show you how to do it with style**

PANTRY SUPPERS

SPUR-OF-THE-MOMENT ENTERTAINING IS MADE A LOT EASIER IF YOU KNOW A RANGE OF EASY DISHES THAT CAN BE RUSTLED UP FROM THE USUAL CONTENTS OF YOUR REFRIGERATOR OR PANTRY.

late night supper

This fish pie is an ideal late-night supper after a theater trip or cocktail party. I have served this on several occasions, and my advice is to set the table before leaving and place the pie in the oven with the timer set. On arriving home, there is just time for a glass of wine before serving supper. SERVES 10

Creamy Fish Pie

Pie Filling
6 cups (1.5 liters) fish stock
7oz (200g) salmon fillet, cut into 1½in (4cm) cubes
7oz (200g) monkfish fillet (or other firm, white fish), cut into 1½in (4cm) cubes
7oz (200g) halibut fillet, cut into 1½in (4cm) cubes
7oz (200g) peeled prawns
7oz (200g) cooked mussels
7oz (200g) baby scallops, shelled with muscle removed
7 tbsp (100g) butter
scant 1 cup (100g) all-purpose flour
1¾ cups (450ml) heavy whipping cream
3 shallots, thinly sliced
2 medium-sized leeks, washed & thinly sliced
vegetable oil for cooking
1 cup (1 glass) white wine
2 tbsp Pernod liquor
salt & ground white pepper
¼ cup (¼ tea cup) snipped chives
¼ cup (¼ tea cup) flat-leaf parsely, washed, dried & chopped

Creamed Potatoes
2½lb (1.2kg) yellow potatoes, quartered
1¼ cups (300ml) heavy whipping cream
2 tbsp unsalted butter
3 egg yolks
salt & ground white pepper

(1d) **To prepare the filling**
Bring the stock to a boil in a large saucepan, then lower the heat and simmer. Poach the fish individually, allowing about 3–4 minutes cooking time. Pass the stock through a fine sieve into a clean saucepan. In a separate saucepan, melt the butter then add the flour to make a roux. Cook for 2 minutes, without browning. Add the hot stock slowly, stirring continually to prevent any lumps from forming. Cook over a low heat for about 10 minutes. Remove from the heat and add the cream. Cover with greaseproof paper and let cool slightly. Sauté the shallots and leeks in oil until transparent, not brown. Add the white wine and Pernod, then reduce until very syrupy. Season and transfer to a container. In an oval dish, approximately 14½in (37cm) long, 11in (28cm) wide and 2½in (6cm) deep, scatter the cooked fish, shellfish, shallots and leeks. Make sure that they are evenly distributed, then season. Add the chopped herbs to the cream sauce, stir and season. Ladle over the filling. Let cool, cover with plastic wrap and chill.

(8h) **To cook the potatoes**
Cook the potatoes in a saucepan of salted water until soft, then drain. Pass through a potato ricer or fine sieve into a bowl. Bring the cream to a boil, add the butter and season. Remove from the heat, pour on to the potatoes and beat. Stir in the egg yolks and season. Let cool, then either pipe, using a pastry bag with a fluted nozzle, or spoon over the pie filling. Cover and refrigerate.

To serve
Preheat the oven to 350°F/180°C. Reheat the pie for 1 hour. If you would like the top brown, broil for a few minutes before serving.

Spiced Baked Apples

1¾ cups (280g) raisins
1 cup (220ml) brandy
1 tsp ground cinnamon
½ tsp ground allspice
½ cup (120g) light brown sugar
10 medium cooking apples
10 whole cloves

(2d) **To soak the raisins**
Place the raisins in an airtight jar, pour in the brandy and store in a cool, dry place until required.

(2h) **To prepare the apples**
Preheat the oven to 325°F/160°C. Place the raisins in a bowl, then add the cinnamon, allspice and sugar. Stir until combined. Core the apples, keeping them whole; do not peel them. Score the outsides of the apples around the middle. Place in an ovenproof dish, large enough that the apples will not touch – this allows them to cook evenly. Fill the apples halfway with the fruit mixture, place a clove in the center of each one, then fill to the top with the remaining fruit. Pour about ½ cup (110ml) cold water in the bottom of the dish, then cover and place in the refrigerator until ready to cook.

(¾h) **To cook the apples**
Bake the apples for about 45 minutes, or until they are soft and slightly puffed but still holding their shape.

To serve
Remove from the oven and let cool for about 5 minutes. Place each apple in a bowl and serve, pouring the syrup that collects at the bottom of the baking pan over the apples.

Spiced Baked Apples

speedy supper

When friends drop in unexpectedly, tortillas (Spanish omelets) are very easy to make and quick to cook. They can be made using any leftovers – meat or vegetables – and form an extremely satisfying and tasty meal. Altogether, you should end up with 4 tortillas – enough for 10 people. SERVES 10

Quick-Fix Tortillas

Vegetable Tortillas

3 roasted red peppers, seeded, skins
   removed and cut into large squares
9oz (250g) grated mahon cheese, or aged
   Cheddar
¼ cup (¼ tea cup) mixed herbs (chopped
   parsley, chives and chervil, washed & dried)
olive oil
1 Spanish onion, thinly sliced
9oz (250g) potatoes, thinly sliced
2 garlic cloves, finely chopped
11oz (300g) Portobello mushrooms, sliced
salt & freshly ground black pepper
7oz (200g) spinach, washed & dried
12 eggs

Chorizo Tortillas

9oz (250g) piece of cooked knuckle of ham,
   roughly chopped
½ chile, seeded & finely chopped (optional)
¼ cup (¼ tea cup) mixed herbs (chopped
   parsley, chives and chervil, washed & dried)
olive oil
1 Spanish onion, thinly sliced
9oz (250g) potatoes, thinly sliced
1 leek, washed & thinly sliced
2 garlic cloves, finely chopped
salt & freshly ground black pepper
9oz (250g) chorizo, thinly sliced & quartered
12 eggs

(2h) **To make the vegetable tortillas**
Preheat the broiler. Divide the peppers, cheese and herbs between 2 bowls. Heat a little oil in a 10in (26cm) sauté pan and sauté the onions until very soft. Add the potatoes, and when soft, add the garlic, then sauté for 2–3 minutes more.

Season and divide between the 2 bowls. Clean the sauté pan with paper towels. Pour in a little oil, sauté the mushrooms and season. Transfer to the bowls. Reheat the sauté pan, add the spinach and cook until wilted, then season, drain and place in the bowls. Beat the eggs lightly with a fork and season. Divide and pour into the bowls. Mix well, checking the seasoning. Heat a little olive oil in a sauté pan and add the mixture. Cook on one side, then place under the broiler until the tortilla is light brown and firm to touch. Leave for about 5 minutes. Slide the tortilla onto a serving platter and let cool. Repeat. Serve hot or at room temperature.

(2h) **To make the chorizo tortillas**
Preheat the grill. Divide the ham, chile and herbs between 2 bowls. Heat a little oil in a 26cm (10in) sauté pan with a metal handle and sauté the onions until very soft. Add the potatoes and leek, and when soft, add the garlic and cook for 2–3 minutes more. Season and divide between the 2 bowls. Clean the sauté pan with paper towels. Sauté the chorizo for about 5 minutes and divide between the bowls. Once again, clean the pan with paper towels. Beat the eggs lightly with a fork and season. Divide and pour into the bowls. Mix well, checking the seasoning. Heat a little olive oil in a sauté pan and add the mixture. Cook on one side then place under the broiler until the tortilla is light brown and firm to touch. Leave for 5 minutes, then turn onto a serving platter and set aside. Repeat.

To assemble
Cut each tortilla into 5 equal portions. Line a large wooden board with vine leaves and arrange the ham, olives, and other optional tortilla extras (below) on it. Garnish with fresh herbs and place the mayonnaise in a sauce boat. Serve hot or at room temperature.

OPTIONAL TORTILLA EXTRAS

CHILI MAYONNAISE; CORNICHONS; CRUSTY BREAD WITH BUTTER; FRESH HERBS; OLIVE OIL; MARINATED GREEN AND BLACK OLIVES; SERRANO HAM; WHOLE SALTED ALMONDS

Crisp Green Salad

Sherry Vinegar Dressing

2 tsp grain mustard
1 tbsp white wine vinegar
1 tbsp sherry vinegar
1 tsp sugar
3 tbsp olive oil
2 shallots, thinly sliced
zest of ½ lemon

1lb (450g) salad leaves, washed & dried
   (a selection of 4 varieties from the following:
   baby bok choy; baby red chard; baby spinach;
   escarole; mustard greens; mizuna; Oak leaf)
½ cup (½ tea cup) flat-leaf parsley, picked,
   washed & dried
½ cup (½ tea cup) picked chervil, washed
   & dried
½ cup (½ tea cup) picked chives, snipped,
   washed & dried
a selection of edible flowers to decorate the
   salad: chives; nasturtiums; pansies;
   rose petals; rosemary; thyme

(1d) **To make the dressing**
Place all the ingredients in a bowl, mix well and season. Pour into a jar with a lid and refrigerate.

(1d) **To wash the salad and herbs**
Wash and dry all the leaves carefully, and place in an airtight box lined with a tea towel. Refrigerate.

To serve
Toss the salad and herbs with dressing. Decorate with edible flowers.

Rhubarb Crumble with Vanilla Cream

4 cups (450g) all-purpose flour, sifted
pinch of salt
1 cup (225g) unsalted butter, cut into cubes
scant 1 cup (225g) sugar
3lb (1.35g) fresh rhubarb
1 cup (250g) sugar
finely grated zest & juice of 2 medium-
 sized oranges

Vanilla Cream

2½ cups (600ml) heavy whipping cream
¼ cup (30g) powdered sugar
1 vanilla bean, split lengthwise, seeded

(1d) **To prepare the crumble**

With an electric mixer, mix the flour, salt, butter and sugar until the texture resembles fine breadcrumbs. Place in an airtight container in the refrigerator.

(6h) **To prepare the rhubarb**

Preheat the oven to 375°F/190°C. Wash the rhubarb, and trim top and bottom. Cut the rhubarb into 2in- (5cm-) long pieces. Mix with remaining sugar, orange zest and juice, then place in an ovenproof dish. Cover the dish with foil, and bake for 30 minutes until the rhubarb is soft but still retains its shape. Let cool, then cover and place in the refrigerator.

(½h) **To cook the crumble**

Preheat the oven to 330°F/170°C. Divide the rhubarb and crumble topping among the serving dishes you are using. Bake for about 30 minutes, until you start to see the liquid bubbling out and the crumble is golden brown. While it cooks, prepare the cream.

(½h) **To prepare the cream**

Place the chilled cream in a mixing bowl, then add the powdered sugar and vanilla seeds. Whisk, by hand or with an electric mixer, until the mixture begins to thicken. If using an electric mixer, do not leave unattended, otherwise you could overbeat the cream and turn it into butter. The vanilla cream is best served as soon as it is made, which takes only a few minutes.

To serve

Place the vanilla cream in a serving bowl. With a damp cloth, clean around the bowl and serve.

garlic and sauté for 2 minutes more, without browning. Add the rice and stir, making sure it is coated with butter. Pour in the wine, and when it is almost absorbed, add a little stock a ladleful at a time. When this is almost absorbed, repeat until all the stock is used. If more liquid is required, add a little boiling water. At this point the rice should be 'al dente' and creamy, not dry or runny. Stir in the remaining butter and the Parmesan cheese, then season. Add the mushrooms and parsley, then stir, taking care not to break the grains. Transfer to a warm serving bowl, drizzle on a few drops of truffle oil and scatter over the shavings of Parmesan. Serve.

PERFECT CREAMY RISOTTO

THE SECRET IS TO COOK ON A MEDIUM-LOW HEAT, NOT SO HIGH THAT THE STOCK EVAPORATES RAPIDLY NOR SO LOW THAT IT'S NOT ABSORBED. KEEP THE STOCK BARELY AT A SIMMER AND ADD IT SLOWLY.

Wild Mushroom Risotto

tuscan supper

A few years ago, I spent a holiday in a Tuscan farmhouse with friends who shared a great love of good food and wines. This is typical of the meals we would create from the local produce. SERVES 10

Wild Mushroom Risotto

1lb (450g) seasonal selection of wild
  mushrooms, large ones broken into pieces
olive oil
salt & freshly ground black pepper
3½ quarts (3.6 liters) vegetable stock
¼ cup (60g) unsalted butter
4 shallots, thinly sliced
3 garlic cloves, finely diced
2lb (900g) Arborio rice
1 cup (1 glass) dry white wine
¼ cup (60g) unsalted butter
1 cup (100g) Parmesan, grated

½ cup (½ tea cup) flat-leaf parsley, washed,
  dried & chopped
a few drops of white truffle oil
shavings of Parmesan

(6h) **To sauté the mushrooms**
Sauté the mushrooms in a little olive oil, season and let cool.

(½h) **To make and serve the risotto**
Bring the vegetable stock to a boil, then reduce the heat and simmer. Melt the butter in a large pan, add the shallots and sauté for 2 minutes, then add the

Rosemary Strawberries with Biscotti

Rosemary syrup
1 cup (250g) superfine sugar
1 cup (250ml) water
3 stems of fresh rosemary

2¼lb (1kg) strawberries, washed & hulled
lemon balm or mint leaves to garnish
40 Pistachio Biscotti (see page 123)
1 bottle Vin Santo 'the wine of the saints'

(2h) **To make the syrup**
Place the sugar and water in a heavy-bottomed pan; leave for 5 minutes. Add the rosemary and bring to a boil, then remove from the heat and let cool. Strain and pour into a bottle with a stopper. Store in a cool place.

To serve
Place the strawberries in a large serving bowl and sprinkle with syrup. Garnish with lemon balm or mint. Place the biscotti in a basket and pour the wine into glasses – guests can dip their biscotti into the wine Tuscan-style.

comfort supper

Tasty, chunky soups are popular with nearly everyone.
Serve the soups straight from the pan on the stove or
ladled into large bowls. They can be prepared ahead of
time, and are warm, comforting and delicious – I hope you
enjoy them. For vegetarians, I have suggested how the
Tuscan Bean Soup can be adapted. SERVES 10

Chicken Pot Pie Soup

3 egg yolks
pinch of salt
12½oz (350g) frozen puff pastry, thawed

Soup
3 quarts (3 liters) white chicken stock
1½lb (675g) chicken breasts, skin &
  bone removed
4 fresh ears of corn
vegetable oil
1 large onion, peeled & thinly sliced
2 medium-sized leeks, washed & sliced
7oz (200g) button mushrooms
14oz (400g) carrots, cut into ¾in (2cm) cubes
7oz (200g) new potatoes, washed & sliced
7oz (200g) fresh peas
¼ cup (60g) unsalted butter
½ cup (60g) all-purpose flour, plus extra
  for dusting
2½ cups (600ml) heavy whipping cream
½ cup (½ tea cup) flat-leaf parsley, washed
  & finely chopped
salt & ground white pepper

(1d) To prepare the pastry
Preheat the oven to 375°F/190°C.
Whisk together the egg yolks and salt.
Line a baking pan with nonstick paper.
On a floured board, roll out the pastry
to a thickness of ⅛in (2mm). Cut out
discs with a 1¼in (3cm) round cutter
and brush with the egg yolks. Place
on the pan and refrigerate for ½ hour,
then transfer to the oven to cook until
golden brown. Let cool, then store in an
airtight container in a cool place.

(1d) To make the soup
Bring the stock to a boil in a large
saucepan. Poach the chicken breasts
for about 6–8 minutes, drain, reserving
the stock and let cool. Cut into ½in
(1.5cm) cubes, cover and refrigerate.
Bring the stock back to a boil, add the
corn and cook until tender. Drain (again
reserving the stock), let cool, then
remove the corn from the cobs, cover
and chill. Pour the stock into a large,
clean bowl. Wash the saucepan then
pour the stock (you should have about
10 cups/2.4 liters) back into it. Heat a
little oil in a sauté pan and sauté the
onions and leeks until soft. Add the
mushrooms, sauté for 2 minutes more,
season and cool. Bring a pan of salted
water to a boil, cook the carrots until
tender, then drain. Repeat with the
potatoes and peas. Cover the vegetables
and refrigerate. Bring the stock to a
simmer. In a large saucepan, melt the
butter, then add the flour to make a
smooth roux. Add the stock slowly,
⅔ cup (150ml) at a time, mixing until
smooth. Cook on a low heat for 10
minutes. Cover with greaseproof paper,
let cool and refrigerate.

To serve
Preheat the oven to 350°F/180°C.
Warm the pastry discs. Bring the soup
to a boil, add the cream, chicken and
vegetables, then season. Add the
chopped parsley just before serving.
Float a few 'pie tops' on the soup.
Serve the rest of the pies separately.

Tuscan Bean & Italian Sausage Soup

Soup
¾ cup (100g) dried chickpeas
¾ cup (100g) dried cannellini beans
¾ cup (100g) dried red kidney beans
¾ cup (100g) dried pinto beans
½ large onion
2 whole garlic cloves
2 bay leaves
4 peppercorns
2 sprigs of thyme
olive oil
1 large onion, cut into chunky dice
3 garlic cloves
6 celery stalks, sliced
12 plum tomatoes, peeled, seeded
  & diced
1 tbsp tomato paste
2 tsp sugar
6 cups (1.5 liters) tomato juice
6 cups (1.5 liters) vegetable stock
½ ham bone or 3½oz (100g) smoked strips
  of bacon
11oz (300g) spicy Italian sausage, quartered
  & sliced
salt & freshly ground black pepper
½ cup (½ tea cup) flat-leaf parsley,
  washed, dried & chopped

handful of washed basil leaves,
  to garnish
crusty Italian bread
bowls of olive oil

VEGETARIAN OPTION
TO MAKE THIS SOUP FOR VEGETARIANS,
OMIT THE SAUSAGE AND HAM BONE, OR
REMOVE A PORTION OF SOUP BEFORE
ADDING THE HAM BONE.

(2d) To soak the beans
Soak the beans separately in water
overnight in the refrigerator.

(1d) To make the soup
Bring a saucepan of salted water to a
boil, then add the onion half, whole
garlic, bay leaves, peppercorns and
thyme. Cook the beans separately until
soft, then set aside. Heat a little olive
oil in a large saucepan, add the diced
onion, garlic and celery, and sweat for
5 minutes without browning. Add the

tomato paste and sugar and cook for
2 minutes. Pour in the tomato juice and
stock, then add the ham bone or bacon.
Bring to a boil, then simmer on a low
heat for 30 minutes. Meanwhile sauté
the sausage and set aside. Add the
beans, tomatoes and sausage to the
soup, and season. Let cool, then place
in an airtight container and refrigerate.

To serve

Bring slowly to a boil, add the parsley,
stir and garnish with basil leaves. Serve
with warm, crusty Italian bread and bowls
of olive oil.

Shrimp with Lemon Grass Laksa

50 medium-sized tiger prawns, with heads
5 quarts (4.8 liters) white chicken stock
7oz (200g) rice noodles
3 shallots, thinly sliced
1½oz (45g) galangal (ginger), peeled & cut
   into fine strips
3 garlic cloves, finely chopped
3 medium-sized fresh red chiles, seeded &
   cut into fine strips
4 lemon grass stems, sliced into thin rings
1 tsp shrimp paste
3½oz (100g) chopped dried shrimp
5 tbsp fish sauce
3 lime leaves, finely chopped
1 tbsp raw sugar or superfine sugar
2 tbsp tamarind paste
3 baby bok choy, washed & cut into squares
½ cup (½ tea cup) cilantro leaves, washed
   & dried

(1d) To prepare the soup base

Peel the prawns, keeping the heads
and shells. Cover and place in the
refrigerator. Bring the chicken stock to
a boil, add the heads and shells, then
simmer for 15 minutes. Strain through
cheesecloth into an airtight container.
Let cool, then cover and refrigerate.

(6h) To cook the noodles

Bring a saucepan of water to a boil,
then add the noodles and cook for 1
minute until soft. Drain and refresh. Cut
into 1in (2.5cm) pieces, cover and chill.

To finish the soup

Bring the broth to a boil, then add the
shallots, galangal, garlic, chiles, lemon
grass, shrimp paste, dried shrimp, fish
sauce, lime leaves, sugar and tamarind
paste. Simmer for 5 minutes, add the
prawns and cook for 2 minutes. Just
before serving, add the noodles, bok
choy and cilantro.

Pecan Tart with Crème Fraîche Ice Cream

Makes 2 tarts in 14 x 4½in (35 x
11cm) fluted, rectangular flan pans.

Sweet Pastry

2½ cups (300g) all-purpose flour, sifted
pinch of salt
1 cup (125g) powdered sugar
½ cup (125g) unsalted butter, cubed
2 eggs

Crème Fraîche Ice Cream

2½ cups (600ml) heavy whipping cream
1¼ cups (300g) superfine sugar
2½ cups (600ml) crème fraîche

Tart Filling

8 eggs
1½ cups (350g) superfine sugar
2½ cups (600ml) light corn syrup or
   golden syrup
pinch of salt
1 vanilla bean, split lengthwise & seeds
   removed
1lb (450g) shelled pecan nuts
powdered sugar, to dust
SPECIAL EQUIPMENT ice cream maker

(1d) To prepare the pastry

Mix the flour, salt, powdered sugar and
butter in an electric mixer until the consistency of breadcrumbs and all the butter
is combined. On a slow speed, add the
eggs slowly, mixing until just combined.
On a floured work surface, divide the
mixture in half, cover with plastic wrap
and chill for 8 hours. The pastry is
sufficiently soft to be rolled out straight
from the refrigerator and can be frozen
for up to 1 month. Defrost it in the
refrigerator overnight when required.

(1d) To prepare the ice cream

In a heavy-based saucepan, heat the
cream gently, then add the sugar and
stir until dissolved. Pour the cream into
a bowl and whisk in the crème fraîche.
Let cool, then churn in the ice cream
maker. Store in a container in the
freezer until required.

(8h) To ball the ice cream

Place the serving dish in the freezer.
Fill a jug with hot water. Dip a scoop
into the water then into the ice cream,
make a ball, place in the dish and
repeat for all the ice cream. Return to
the freezer.

(6h) To make the pie

Preheat the oven to 325°F/160°C. Roll
out the sweet pastry, line the 2 flan
pans with parchment paper and fill with
baking beans. Let rest in the refrigerator
for about 30 minutes. Before baking,
examine the tart shells closely to make
sure that there are no holes. This is
important, as holes will allow the filling
to run out of the tart into the mold,
making the tarts very difficult to remove
from the pans. If there are any small
holes, plug them with a little of the
remaining pastry. Bake the tart shells
for about 30 minutes, then remove the
beans and the paper and continue
cooking for 10 minutes, or until golden
brown. Remove the shells from the oven
and put to one side. Now raise the oven
temperature to 350°F/180°C for the
filling. Beat the eggs lightly in a bowl,
then add the sugar, syrup, salt and
vanilla, and stir in the pecan nuts.
Divide the filling between the 2 tart
shells and cook for about 30 minutes,
or until set. Let cool, then store in an
airtight container in a cool place.

To serve

Place the tarts on a large wooden board
and dust with powdered sugar. Place the
bowl of ice cream next to the tarts or
offer separately.

From top: *Chicken Pot Pie Soup, Shrimp with Lemon
Grass Laksa, Tuscan Bean & Italian Sausage Soup*

Giving a party outside should be a leisurely affair. In summer, a lovely yard or terrace can be transformed into an outside dining room. Tablecloths and napkins can be bold in color, with flowers and foliage, and perhaps even fruit and vegetables, picked from the garden and used to decorate tables.

for eating outdoors

Guests can relax on cushions, blankets and rugs distributed on the lawn. Lunch or dinner outdoors can be as simple as you want it to be – excellent pasta, mouthwatering sandwiches, cheese and fruit. The recipes that follow are for people who enjoy cooking outdoors on barbecues and sitting in a shady spot in the yard to eat easy-to-prepare, delicious food in the company of friends.

Food for Thought

Plan to take the type of foods that will survive the rigors of a car journey and heat. If necessary, the picnic must be small enough to tuck under a seat at a sporting event. When I first started to prepare picnics to take to cricket matches at Lords, I remember serving a great variety of foods and how difficult it was to transport and store them. I have now discovered wraps (see pages 90–91), which are extremely transportable and easy to eat in a small space.

Cooling Drinks

To chill drinks, you can pack ice in a cooler, but this is heavy to carry and bulky to store. Make fresh fruit drinks and transport them in Thermos flasks. Sleeves are available that can be kept in the freezer until required, then placed over bottles just before you leave. Wrap the bottles in their sleeves in paper to transport them. Inflatable ice buckets are another lightweight means of cooling drinks; fill them with ice when you arrive at your destination.

Best Barbecues

Keep the food simple. Light the coals on the barbecue at least three quarters of an hour before starting to grill food. Try not to use lighter fluids as they can taint the flavor of the food. Arrange the grill grate so that it can be raised and lowered over the heat. Place your buffet table and bar near the barbecue so that guests can help themselves to salads and drinks easily.

Professional Tips

• Don't forget the essentials: bottle opener; corkscrew; insect repellent; lotion for stings and bites; sun block and hats
• Make sure that you can carry everything – blankets, rugs or quilts are very portable
• Restrict yourself to lightweight china, glassware and cutlery: plastic containers can be a godsend on a picnic
• Remember to pack paper napkins and garbage bags, too.
• A picnic that starts in daylight may finish in darkness; keep a flashlight handy

WINTER WONDERS

FOR WINTER PICNICS, PREPARE STEWS AND HEARTY SOUPS, STORING THEM IN WIDE-NECKED THERMOS FLASKS SO THAT THEY WILL BE WARM AND REVIVING.

summer garden lunch

What could be more heavenly than sitting in the shade of a tree, on a lovely summer's day, enjoying a lunch with flavors from the Mediterranean? We have given this classic tuna salad a fresh and modern twist, and if you can find fresh anchovies, they make it all the more sublime. Both it and the delicious dessert, cooked with olive oil, are always popular at summer lunch parties, and like most of the menus in this book, are easy to prepare ahead of time – leaving you free to relax in the company of your guests. SERVES 10

Salad Niçoise with Grilled Tuna

Dressing

2 tsp Dijon mustard
1 tbsp white wine vinegar
1 tbsp balsamic vinegar
1 tsp sugar
3 tbsp olive oil
2 shallots, thinly sliced
salt & freshly ground black pepper

Salad

1lb (500g) fresh tuna, preferably with the
  tail, cut into 10 equal portions
olive oil
salt
freshly ground black pepper
30 small vine tomatoes
2 garlic cloves, sliced
a little sugar
2 tsp thyme, finely chopped
1½lb (750g) red potatoes, cooked, cut
  lengthwise & grilled
9oz (250g) extra-fine French beans, topped
  not tailed, blanched & refreshed
1 cucumber, peeled, seeded & sliced
7oz (200g) large black olives
36 quails' eggs, hard boiled
3½oz (100g) capers
5 roasted artichoke hearts, cut into
  halves
½ cup (½ tea cup) picked flat-leaf parsley,
  washed & chopped
½ cup (½ tea cup) snipped chives
two 1¼oz (50g) cans of anchovy fillets, or
  2½oz (100g) fresh anchovies, sautéed in
  a little vegetable oil

Accompaniments

crusty country bread
unsalted butter
olive oil

(1d) **To make the dressing**
Combine all the ingredients for the dressing in a bowl, season and pour into a jar. Replace the lid and store in the refrigerator or in a cool place.

(4h) **To cook the tuna**
Heat a grill pan, brush the tuna with a little olive oil and season with salt and freshly ground black pepper. Grill for no longer than 30 seconds each side. Place on a pan, cover with plastic wrap and refrigerate.

(4h) **To prepare the tomatoes**
Preheat the oven to 325°F/160°C. Place the tomatoes on a metal baking pan, brush with 1 tablespoon olive oil and garlic, sprinkle with the sugar and thyme, then season. Place in the oven and cook for 5 minutes. Store in an airtight container and refrigerate.

To assemble

Place the potatoes, French beans, cucumber, olives, quails' eggs, capers, artichokes, parsley and chives in a large bowl, then pour over ¾ of the dressing, toss well and season. Transfer to a large serving bowl, arrange the tuna, tomatoes and anchovies, then pour on the remaining dressing. Serve with warm bread, butter and olive oil.

Sauternes Cake with Poached Peaches

Make in a 10in (25cm) round cake pan.

Sauternes Cake

1 tbsp butter for greasing
6 egg yolks
¾ cup (180g) superfine sugar
zest of 1 large orange, finely grated
zest of 2 lemons, finely grated
½ cup (120ml) extra-virgin olive oil
⅔ cup (150ml) Sauternes wine
8 egg whites
½ tsp cream of tartar
¾ cup (170g) all-purpose flour
¼ tsp salt
powdered sugar, to dust

Poached Peaches

10 large, ripe peaches
2½ cups (600ml) water
2 cups (450g) superfine sugar
1 bottle (750 ml) sweet sparkling wine
2 vanilla beans, split lengthwise
zest of 1 orange, finely grated
zest of 1 lemon, finely grated
2½ cups (600ml) crème fraîche or
  whipped cream

(3d) **To prepare the cake**
Preheat the oven to 350°F/180°C. Grease a loose-bottomed cake pan with butter and line with parchment paper. Whisk the egg yolks and half the sugar in an electric mixer on a high speed, until light in color, thick and creamy.

Salade Nicoise with Grilled Tuna

Whisk in the finely grated orange and lemon zest. Add the olive oil slowly, followed by the Sauternes, whisking continually. In a bowl, beat the egg whites with the cream of tartar until the mixture holds soft peaks. Whisk in the remaining sugar, continuing until the mixture holds stiff peaks. Sift the flour and salt together, then fold gently into the egg-yolk mixture; add the egg-white mixture, and mix thoroughly so that there are no pockets of flour. Pour the mixture into the cake pan, place on a baking tray in the center of the oven. After 20 minutes, lower the oven temperature to 300°F/150°C, and bake for 20 minutes more, turning the cake if it appears to be browning more on one side. Remove and cool in the pan on a rack. Remove from the pan and store in an airtight container in a cool place.

(2d) To prepare the peaches

Bring a saucepan of water to a boil; fill a large bowl with ice-cold water. Plunge the peaches, 2 at a time, in the boiling water for about 20 seconds. Remove with a slotted spoon, then place immediately into the ice-cold water. Peel off the skins, then put the peaches to one side. To prepare the syrup, place the water and sugar into a saucepan large enough to accommodate all the peaches. Bring to a boil slowly, then add the sparkling wine, vanilla beans, orange and lemon zest. Return to a boil, then lower the heat and barely simmer. Place the peaches in the syrup and poach gently for about 15 minutes. Remove from the heat and let the peaches cool in the syrup; remove them from the syrup when cool. With a small knife, make a cut halfway through each peach and remove the pit gently. Place in a shallow dish and pour on a little of the syrup. Cover with plastic wrap and place in the refrigerator. Remove several hours before required.

SKINNING PEACHES

IF THE SKINS ARE STILL A LITTLE DIFFICULT TO REMOVE AFTER THE PEACHES HAVE BEEN TRANSFERRED FROM THE BOILING TO THE COLD WATER, THEN DIP THEM INTO THE BOILING WATER ONCE AGAIN FOR A FEW MORE SECONDS.

To serve

Place the cake on a stand; dust with powdered sugar. Fill a glass vase or bowl with the peaches and pour on the syrup. Divide the crème fraîche between 2 small bowls. Serve.

brilliant barbecue

Barbecues always remind me of enjoying hot, sunny weather in the company of friends. As a change from the traditional meat, I've designed my ultimate seafood barbecue. Ideally of course, I'll have helped to catch the fish that morning, but when that really isn't possible, this tantalizing feast will help recreate a seaside atmosphere at home. If you really wish to replace any of the suggested recipes, try the chopped steak or grilled ribs from the buffet menus – they are just as good cooked on the barbecue. SERVES 10

Vegetables with Salsa Verde

Choose 3 to 4 of the following:
 10 red peppers, quartered & seeds removed
 30 asparagus spears, blanched & refreshed
 30 baby fennel, blanched & refreshed
 4 large zucchini, cut into ½in (1.5cm)
  slices
 2 medium eggplants, sliced & sprinkled
  with salt
 5 medium red onions, quartered & blanched
olive oil
salt & freshly ground black pepper
a selection of fresh herbs to garnish
double quantity of Salsa Verde (see
 page 121)

To grill the vegetables
Place your chosen vegetables on a pan, brush with oil, season and grill or barbecue on both sides for 10–15 minutes until soft and grill marks are visible. Arrange on a serving dish and decorate with a selection of herbs.

To serve
Drizzle the vegetables with a little Salsa Verde, placing the remainder of the salsa in a bowl.

Lobster with a Tamarind Dressing

Tamarind Dressing
⅔ cup (150ml) olive oil
2 tbsp tamarind pulp
2 tsp palm sugar (coarse raw sugar)
zest & juice of 1 lime
2 tbsp chopped ginger
3 garlic cloves, sliced
2 shallots, thinly sliced
¼ cup (¼ tea cup) cilantro, washed,
 dried & chopped
3 lime leaves, finely shredded
salt & freshly ground black pepper

five 1½lb (675g) lobsters, cooked and split
 in half with tail meat removed, sliced &
 returned to the shell
seaweed to garnish

ⓓ **To make the dressing**
Blend the olive oil, tamarind pulp, sugar, lime zest and juice and ginger in a blender for about 30 seconds, or until a smooth liquid is formed. Pour into a clean jar with a lid; add the remaining ingredients for the dressing, season with salt and pepper and store in the refrigerator.

To grill the lobsters
Place the lobster halves on a pan and spoon a little dressing over each one. Grill, shell side down, for about 5–10 minutes until the meat is hot and the shell is brown. Remove and place on a serving platter lined with seaweed.

BBQ TIPS
MAKING SURE THAT THE COALS ARE HOT BEFORE STARTING TO COOK THE FOOD AND HAVING THE RIGHT UTENSILS ON HAND MAKES LIFE EASIER. PLACE A JUG OF HOT WATER BY THE GRILL TO DAMP DOWN FLAMES IF NECESSARY.

Swordfish with Red Onion & Mango Salsa

Red Onion Salsa
¾ cup (120g) dried black-eyed peas, soaked
 in water for 12 hours
6 ripe mangoes
5 plum tomatoes, skinned, seeded & diced
1 cup (1 tea cup) cilantro, washed, dried
 & chopped
½ cup (½ tea cup) parsley, washed, dried
 & chopped
4 garlic cloves, finely chopped
4 medium red chiles, seeds removed then diced
4 red onions, finely diced
zest & juice of 6 limes
1¼ cups (300ml) olive oil
salt & freshly ground black pepper

Flavored Oil
1¼ cups (300ml) olive oil
1 stem of dill weed, chopped
2 star anise
½ head of garlic
2 shallots, sliced
3 lemon peel slices

ten 6oz (180g) swordfish steaks
salt & freshly ground black pepper
dill weed flowers & stalks
lime halves

ⓓ **To make the salsa**
Drain the beans. Bring a pan of vegetable stock or salted water to

Lobster with a Tamarind Dressing

Grilled Swordfish with Red Onion & Mango Salsa

a boil, then reduce the heat, add the beans and simmer until tender. Drain and let cool. Peel the mangoes (over a sink!) and cut the flesh away from the pit. Purée half the mangoes in a blender or by hand until very smooth. Dice the remaining mangoes finely and place in a large bowl with the purée. Add the beans and remaining salsa ingredients; season. Cover and place in the refrigerator.

(1d) **To infuse the oil**
Place all the ingredients for the flavored oil in a saucepan over a low heat for about 10 minutes. Remove from the heat and let cool. Pour flavored oil into a jar with a lid and store in a cool place.

To cook and serve the swordfish
Place the fish on a tray, brush with the herb-flavored oil and season. Grill or barbecue on each side until cooked, then remove and place on a serving platter. Garnish with the dill flowers and stalks and the halved limes. Place the salsa in bowls and serve at once.

GETTING RID OF GARLIC
AS YOU WILL HAVE NOTICED I LOVE THE PIQUANT FLAVOR OF GARLIC IN FOOD AND MANY OF THESE BARBECUE RECIPES INCLUDE IT. ITS ODOR CAN STICK TO YOUR HANDS HOWEVER. MY FOOLPROOF METHOD OF REMOVING IT IS TO PLACE A STAINLESS STEEL SPOON UNDER RUNNING WARM WATER AND RUB YOUR HANDS OVER THE SPOON UNDER THE WATER.

Sweet Potatoes with Green Onions

Green Onion Dressing
⅔ cup (150ml) seasoned rice vinegar

1 tbsp sugar

1¾ cups (450ml) unsweetened coconut milk

1 bunch of green onions, washed, roots removed & chopped

½ cup (½ tea cup) chopped chives

3 tbsp toasted sesame seeds

2 tbsp sweet chili sauce (optional)

salt & freshly ground black pepper

10 small orange sweet potatoes

(1d) **To make the dressing**
Blend the vinegar and sugar in a food processor for about 10 seconds. Add

the coconut milk slowly, and when emulsified, remove and pour into a bowl. Add the remaining ingredients and season. Cover and place in the refrigerator.

(1d) **To prepare the potatoes**

Scrub the skins of the potatoes and dry with a clean tea towel. Prick the skins with a fork, wrap in foil and refrigerate.

To grill the potatoes

Place the potatoes on the grill or barbecue, and after 50 minutes, remove the foil. Return to the grill and cook until the skins are crisp.

To serve

Cut the potatoes in half, place in a serving bowl and drizzle on some dressing. Serve the remainder of the dressing in a jug.

Sweet Corn with Black Pepper Butter

Black Pepper Butter
1 cup (250g) soft, unsalted butter
2 tsp crushed black pepper
sea salt flakes

10 ears of corn in their husks
dried corn husks to garnish

(1d) **To make the butter**

Beat the butter in an electric mixer until pale. Remove, then add the pepper and salt flakes. Mix, making sure that the pepper is evenly distributed. Place in a piping bag with a 1in (2.5cm) plain nozzle and pipe onto plastic wrap. Roll into a cylinder and place in the freezer.

To prepare and cook the corn

Remove the butter from the freezer, cut it into even slices and place in a bowl of iced water. Soak the corn in cold water for 10 minutes, then remove and drain. Place on the grill, cooking on all sides until soft. Transfer to a basket lined with dry corn husks and serve with the butter.

Marinated Prawns with Chipotle Mayonnaise

Prawn Marinade
40 skewers or vine sticks soaked in water
40 medium fresh tiger prawns
5 tbsp olive oil
5 shallots, chopped
8 garlic cloves, chopped
¼ cup (¼ tea cup) fresh thyme, chopped
1 tbsp paprika
juice & zest of 3 limes
1 tbsp sugar
salt & freshly ground black pepper
sea salt flakes

Mayonnaise
3 tbsp white wine vinegar
juice of 2 limes
3 garlic cloves, finely chopped
2 chipotle chiles (smoked jalapeños), soaked & seeds removed
3 shallots, finely chopped
1 tbsp sugar
6 fresh free-range egg yolks
4½ cups (1.2 liters) vegetable oil
⅔ cup (150ml) boiling water
salt & freshly ground black pepper

Sweetcorn with Black Pepper Butter

Garnish
stems of fresh rosemary or sage
fresh red chiles

(6h) **To marinate the prawns**

Skewer the prawns and place them in a pan. Blend all the marinade ingredients until smooth; season. Coat the prawns in the marinade, then cover and chill.

(6h) **To make the mayonnaise**

In a pan, heat the vinegar, lime juice, garlic, chiles, shallots and sugar, reduce by half; let cool. Blend the mixture with the egg yolks in a food processor for about 30 seconds. Pour in the oil, in a slow steady stream, stopping to scrape the sides of the bowl. When emulsified, add the boiling water and process for 10 seconds; season. Chill in an airtight container.

To grill and serve the prawns

Grill or barbecue the prawns until the shells are brown; season with salt flakes and place on a platter lined with fresh chiles and herbs; pour the mayonnaise into a bowl.

perfect picnic

Designed to be easily portable, this is my any-occasion picnic for 10 people. All the dishes are simple to prepare but truly delicious – I love the original combination of sharp feta with sweet red onions. Each cold dish can be boxed individually, with extra salad greens added at the last moment. The squid ink pasta salad also makes a lovely main-course salad for a summer lunch at home. SERVES 10

Squid Ink Pasta with Prawn Salad

Dressing
3 tbsp white wine vinegar
1 tbsp sugar
5 tbsp extra-virgin olive oil

Salad
30 fresh medium tiger prawns, peeled
olive oil
salt & freshly ground black pepper
1lb (500g) fresh squid ink fettuccine
30 asparagus spears, peeled & blanched
1 bunch of green onions, washed, roots
  trimmed, thinly sliced
10 plum tomatoes, skinned, seeded &
  diced
2 red chiles, seeded & thinly sliced
1/2 cup (1/2 tea cup) snipped chives

(1h) **To prepare the dressing**
Blend the vinegar and sugar in a blender or food processor for 20 seconds. Add the oil slowly in a steady stream until emulsified. Pour into a jar with a lid and store in a cool place.

(1d) **To prepare the salad**
Preheat a grill or grill pan. Brush the prawns with olive oil, season, place on the grill and cook evenly on all sides. Remove, cover and let cool before

Squid Ink Pasta with Prawn Salad

placing in the refrigerator. Bring a saucepan of salted water with a little olive oil to a boil, cook the pasta al dente, drain and refresh. When cold, cut the pasta with sissors into 4in (10cm) lengths. Cover and refrigerate.

To finish the salad
Place the prawns, pasta and asparagus in a large bowl and pour over the dressing. Add the green onions, tomatoes, chiles and chives; toss well. Season and pack into containers.

Feta Cheese, Black Olives & Caper Salad

3 small red onions, each onion cut into
  8 pieces
2/3 cup (150ml) aged balsamic vinegar
3 tbsp extra-virgin olive oil
2 tsp Demerara raw sugar
5 sprigs of thyme, finely chopped
salt & freshly ground black pepper
1lb (500g) good-quality fresh feta cheese,
  cut into cubes
11oz (300g) extra-fine French beans,
  blanched
9oz (250g) large, marinated black olives
3 1/2oz (100g) capers
20 yellow pear tomatoes, washed, dried &
  cut in half
2 cups (2 tea cups) picked flat-leaf parsley,
  washed & dried

(1d) **To roast the red onions**
Preheat the oven to 375°F/190°C. Place the onions in a baking pan; pour over the vinegar, oil, sugar and thyme. Season and roast in the oven for about 15–20 minutes until the onions are soft and glazed. Transfer the onions and vinegar mixture (this will be the dressing for the salad) into an airtight container; when cold, refrigerate.

To finish the salad
Place the onions and dressing in a bowl, add the remaining ingredients, season, toss and pack into containers.

Marinated Chicken & Jewelled Rice

Chicken Marinade
1oz (30g) dried sorrel flowers
3 garlic cloves, chopped
2 jalapeño chiles, seeded & finely chopped
1/4 cup (1/4 tea cup) cilantro, washed, dried
  & chopped
1 lime, sliced
5 free-range or corn-fed chicken breasts,
  skin removed
salt & freshly ground black pepper
vegetable oil for cooking

Jewelled Rice
6 cups (1.4 liters) vegetable stock
olive oil
1 onion, finely diced
3 garlic cloves, finely chopped
1/2 teaspoon saffron strands
5 green cardamom pods, crushed
2 cinnamon sticks
1 1/2lb (675g) basmati rice
vegetable oil
peel of 2 oranges, pith removed & very
  thinly sliced
4oz (115g) carrot, finely shredded
2 tbsp sugar
1/3 cup (60g) barberries (or dried cranberries),
  rinsed, stem removed & soaked for 12 hours
1 cup (150g) large golden raisins
1 cup (150g) pistachio nuts, shelled, peeled
  & roasted
1 cup (150g) unsalted roasted cashew nuts
2 cups (2 tea cups) cilantro leaves, washed
  & dried
salt & freshly ground black pepper

(2d) **To marinate the chicken**

In a large pan, bring 2½ cups (600ml) water to a boil. When boiling, add the sorrel and reduce by half. Strain through a fine sieve into an airtight container large enough to hold the chicken; cool. When cold, add the garlic, chiles, cilantro, sliced lime and chicken breasts, making sure that the chicken is covered with the marinade. Cover and refrigerate for 12 hours.

(1d) **To cook the chicken**

Preheat the oven to 375°F/190°C. Remove the chicken from the marinade, pat dry, season and place on a tray. Heat a little oil in a sauté pan and sear the chicken on both sides. Transfer to the oven to cook for about 10–12 minutes; remove and let cool. Cover and refrigerate.

(1d) **To cook the jewelled rice**

Preheat the oven to 350°F/180°C. Bring the stock to a boil, then reduce the heat to simmer. Heat a little olive oil in a large, ovenproof pan and add the onion, garlic, saffron, cardamom and cinnamon sticks; sauté for about 2 minutes. Add the rice, stir well and do not allow to color. Add the hot stock, stir, bring to a boil and cover with parchment paper then a lid. Place in the oven for about 20–25 minutes, or until the rice is tender and all the stock has been absorbed. Let cool, then cover and place in the refrigerator. Heat a little oil in a sauté pan. Add the orange peel and carrot and sauté on a low heat for about 5 minutes; do not allow to color. Add the sugar, cook for 5 more minutes and remove from heat. Let cool and place in an airtight container. Cover and refrigerate.

To finish the chicken and rice

Drain the berries. Place the rice in a large bowl, add the remaining ingredients, season and mix well. Pack into containers. Slice the chicken breasts and place on top of the rice; cover.

Spicy Vegetables

¾ cup (100g) dried chickpeas, soaked
2 tsp palm oil or vegetable oil
9oz (250g) baby onions, peeled
3 garlic cloves, sliced
2 tbsp garam marsala paste
5 plum tomatoes, skinned, seeded & diced
1¼ cups (300ml) vegetable stock
salt & freshly ground black pepper
1 medium eggplant, diced
10 baby corn, cut in half & blanched
11oz (300g) sweet potato, blanched & diced
11oz (300g) button mushrooms, stalks removed, & cleaned
4oz (115g) baby spinach, washed & dried

Raita Dressing

1¼ cups (300ml) plain yogurt
½ cup (½ tea cup) mint leaves, washed, dried & finely shredded
¼ cucumber, peeled, seeded & finely diced
salt & freshly ground black pepper

(1d) **To make the spicy vegetables**

Cook the chickpeas until tender in a pan of boiling salted water. Drain and set aside. Heat the oil in a large sauté pan, add the onions and sauté for about 5 minutes. Add the garlic, garam masala paste and tomato and sauté for 5 minutes more. Pour in the stock and reduce by half. Season and cool. Rinse and dry the pan, then use it to heat a little oil. Sauté the remaining vegetables, excluding the spinach, for about 5 minutes. Remove from the heat, stir in the spinach, season and let cool. When cold, add the vegetables and chickpeas to the sauce, stir and season. Place in containers, cover and refrigerate.

(1d) **To make the dressing**

Place all the ingredients in a bowl, season, stir well and place in a container in the refrigerator.

To serve

Offer the vegetables and dressing separately.

ALL-YEAR ROUND

IF THE WEATHER IS LESS THAN IDYLLIC AND WARMING FOOD IS MORE DESIRABLE, WHY NOT SUBSTITUTE A LARGE THERMOS FILLED WITH TUSCAN BEAN SOUP (SEE PAGE 151) FOR ONE OF THE SALADS?

Lemon Cookies

14 tbsp (200g) unsalted butter
1 cup (120g) powdered sugar
1 egg yolk
zest of 2 lemons
2 tsp lemon juice
2¼ cups (250g) all-purpose flour
superfine sugar

(2d) **To make the cookies**

Cream the butter and sugar in an electric mixer until soft and creamy. Add the egg yolk, beat until smooth, then add the lemon zest, juice and flour. Continue to mix until all the dough ingredients are well combined. Cover the work surface with a sheet of plastic wrap and place the dough on top; cover with a second sheet of plastic wrap. Roll the dough to a thickness of ¼in (7mm). Place in the refrigerator for 1 hour. Preheat the oven to 350°F/180°C. Line a baking sheet with parchment paper. Lightly flour a cool work surface. Transfer the dough from the refrigerator to the floured surface and use a cutter to cut out about 20 heart shapes, placing them on the baking sheet. Bake for about 10 minutes or until the heart shapes turn a golden color. Transfer the hearts to a cooling rack and sprinkle with sugar. When cold, pack carefully in airtight containers.

Top to bottom: Feta Cheese, Black Olives & Caper Salad, Marinated Chicken & Jewelled Rice

Walnut, Pecan & Chocolate Brownies

¾ cup (85g) all-purpose flour
1 tsp baking powder
½ tsp salt
⅔ cup (115g) shelled pecan nuts, roughly chopped
⅔ cup (115g) shelled walnuts, roughly chopped
10oz (285g) unsweetened chocolate, chopped into small pieces
14 tbsp (200g) unsalted, soft butter
3 eggs
1¼ cups (285g) dark brown sugar
cocoa powder for dusting (optional)

(1d) **To make the brownies**

Preheat the oven to 325°F/160°C. Line a deep baking pan, about 10 x 10 x 1½in (26 x 26 x 4cm) with parchment paper. Place the flour, baking powder, salt, nuts and half the chocolate in a bowl; mix and set aside. Half-fill a saucepan with water, find a mixing bowl to fit on top of the saucepan and bring to a gentle simmer. Place the butter and the remaining half of the chocolate in the bowl to melt over the heat. Meanwhile, whisk the eggs and sugar in an electric mixer until creamy. Remove the bowl from the mixer and pour in the melted chocolate and butter; mix until smooth. Add the remaining ingredients and mix with a rubber or plastic spatula. Pour into the prepared pan, smooth the top and bake in the oven for about 30–40 minutes or until just set. Let cool for 5 minutes then remove from the pan and place on a cooling rack. When cold, remove the paper and cut the brownies into squares (you should get about 20); dust the tops with cocoa powder if using. Pack into airtight containers lined with parchment paper.

LEFTOVER EGG WHITES

IF YOU DO NOT WANT TO WASTE EGG WHITES LEFT FROM THOSE RECIPES THAT ONLY REQUIRE EGG YOLKS (LIKE THE LEMON COOKIES ON THIS PAGE), YOU CAN FREEZE THEM FOR UP TO 1 MONTH FOR USE IN OTHER RECIPES.

cheeseboard

Today the range of cheeses available can be confusing. It includes cheeses made from cows' milk, goats' milk and sheep's milk, and textures vary from hard to semi-soft and soft, with rich, smooth triple-cream types also available. In addition, there are seasonal cheeses, such as Terry's favorite, Vacherin. I would recommend buying cheese from a specialized cheesemonger who will also be able to supply a good selection of crackers and breads, as well as baskets, mats and paper leaves for serving. They will advise you on what cheese is at its peak, in season and ready to serve.

Storing Suggestions

Wrap cheese in greaseproof paper covered with a piece of cheesecloth before storing in a plastic bag or wrapping in plastic wrap. The best place to keep it is on the top shelf of the refrigerator (so any strong-smelling cheese will not taint other foods), in a cool cupboard, or if you are lucky enough to have a cellar, store it there in a cheese safe.

A Selection to Serve

For a buffet party, we generally provide a selection of up to 6 cheeses, depending on the number of guests. My recommendations for an interesting basket of cheeses would be a raw milk brie with a goat cheese (preferably a cylinder rolled in ash), a triple cream, a blue cheese, a mild washed rind and a cheese wrapped in leaves.

For a dinner party we offer a selection of 3 cheeses. Try to avoid hard cheeses that are difficult for guests to cut as well as cheeses with inedible rinds or pungent odors – not everyone will be a cheese-lover.

A Feast for the Eyes

Many years ago, I planted a grapevine in my garden, so in the summer we have glorious fresh vine leaves with which to line the cheese baskets. In September, the vine produces small bunches of very sweet black grapes which I also cut to arrange on baskets. From mid-October, we use colorful autumnal leaves. If you do not have access to a vine, you can substitute any non-poisonous leaves from trees such as fig, maple, sea grape, plane, lemon, lime or orange. A straw or bamboo mat also makes a suitable liner for any basket or board. Arrange the cheeses to look appetizing and attractive on the board, in the basket or on individual plates, surrounding them with accompaniments such as halved figs, bunches of grapes, small apples, slices of oven-dried pears (see page 169), quince 'cheese' oatmeal biscuits, fig and walnut bread, or sesame wafers. If you would like to serve the cheese in individual portions on plates, arrange each serving with half a fig, a small bunch of grapes, a slice of oven-dried pear or apple, a sprig of parsley or lovage and then a few crackers and a slice of bread.

Experiment with marinating small goat cheeses in very good quality olive oil with herbs and spices; offer these in jars, with a pair of long cornichon tongs for easy serving. You can also add flavorings by rolling individual goat cheeses in herbs, nuts or cracked peppercorns. It is fun to develop your own range of cheeses.

Sesame Wafers

These are easy to make and it is worth keeping a packet of spring roll wrappers in the freezer so that these wafers can be made quickly for unexpected guests. The wafers are also a delicious accompaniment for chicken liver parfait or foie gras terrine. MAKES 40

Cheese Basket

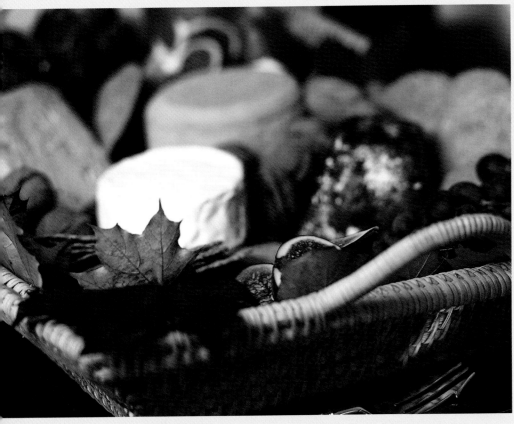

20 spring roll wrappers, 5 x 5in (125 x 125mm)

1 egg white

1 tbsp sesame seeds

(1d) **To make the wafers**

Preheat the oven to 350°F/180°C. Cut the
spring roll wrappers in half to form
triangles. Brush with egg white and
sprinkle with sesame seeds. Place on a
baking pan in the oven for about 10
minutes until golden brown. Remove and
cool. Store in an airtight container.

Oatmeal Biscuits

Maureen Chalander, who used to
be our head chef, developed these
delicious biscuits. They are easy to
make and store well. MAKES 25

2½ cups (210g) oatmeal

1 cup (100g) whole wheat flour

1 cup (100g) all-purpose flour

1 tbsp sugar

½ tsp salt

½ tsp baking powder

15 tbsp (210g) unsalted butter, cubed

4 egg whites

(2d) **To make the biscuits**

Mix the dry ingredients in an electric
mixer, then add the butter and continue
to mix until the consistency resembles
breadcrumbs. Add the egg whites and
mix until it forms a smooth dough. Roll
into a smooth ball, wrap in plastic wrap
and place in the refrigerator for about
2 hours. Alternatively place in the freezer
for use at a later time.

(2d) **To cook the oatmeal biscuits**

Preheat the oven 350°F/180°C. Line
2 baking pans with parchment paper
or a silicon mat. Remove the dough
from the refrigerator and place on a
floured board. Roll out as thinly as
possible, then cut into rounds with
a 3–4in (7.5–10cm) fluted cutter.
Place on the baking pans and bake
for 10–15 minutes, or until golden
brown. Remove and place on cooling
racks. When cold, layer with greaseproof
paper and store in an airtight container
in a cool place.

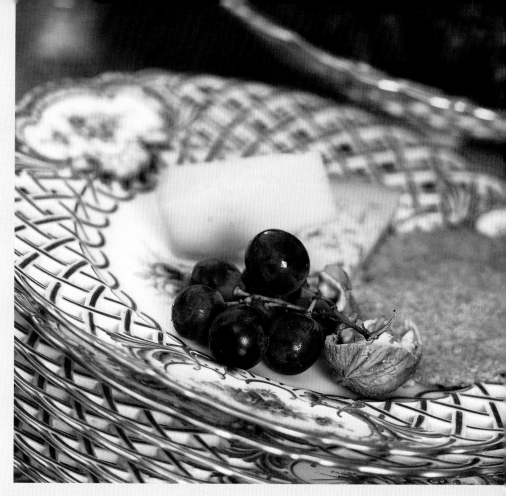

Oatmeal Biscuits with Cheese

Fig & Walnut Bread

Years ago, Terry started to
experiment with various breads to
accompany cheese and this is his
favorite. We make it in a 15in-
(38cm-) long cylindrical pudding
mold. MAKES 1 LOAF

2 tbsp butter, melted

2½ cups (280g) rye flour, sifted

2½ cups (280g) bread flour, sifted

2 tbsp salt

2 tbsp unsalted butter

1 tbsp fresh yeast

1 tsp black molasses

1 tbsp liquid honey

2 cups (450ml) milk

½ cup (60g) chopped walnuts

8oz (230g) dried figs

(1d) **To make the bread**

Grease a mold with the butter. In an
mixer with a dough hook, combine the
flours, salt and butter. Place the yeast,
molasses and honey in a ceramic mixing
bowl. Warm the milk in a pan to blood
heat then whisk into the yeast mixture
until the yeast dissolves. Add to the
flour and continue to mix for 5 minutes
or until a smooth dough is achieved.
Transfer the mixture to a floured surface;
knead for 4–6 minutes until the dough is
firm, elastic and no longer sticky. Place
in a warm bowl and cover with plastic
wrap or an oiled plastic bag and a damp
tea towel. Leave space for the dough to
rise. Leave in a warm place until the
dough has doubled in size. Knead the
dough smooth on a floured surface,
then turn into a 14 x 8in (35 x 20cm)
rectangle. Sprinkle on the nuts and place
a line of figs along one of the long sides.
Roll the dough over the figs like a jelly
roll and place in the mold. Cover and
leave in a warm place until the dough has
again doubled in size (30–45 minutes).
Preheat the oven to 425°F/220°C. Bake
for 40 minutes or until golden brown and
hollow-sounding when tapped. Remove
from oven, and once the pan is cool
remove the bread. Leave the bread to cool
then store in an airtight container.

basic recipes

Vegetable Stock
MAKES 5½ CUPS (1.4 LITERS)

4 onions, cut into quarters
2 leeks, white part only, washed & sliced
5 medium carrots, peeled & chopped
½ head of garlic
10 celery sticks, washed & chopped
5 sprigs of thyme
2 bay leaves
1 bulb fennel, washed & chopped
3 peppercorns
1 star anise
11 cups (2.8 liters) water
salt & freshly ground black pepper

(1d) **To make the stock**
Place all the ingredients in the stockpot, bring to a simmer and cook for about 1 hour. Remove from the heat and pass through a fine sieve into a clean saucepan. Return to the heat and reduce until a good flavor is achieved. Season and let cool. When cold, place in the refrigerator or freezer.

Brown Chicken Stock
MAKES 7 CUPS (1.8 LITERS)

6½lb (3kg) chicken bones, all fat removed
1 onion, cut into quarters
3 medium carrots, cut into large chunks
4 stems of celery, washed & sliced
1 leek, washed & sliced
10 sprigs of thyme
4 garlic cloves, crushed
7 quarts (7.2 liters) water
2 tbsp tomato paste

(1d) **To make the stock**
Preheat the oven to 375°F/190°C. Place the bones in a roasting pan and roast for about 45 minutes, until the bones are deep golden brown. While the bones are roasting, place the onion in a sauté pan without oil and cook for about 10 minutes. Add to a large stockpot with the bones and remaining ingredients. Bring to a boil and simmer for about 5 hours, skimming any scum

from the top. Strain through a fine sieve into a clean saucepan. Return to the heat and reduce to the required amount (tasting to ensure the flavor is acceptable). Let cool, cover and refrigerate or freeze.

WHITE CHICKEN STOCK
MAKE WHITE CHICKEN STOCK IN THE SAME WAY AS FOR BROWN CHICKEN STOCK BUT DO NOT ROAST THE BONES AND OMIT THE TOMATO PASTE.

Fish Stock
MAKES 2 QUARTS (2 LITERS)

6½lb (3kg) fish bones, sole are the best, cut into thirds
vegetable oil
1 leek, white part only, thinly sliced
1 onion, thinly sliced
½ bulb fennel, sliced
2 garlic cloves
5 sprigs of thyme
5 peppercorns
½ cup (½ tea cup) parsley stalks
1 bay leaf
1 cup (1 glass) dry white wine
4½ quarts (4½ liters) water

(1d) **To make the stock**
Remove the head and any blood from the fish, then soak in cold water for 20 minutes. Heat a little oil in a stockpot and sauté the leek, onion, fennel and garlic. Cook until soft, then add the bones, thyme, peppercorns, parsley stalks, bay leaf and white wine; cover and leave for about 5 minutes. Pour in the water, bring to a boil, then reduce the heat and simmer for 20 minutes. Keep skimming from time to time to prevent scum from forming on top of the stock. Remove from the heat and strain through a fine sieve into a clean saucepan. Return to the heat and reduce until a good flavor is achieved. Let cool, cover and place in the refrigerator or freezer.

Pesto
MAKES 1½ CUPS (350ML)

3 cups (3 tea cups) basil leaves
1 garlic clove, chopped
salt & freshly ground black pepper
1¼ cups (300ml) olive oil
3 tbsp toasted pine nuts
1 cup (120g) Parmesan, grated

(1d) **To make the pesto**
Place the basil, garlic, salt, pepper and half the oil in a food processor. Process until the basil is roughly chopped. Add the pine nuts, Parmesan and remaining oil. Process for a further 10 seconds. Pesto keeps for several days covered with a layer of oil.

Red Onion Jam
MAKES 5 TABLESPOONS

vegetable oil
2 red onions, thinly sliced
2 tbsp brown sugar
1 cup (250ml) red wine
1 tbsp red wine vinegar

(1d) **To cook jam**
Heat a little oil in a sauté pan over low heat, add the sliced red onions, and cook slowly until very soft. Add the sugar, wine and vinegar, and continue to cook for about 30 minutes or until it reaches a jam-like consistency. Place in an airtight container and refrigerate.

Cassis & Red Wine Dressing
SERVES 10

2 shallots, finely chopped
⅔ cup (150ml) red wine, reduced by half
1 tbsp sherry vinegar
1 tbsp crème de cassis
3 tbsp extra-virgin olive oil
salt & freshly ground black pepper

(1d) **To make the dressing**
Mix all the ingredients in a bowl, season and pour into a jar with a lid. Chill.

Crystallized Flowers

MAKES AS MUCH AS YOU WANT

good handful of perfect flowers or petals,
  washed & dried

1 egg white

1 cup (250g) superfine sugar in a sifter

(1d) To crystallize the flowers

If using flowers (rather than petals), cut the stems almost to the base and cut away any pieces of green. Line a baking pan with parchment paper. Place the egg white in a bowl and beat for about 20 seconds. Pick up a single flower or petal gently with the tweezers, taking care not to bruise it. Holding the flower, brush gently with egg whites and sift with the sugar; turn over and repeat. Tap the tweezer to remove any excess sugar, place on the paper and let dry in a warm, dry place for 8–10 hours. Store in an airtight container in a cool place.

GOOD ENOUGH TO EAT

EDIBLE FLOWERS SUCH AS ROSE PETALS, PANSIES, VIOLAS AND VIOLETS CAN BE USED TO DECORATE CAKES, MOUSSES, MERINGUES AND TARTS. THE TECHNIQUE REQUIRES PATIENCE, BUT IT IS REWARDING.

Oven-Dried Fruit Slices

MAKES 2LB (900G)

choice of fruits: oranges, limes, lemons,
  apples, pears, strawberries, mango & rhubarb

1¼ cups (300ml) sugar syrup (see page 74)

(1d) To make the oven-dried fruit

Select any of the above fruits, leaving the peel on the citrus fruits, pears and apples. Slice thinly lengthwise on a mandolin, making sure that each slice is whole and the same thickness. For rhubarb or mango, peel and slice lengthwise with a knife. Preheat the oven to 225°F/110°C. Line the baking tray with parchment or greaseproof paper. Dip the sliced fruit into the sugar syrup, shake to remove any excess and place on the paper; repeat. Place in the oven for 2–3 hours until the fruit is crisp and dry. Remove, let cool and layer with parchment paper in an airtight container. Store in a cool, dry place.

OVEN-DRIED FRUITS

SLICES OF OVEN-DRIED FRUITS MAKE AN EXCELLENT GARNISH FOR DESSERTS OR TO SERVE WITH CHEESE.

Sugar Cobwebs

MAKES 10 (ALLOWING FOR BREAKAGES)

9oz (250g) sugar cubes

1 tbsp liquid glucose or corn syrup

⅔ cup (150ml) water

(8h) To make the sugar cobwebs

Line a tray with greaseproof paper and fill a bowl with ice-cold water. Heat the sugar cubes, glucose and water in a heavy-based pan, stirring until the sugar dissolves. Bring to a boil and continue stirring over the heat to form a light caramel, or to a temperature of 325°F (165°C). Wrap your hand in a tea towel to protect it. Remove the pan from the heat, dip the base into the ice-cold water for about 20 seconds and let cool for 2 minutes. Dip a spoon into the caramel and make a cobweb pattern on the paper, about 4in (10cm) round. Leave to set for 5 minutes. Layer the cobwebs between nonstick paper and store in an airtight container.

Diplomat Cream

SERVES 10

1¼ cups (300ml) milk

2½ cups (600ml) heavy whipping cream

6 egg yolks

½ cup (125g) superfine sugar

⅔ cup (75g) all purpose flour

3 tbsp Grand Marnier

(8h) To make the diplomat cream

Line a tray with plastic wrap. Boil the milk with half the cream in a pan. In a mixer, whisk the egg yolks and sugar until light and creamy. Add the flour and whisk again. On a slow speed, pour in half the cream and milk mixture and whisk. Add the rest of the mixture and whisk until combined. Return to the pan over medium heat and whisk until the mixture starts to boil. Remove from heat and pour onto the tray. Cover with plastic wrap to prevent a skin from forming. Let cool.

Return the mixture to a bowl and whisk. Whip the remaining 1¼ cups (300ml) of cream and fold this, with the Grand Marnier, into the mixture, taking care not to overbeat. Refrigerate in an airtight container.

Macadamia Nut Brittle

MAKES 10 (ALLOWING FOR BREAKAGES)

vegetable oil for greasing tray

1 cup (200g) superfine sugar

⅓ cup (75ml) water

¼ tsp vinegar

1 cup (100g) unsalted macadamia nuts

(5d) To prepare the brittle

Brush a shallow metal pan (not non-stick) lightly with oil. Grease well into the corners, as the sugar will spread when hot. Place the sugar, water and vinegar in a clean and grease-free (preferably copper) saucepan. (Brush the pan first with cold water to remove any sugar crystals as they could cause the caramel mixture to crystallize and you would have to start again.) Let the sugar dissolve for about 5 minutes. Bring to a boil, continuing to boil until the sugar is a deep amber color or reaches a temperature of 325°F (160°C). Turn off the heat and leave for about 2 minutes. Add the macadamia nuts and pour onto the prepared pan. Let cool completely before removing from the pan. Store in an airtight container in a cool place. It does not matter if the nut brittle is broken into pieces.

(5h) To make the brittle

Preheat the oven to 300°F/150°C. Line a baking tray with parchment paper. Using the metal blade in a food processor, process the brittle to a fine dust. Sprinkle onto the paper in an even, thin layer, making sure that there are no gaps. Place in the oven for approximately 5 minutes or until the brittle has melted – it should not continue to color. Remove and leave for 2 minutes until cool enough to handle. Using a knife, cut the brittle carefully into tall triangles. Layer in greaseproof paper and store in an airtight container.

essential equipment

As a professional caterer and home cook, this is my wish list of equipment that I consider essential and practical in the kitchen. Some you may already own, others, you can always borrow. Life is always made a lot easier if you have the tools of the trade. Make hints at birthday and Christmas for those special items you really want.

Do not panic if you find yourself without the special equipment I recommend. There are always ways to improvise. For example, if you haven't got an electric carving knife to cut foods like cheese and butter, dip a sharp knife into a jug of very hot water before slicing. Ice cream can still be made without an ice-cream maker. Instead of putting the mixture into the ice-cream maker, once it is all combined, put it directly in the freezer and then, every hour until it is properly frozen take the mixture out and churn it up with a fork to make sure all the ingredients are distributed evenly and there no crystals.

Utensils

If you have a choice, I recommend (except where specified) that you try to buy stainless steel utensils.

airtight containers, plastic (capacity 1/2–12 cups/0.25–14 litres)
apple corer
balloon whisks, small, medium and large
3 1/2 cups (500g) ceramic baking beans (or dried pulses or beans which are a good subsitute)
blow torch
bottle pourers and stoppers
box grater
can opener
candy thermometer
cheese shaver
chopping boards, wooden (various sizes)
claw hammer
fish slicer
flour and sugar dredgers
funnels, plastic and metal

glass jars with lids, selection of
ice-cream scoop
ladles, large and medium
mandolin
mezzaluna herb chopper
mixing bowls, set of graduated sizes
mortar and pestle (ceramic)
nonstick baking mats
parchment paper
pastry cutters, sets of round, fluted, heart and square shapes
plastic food covers
rolling pin, wooden without handles (18in/46cm)
rubber scrapers
refrigerator thermometer
salad spinner
sauce gun or squeeze bottle
scissors
slotted spoons
skimmers for straining
spoons
timer
tongs
vegetable peeler
wooden spoons
zester

Knives

Buy stainless-steel knives in a variety of sizes, and store them in a wooden knife block or canvas knife wallet. The essentials are:

4in (10cm) paring knife
4in (10cm) vegetable knife
10in (25cm) carving knife
10in (25cm) cook's knife
8in (20cm) chopping knife
6in (15cm) all-purpose knife
5in (12.5cm) serrated knife
9in (23cm) bread knife
7in (18cm) prong carving fork
8in (20cm) sharpening steel

PALETTE KNIFES

I ALSO ALWAYS KEEP A PALETTE KNIFE HANDY IN THE KITCHEN FOR LEVELING OFF THE TOPS OF DESSERTS SUCH AS THE GINGER TIRAMISU ON PAGE 135.

Pots and Pans

I recommend that you start a collection of heavy-based stainless-steel saucepans and strainers (including one that is cone-shaped). You will need various sizes. Also invest in sauté pans, nonstick milk pans, grill pans and an omelette pan.

Baking Pans

baking pans, nonstick (14 1/2 x 11in/ 37 x 28cm)
cake pans, various sizes, with removable bases
muffin pans (14 1/2 x 10 1/2in/37 x 27cm)
cooling racks (18 x 12 1/2in/46 x 32cm)
roasting pans, deep anodized (14 1/2 x 10 x 3in/37 x 26 x 8cm)

Nozzles and Brushes

piping nozzles, plain and fluted, selection of plastic piping for cutting into ring molds
plastic spray bottles for oil and melted butter
stainless-steel ruler
14in (36cm) plastic pastry bag and nozzles
brushes, 1/2in (1.25cm) and 1in (2.5cm)

Scales and Measures

cup measures
scales, electronic or manual (weighs to 21lb/10kg)
stainless-steel spoon measures
round weights
plastic measuring jug (2 quart/2.2 liter)
plastic measuring jug (1 quart/1 liter)

Electrical Appliances

blender (1 quart/1 liter capacity)
deep-fat fryer
electric carving knife
electric juicer
electric coffee grinder
food mixer (6 1/2 quart/6.4 liter capacity)
food processor (1 1/2 quart/1.4 liter capacity)
ice cream/sorbet maker

acknowledgements

I would like to thank the following people:

My business partner, Terry Shaw, who has been the most incredible support for 18 years, his friendship, judgement, and advice will always be immeasurable. Steve Bailey, our executive chef who, with Richard Cubbin and Dave Lee, manage to put up with me and some of my crazy ideas. They run the kitchen with such professionalism and dedication; nothing is ever too much trouble. Dave Withers has been responsible for testing all the recipes apart from the desserts. He has worked tirelessly for six months with creativity and so much attention to detail and skill. We have both had the most wonderful time.

Paul North and Liz Taylor for testing the seasonal desserts and dessert buffet. Jane Grafton for interpreting my ideas on desserts so brilliantly and testing them. John Hopkins and Will Yap for running around town picking up all the bits and pieces I wanted. Luis for his hard and loyal work. Phillipa Candy for keeping the office going, being so patient and minding the books. Nicola Edwards has worked with me on this project from the beginning – she is the most wonderful assistant; nothing is too much trouble and her efficiency is legendary. Her wit, humor and ideas have been a great source of support. All the team have been extremely encouraging through the months it has taken us all to develop these recipes. Their loyalty and enthusiasm know no bounds.

Sir Elton John and David Furnish for giving us the opportunity and trust to create very memorable parties and for letting us raid the contents of their china and linen cupboards and for the generous use of their home. George Quinlan for letting us disrupt his day and being so incredibly kind and helpful. Bob Stacy for his help and great sense of humor. Bryan and Nanette Forbes for their support and encouragement and letting us use their lovely lake and gardens.

Kyle Cathie who made this all possible, my editor Sophie Bessemer who, for the past 18 months, has held my hand through what I feel is uncharted waters – thank you for being so patient. Samantha Gray, my copy-editor, for lots of encouragement and Mark Latter at Vivid for his innovative design and constant good humor through everything. Wei Tang, whose styling is so inspiring – we have both had a tremendous time and you have taught me what works through a camera lens. Jeremy Hopley for the most wonderful photographs and for making the days in the studio enjoyable for all. I have gained so much from just being there.

To Charlie Woodward Fisher, a good friend and support, and his team at Fisher for being true professionals. Ken Turner, Detta Phillips, Michael Mathews, Simon Lycett and Rob Van Heldon – all creative floral designers from whom I have gained much knowledge and the memory of wonderful parties.

John Reid, who has been the most incredible support over the last 15 years, and who is always a great source of encouragement, guidance and advice. Lady Elizabeth Anson at Party Planners – we have had years of wonderful parties and enjoyed every moment, especially our away-day picnics! Joseph, Franklin and Maurice Ettedgui for letting me create L'Express and Joe's. All our customers over the years for their loyalty and trusting us to create their dreams. Our oldest customer, in the nicest way, John Bayman, for always being fun and a friend, watching the children grow up – we did the christenings and 18th birthday parties.

Gabriel and Lynne, Olivia and Lauren Alvarez, who are always there for me; Gabriel for introducing me to Mexican food; Rod and EM Grimes Graeme for being wonderful friends, great supporters and testers of recipes. Rod taught me everything I know about barbecuing. Roddy Grimes Graeme helped me to understand the mysteries of e-mail and the Internet. Frank and Carolyn Mercurio who have brought so much into my life. Joan White for proof-reading and being a good friend for nearly 30 years. Alison and Stephen Camacho for the rum punch recipe and their encouragement. Bill Minors for teaching me to fish although I still cannot eat the barracuda we catch. Irene Hopton Scott for reading the first drafts. Christine for always being happy, helpful and keeping my home together for me. John Hird for encouragement and patience. Sarah and Brian St Pierre for their advice and help. My friends, who I have not been able to see, thank you for being so understanding. Sheila Keating who wrote the article that started this project.

Tiles of Newport, for the loan of tiles for our Moroccan evening. Lucy and Phillip at The Icebox, for the ice bar. Guinivere, Mark, Heather and Kevin Weaver for letting us borrow such wonderful items from your Aladdin's cave in the King's Road. Graham Jones, Terry Jones, Sophie and Jerry of Jones Hire, for listening and their generosity in letting us rummage through their warehouse and borrow equipment. William and Annie Mellon of Top Table who listen and supply beautiful china, glassware, cutlery and linen – thank you for taking us seriously. Trade and Care for the loan of their beautiful lacquerware. Also all at Wedgewood for much of their china that we used in the photographs and VV Rouleaux for their fabulous ribbons. Julian Posner at Banana Split for letting us photograph their magnificent tent. Julian Chamberlen for the wine suggestions. Pedro Oliveira for testing the cocktails and Steve White for folding the napkins.

index